GOLD COINS
of
The Carson City Mint
1870-1893

By: Douglas Winter

Copy #_____ of 500 printed

GOLD COINS
of
The Carson City Mint
1870-1893

Written by: Douglas Winter

With Contributions by
Dr. Lawrence E. Cutler

Edited by: James L. Halperin

www.carsoncitygold.com

Carson City Gold Coins, 1870-1893

www.carsoncitygold.com

Library of Congress Control Number: 2001089867

ISBN 0 - 9651041-3-3 (Softbound)
ISBN 0 - 9651041-4-1 (Hardbound)

PUBLISHED: BY IVY PRESS / DWN PUBLISHING
100 Highland Park Village • 2nd Floor
Dallas, TX. 75205-2788

TABLE OF CONTENTS

ABOUT THE AUTHOR

Douglas Winter was born in New York City. He became interested in coins at an early age. By the time he was thirteen, Winter was a fixture at Eastern coin conventions where he would exhibit his collection and buy and sell coins.

After graduating from college, Winter went to work for Heritage Rare Coin Galleries of Dallas, Texas. He served as Director of Research and was responsible for many of its auction catalogs, fixed price lists and promotional material. In 1985 he established his own firm, Douglas Winter Consulting, which acted as a consultant to many of the major United States auction and retail firms. In 1989 he opened Douglas Winter Numismatics, a firm that specializes in choice and rare United States gold coinage. Today, this firm is a leader in this area and Winter is regarded as a leading expert in the area of 19th century branch mint gold issues.

In addition to buying and selling coins to collectors and other dealers, Winter's professional activities include writing and research. He has now written the standard references on the gold coinage from four branch mints (Carson City, Charlotte, Dahlonega and New Orleans) as well as two books on Liberty Head double eagles.

Douglas Winter is a member of all leading numismatic organizations including the Professional Numismatic Guild (PNG). He lives with his wife, Mary, in Dallas.

Questions and comments regarding this book can be addressed to the author at PO Box 7827, Dallas, TX. 75209 or via email at dwn@ont.com.

ABOUT THE EDITOR

James L. Halperin may be the most successful coin dealer of all time. PCGS founder and CEO David Hall called him "the Michael Jordan of numismatics." Jim and traders under his supervision have transacted billions in coin business, and have outsold all other numismatic firms each year for almost 20 years. An astonishing percentage of America's most successful coin dealers learned their craft by working for Jim at one time or another. An avid futurist, Jim has also written two best-selling science fiction novels, invests in technology companies, and endows a multimillion-dollar health education foundation.

James Halperin can be contacted c/o Heritage Numismatic Auctions, 100 Highland Park Village, Suite 200, Dallas, Texas 75205 or via email: Jim@HeritageCoin.com

ACKNOWLEDGEMENTS

Parts of this book are based on research by Dr. Lawrence E. Cutler for the 1994 book "Gold Coins of the Old West-The Carson City Mint 1870-1893," published by Bowers and Merena Galleries.

The author would like to thank the individuals who allowed him to have access to coins in their collections. The author and editor would each like to thank those collectors who have entrusted us with the responsibility and privilege of assembling, purchasing or auctioning their sets of Carson City gold coins.

The majority of the photographs in this book were taken by PCGS and consist of outstanding coins from the Nevada Collection. Special thanks go to Rick Montgomery of PCGS for assisting me in this area.

I would like to thank dealers Paul Nugget, Lee Minshull and Mike Fuljenz for their assistance with the Condition Census and rarity information in this book.

Special thanks go to Greg Rohan and to Heather Foose of Heritage Rare Coin Galleries and Heritage Numismatic Auctions for their help with this project.

The design and layout of this book was completed by Cathy Hadd, Carl Watson, Marsha Taylor, Jody Garver and Carlos Cardoza of Heritage Rare Coin Galleries. Line editing was completed by Heather Foose.

OTHER BOOKS BY DOUGLAS WINTER

Published by DWN Publishing, Dallas, TX.
- *Gold Coins of the Charlotte Mint 1838-1861*: Annual Rarity and Condition Census Update (s) (published 1998-2000)
- *Gold Coins of the Charlotte Mint, 1838-1861* (published 1998)
Carson City Gold Coinage 1870-1893: Rarity and Condition Census Update (published 1998)
- *Gold Coins of the Dahlonega Mint 1838-1861*: Annual Rarity and Condition Census Update (s) (published 1998-2000)
- *Gold Coins of the Dahlonega Mint, 1838-1861* A Numismatic History and Analysis (published 1997)

Published by Universal Coin and Bullion, Beaumont, TX. and DWN Publishing
- *Indian Head Quarter Eagles, 1908-1929.* A Collector's Guide (with Michael Fuljenz, published 2001)
- *Type Three Double Eagles 1877-1907*: A Numismatic History and Analysis (with Michael Fuljenz, published 1998)
- *Type Two Double Eagles 1866-1876*: A Numismatic History and Analysis (with Michael Fuljenz, published 1996)

Published by Bowers and Merena Galleries, Inc., Wolfeboro, N.H.
- *Gold Coins of the Old West: The Carson City Mint 1870-1893* (with Dr. Lawrence Cutler, published 1994)
- *New Orleans Mint Gold Coinage: 1839-1909* A Numismatic History and Analysis (published 1992)
- *Charlotte Mint Gold Coins: 1838-1861* A Numismatic History and Analysis (published 1987)

To purchase any of these books, please visit our website at www.raregoldcoins.com and click on the icon marked "my books"

OTHER BOOKS BY JAMES L. HALPERIN

- *How to Grade U.S. Coins*, Ivy Press, published 1986 and 1990
www.CoinGrading.com
- *The Rare Coin Estate Handbook*, with co-authors Steve Ivy & Greg Rohan, Ivy Press, Published 2000, www.HeritageCoin.com/sales/estatebook.asp
- *The Truth Machine*, Ballantine/Random House, Published 1996 & 1997
www.TruthMachine.com
- *The First Immortal*, Ballantine/Random House, Published 1997
www.amazon.com/exec/obidos/ASIN/0345421825

FOREWORD

Upon opening my first store in 1968 at the tender age of 15, I quickly discovered that certain coins are magic. While some items would languish in inventory for weeks or months, 1916-D dimes, 1909-S VDB cents, Fugios, Educational Series currency, and Carson City coinage of any description generally lasted about 24 hours.

Especially Carson City coinage -- whether dimes, double eagles, or any denomination betwixt. Was it because of emotional and cerebral connections to westward expansion and manifest destiny, the neighboring Sierra Nevada mountains, Lake Tahoe and Reno, the Comstock Lode? Perhaps these coins also conjured images of Colonel Kit Carson, the Nevada state capital's namesake, with his own rich history as explorer, guide, Indian fighter and sympathizer, Union soldier for 1st New Mexico Volunteers, and final career as Colorado Territory Superintendent of Indian Affairs. And let's not forget Virginia City and nearby fictional ranch, the Ponderosa -- in those days, almost everyone watched "Bonanza" on TV.

Yes, even back in 1968, a coin minted at Carson City was far more likely than most to grab the attention and open the wallet of the next collector, or non-collector, who walked in to Jim's Stamp & Coin Shop -- of Cochituate, Massachusetts no less! As far northeast as New England, numismatic novices and experts alike seemed to develop an instant affinity for those semi-scarce-to-rare, and usually well-circulated coins from the old west with the "CC" mintmark on the back.

I would later discover that the same attraction holds throughout Europe, Asia and South America. People everywhere have long hungered to see and own such coins because of the history and romance implied by those two initials. Such images of and ties to America's checkered yet often-heroic history cast a wide wave that does not wane.

Thus, Carson City coinage is seldom undervalued, at least by traditional standards of price versus rarity. If you don't believe me, simply compare the Coin World Trends value of any gold coin from another mint against a Carson City gold coin of the same denomination, era, and the number certified by independent third-party grading services like NGC and PCGS. The similarly rare CC coin will invariably be more expensive. This was true ten years ago, is true now, and will likely be true ten years from now. The premium for Carson City coinage endures, year after year, decade after decade -- and rightly so. No other mint has captured as much of the numismatic public's imagination, and no other mintmark from any nation has ever been as eagerly collected.

Therefore if you are a so-called value buyer, I suggest you seek your bargains elsewhere. And if you already collect Carson City coinage, you know how difficult it is to buy and how easy it is to sell nice, original examples from this mint. But if you want pieces of American history you can hold and enjoy, and a vehicle through which to learn, or perhaps to teach others about those intrepid pioneers who sought their fortunes in the wild west, look no further than the coinage described in this terrific book.

Douglas Winter is a scholar who knows the series well, having diligently studied it for many years, during which he has handled hundreds of the very best examples known. Admittedly, vast information within the topic remains unknown or in dispute. Disagreements abound between experts on a particular coin's true grade, originality, conditions of manufacture, circulation patterns, and rarity. Countless specimens and perhaps many hoards of CC coins are yet to be discovered. The lore is incomplete. But although much of what is written about Carson City coinage must by necessity be speculative, Doug's opinions carry weight, perhaps more than those of any other expert in the field. Which is why Gold Coins of the Old West: The Carson City Mint 1870-1893 (with Dr. Lawrence Cutler) became an instant classic when first published in 1994, and why the present revision is even better. It has been a privilege to be involved with this project. I learned a lot from this book. You will, too.

James L. Halperin
February 2001

THE HISTORY OF CARSON CITY
AND THE CARSON CITY MINT

The history of the Old West, and of early Nevada, is a tale of pioneers and frontiers, gold and silver rushes, mining booms and busts, ghost towns and cowboys and Indians. Coins manufactured in the Old West capture the spirit and adventure of that special time in the history of the United States.

The Carson City mint produced silver and gold from 1870 until 1893 in dime, twenty cent, quarter dollar, half dollar, silver dollar, trade dollar, half eagle, eagle and double eagle denominations. Gold coinage produced totaled $23,823,425 in face value. All coins struck in Carson City have a "CC" mintmark located on the reverse.

Both Carson City and its mint owe their existence to the determination and the foresight of Abraham Curry. In fact, Abe Curry played such a central role in the establishment, construction and administration of the Carson City mint that it has been said, only partly in jest, that the mintmark "CC" stood as much for "Curry's Compliments" as for "Carson City."

The Carson City mint exemplifies the history of the western gold and silver rushes as well as the history of United States coinage and its related laws. The history of the mint also provides important insights into the mintage figures of the coins struck during the mint's active life, as well as a historical perspective for studying these special coins.

Westward Migration and Curry's Purchase of Carson City

Like much of the early history of the West, the history of Carson City begins with westward migration due to the California gold rush of 1848. By 1851, there was a small settlement in Eagle Valley (the valley which was later to contain Carson City) that sold supplies to emigrants stopping on their way to California just before crossing the imposing Sierra Nevada Mountains.

Abraham Curry had traveled west from his native New York. In 1858, finding California land prices exorbitant, Curry and three other families traveled back to Mormon Station (now Genoa) in western Utah Territory, where there was an active town and trading post. There, Curry had hoped to establish a general store of his own. But he balked at the asking price of $1,000 for a plot of land and, instead, vowed to start his own town.

Curry and his associates then traveled north to Eagle Valley, which was then part of Carson County in western Utah Territory. Carson County had been named for Kit Carson, the famous explorer and scout. Here, Curry was able to purchase Eagle Valley from its owner, John Mankin, for $500 and a few horses.

Curry dreamed of turning his little town into a thriving city that would one day become a state capital. He named the town Carson City and hired a surveyor to lay out the streets and the building sites. In exchange for his services, Curry offered the surveyor a choice block in the new town. The surveyor, thinking that the town was doomed from the start, refused and insisted on being paid in cash. It was hard to fault him, as the new town grew very slowly at its inception.

The Gold and Silver Rush

While gold was discovered in Nevada in 1849, for the following decade the state served only as a highway for emigrants to California. In 1859, the first veins of the fabulous Comstock lode of rich silver and gold ore were discovered on the eastern side of Mount Davidson, only fifteen miles from Carson City. The Comstock Lode became the greatest source of silver and gold ever discovered in the United States. Its prime years of production ran from 1859 until the late 1870's.

Mining in the area later known as the Comstock Lode began as early as 1852. A man named Clark built the first cabin in the area. He did not stay long before being driven away by Washoe Indians. The next wave of miners in the area included James Fennimore (or Finney) whose nickname was "Old Virginia." Most of the miners in the area at this time were only searching for gold. They bitterly complained of a heavy metallic substance which covered the bottom of their rockers and called it "that infernal blue stuff." They believed this material worthless and that it interfered with the more lucrative gold mining.

James Finney was the first miner to put his location notice on the ledge destined to start the new rush and which later became the home of the Ophir Mine, but he was too lazy to work the area. Patrick McLaughlin and Peter O'Riley prospected Finney's claim and soon found a good quantity of gold. Within weeks, they were recovering $500 to $1,000 a day. Henry Comstock, the namesake of the famous Lode, somehow bluffed the two miners into a share of the soon-to-be-famous mine. By early 1859, there was a rush from all over the Territory to the new gold find.

"Infernal Blue Stuff" Proves Valuable

In July, 1859, a rancher by the name of W.P. Morrison went to see the mining operation. He picked up a sample of the despised "blue stuff" for assay. He forgot about it for many months and finally had the sample analyzed in an assay office in Grass Valley, California. It was estimated to yield almost $1,600 a ton in gold and twice as much in silver. Thus, the ore that the miners had been throwing away to get at the gold was, in fact, composed of silver and gold worth $4,971 a ton.

Once it was learned that the "blue stuff" was just lying around in heaps, the rush for riches was really on. Within days, the area around Grass Valley pulsed with excitement not seen since the early days of the California Gold Rush. The rush to Washoe, as the area was then called, emptied California's now played-out mining camps.

The goal of most of the emigrants to Nevada was neither the settlement of new territories nor the slow, gradual development of wealth. Instead, most of these men desired to quickly obtain overwhelming riches and then return as soon as possible to their former homes far from the barren Nevada desert. Some of these miners did make their fortunes and left to build other cities such as San Francisco. But a few stayed and made Nevada their new home.

The mining camp that grew up around the rich strike was first called Pleasant Hill and then Ophir. The name that stuck was Virginia City. This name was given by James Finney—better known as "Old Virginia—" who was one of the original discovers of the Lode.

Mining Success Spurs Cities' Growth

It soon became clear that most of the rich minerals lay deep underground and were difficult to reach. Even as early as 1860, the pace of the mining was slowing noticeably. The deposits of silver measured as great as 200 feet across in places and, at times, a quarter of a mile straight down. The mining soon entailed digging shafts and offshoot tunnels, which in turn required dynamiting through solid rock. The ore itself was often very soft and this gave the earth a tendency to slide during excavations. As a result, cave-ins were common. To minimize the danger of shifting earth during deep underground mining, Philip Deiderheimer, a German mining engineer, developed square-set mine timbering, whereby cubes of timber were lowered into the mines and placed in a honeycomb pattern. This new technique was successful and soon used in mines all over the world.

Along with the riches from the mines, Virginia City grew rapidly. After 1860, good roads were built across the Sierra Nevada Mountains to link up with the West Coast. Virginia City and its smaller neighbor, Carson City, immediately became major supply centers for the miners and the owners of the mines. Business boomed and the towns flourished.

By 1860, Carson City boasted two boarding houses, three restaurants, seven hotels, ten saloons and six breweries. There were five doctors, one school teacher five lawyers, one jeweler, six barbers, twenty carpenters and forty-six teamsters and blacksmiths. A farm hand was paid $3.00 a day, while carpenters earned $7.00 when lumber was available. The Virginia City miners were the highest paid in the world, earning up to $5.00 per day (in comparison, European miners made less than $1.00 per day.) But since a room cost $4.00 per day (or about $20.00 per week for those able to pay in advance) even the thriftiest Virginia City miners had a hard time saving money.

While it spurred the growth of Virginia City and Carson City, it is important to note that mining was hard and dangerous work. The conditions in the mines were miserable with temperatures rising at times to 130 degrees. The miners would work in shifts when temperatures rose to this level. They would recover by drinking fluids and chewing ice. Knowing the danger of their work, the miners had their own type of insurance policy to help take care of their families in case of a disaster. If a miner were maimed or killed in the mines of the Comstock (and about 10,000 of them were) the miners would take a collection directly out of their paychecks to give to the surviving widow's family. The collection could amount to $1,500, which was several years pay for most miners.

Home To Giants of American Literature

Virginia City boasted the Territorial Enterprise, the most famous newspaper in the West. The Enterprise was started in Genoa and moved to Virginia City in 1860. On its payroll were some of the most brilliant names in American journalism, including Mark Twain and Dan De Quill. The popularity of this paper was due, in part, to the fact that its journalists had enormous poetic license, fashioning stories out of little more than clever fiction.

The young Mark Twain (pen name for Samuel Langhorne Clemens) actually got his start in journalism by writing for the Enterprise. He had traveled from Hannibal, Missouri to Nevada to find his fortune and to escape the Civil War.

When his brother Orion was appointed Secretary of the Nevada Territory, Samuel tagged along to Carson City. He set out to make his fortune speculating in lumber, forming a partnership and attempting to purchase some timber near Lake Tahoe. When the deal fell through and left him broke, he then turned to prospecting. The young Twain was barely able to earn his keep as he worked on his small claim. It was only his hidden passion for writing that kept him from starving. Twain would send short stories signed "Josh" to the editors of various western newspapers. The editor of the Enterprise was so taken with Clemens' wit and humor that he offered him a full-time position. He took the pen name Mark Twain and American literature would be forever enriched by his brilliance.

Civil War Helps Curry's Campaign For Carson City Mint

In 1862, more than a year after the Civil War began, the United States House of Representatives considered establishing a branch mint in the Territory of Nevada. It was hoped that having such a mint near the Comstock Lode would decrease the cost of transporting bullion to San Francisco and that it would keep the bullion from being transported overseas. Another factor which may have worked in favor of establishing a new Western mint was the loss of the Southern branch mints in New Orleans, Charlotte and Dahlonega. There was an objection to the proposed Nevada facility by the Director of the Mint, James Pollock, on two grounds: the branch mint system was already too much of a burden and the Nevada mines were, as yet, unproven. Despite Pollack's objections, Congress passed legislation on March 3, 1863 establishing a mint in the Territory of Nevada.

Abraham Curry lobbied to establish the new mint in Carson City, emphasizing the town's central location to all the major mining districts, a rich agricultural setting and a population full of fine, enterprising people. He also argued (although it was not true) that there was a total absence of coins in the area and, thus, a need for a mint. In late 1863, Carson City was selected as the site for the new facility. Because of the Civil War, however, further plans were put on hold.

By 1863, Virginia City had mushroomed to a population of between 15,000 and 20,000. As large as the city was, each of its six mines contained more timber below ground than all of the city's surface structures combined. Nearby timberlands were quickly stripped bare. Even to this day, the forest on the eastern shore of Lake Tahoe is not nearly as lush as the more distant and relatively unfarmed western side.

With the Civil War draining the Union treasury and the Comstock Lode producing millions of dollars per year, Abraham Lincoln and his fellow Republicans felt it imperative to incorporate the rich state of Nevada into the Union. They also wanted another state with Northern sympathies to vote favorably for the 13th amendment to the Constitution to abolish slavery. Although the Territory of Nevada did not meet the 60,000 person population requirement for statehood, on October 31, 1864, it became the 36th state. A strong argument can be made that the gold and silver mined in Nevada changed the course of the Civil War as it provided the Union with a much-needed surplus of cash.

When the Civil War finally ended, attention again focused on the establishment of the branch mint in Carson City. In 1865, a plot of land measuring 170' x 170' was purchased and a commission of three men appointed to officially establish the mint. To no one's surprise, one of the commissioners was Abraham Curry.

When the plans for the mint finally arrived, Curry submitted his bid and was named contractor.

Construction of the Carson City mint progressed slowly from 1866 through 1869. Delays in funding led to work stoppages; other delays were caused by severe winter weather and a shortage of materials. By the end of 1869, construction was complete and all of the machinery was installed. The mint had cost $426,787.66 to build; almost three times the original estimate of $150,000. On December 28, 1869, when a large earthquake shook Carson City the mint was not damaged, a testament to its solid--if overpriced--construction.

Abraham Curry, named as the first Superintendent of the Mint, was central to the mint's establishment, construction and administration. As previously mentioned, it was said, only half in jest, that the mintmark "CC" stood for "Curry's Compliments."

Inside The New Mint

The first floor of the new mint contained a paying teller's office, the deposit weighing room, the coin press room, gold and silver melting rooms, the coiner's office, the treasurer's office, the melter and refiner's office, fire vaults, an engine room and the boiler room. The second floor consisted of the adjusting room, the refinery, the assayer's office, the humid assay room, two other assay rooms, the superintendent's office, the clerk's office, a watchman's room, a ladies' dressing room and various storerooms. The basement was divided into vaults.

On January 6, 1870, the mint officially opened its doors and almost immediately received its first shipment of bullion. However, the dies needed to strike coins did not arrive until four days later at the Wells Fargo office in Carson City.

The First Coins

On February 11, 1870, 2,303 Liberty Seated silver dollars, the first coins to be issued with the mintmark "CC," were released into circulation. The next coins struck were ten dollar gold pieces or eagles. These were produced on February 14, 1870. On March 2, 1870, the first five dollar gold pieces or half eagles were struck. These were followed by twenty dollar gold pieces or double eagles in March, 1870. Quarter dollars and half dollars were also struck in the first year of production at the mint.

Even as the first coins were being struck at the new facility, attempts were being made to close the Carson City mint. George S. Boutwell, the Secretary of the Treasury, had publicly stated that he wanted only the Philadelphia and the San Francisco mints in operation. A bill was brought before Congress which stated that bullion would be refined only by private reduction works; effectively closing the new mint. This measure failed but attempts by opponents to restrict the refining and minting capacity of the Carson City mint continued for decades.

In September, 1870, Abe Curry resigned as superintendent to seek, unsuccessfully, the Republican nomination for Lieutenant Governor. The local Wells Fargo agent, H. F. Rice, was appointed as the new superintendent.

With adequate funding and bullion deposits, coinage figures approximately doubled in 1871 and 1872. Excessive snow in the winter of 1871-72 led to the blocking of the Union Pacific railroad and the subsequent delivery of the 1872-date dies from Philadelphia. A set of obverse dies was borrowed from the San Francisco mint. Since the Carson City mint could not use the San Francisco mint's reverse dies, only one side of the new coins was actually struck. In February 1872, the new dies finally arrived and the half-finished coins were completed.

New Coinage Laws Shape The Mint's History

1873 saw another increase in production. However, coinage laws passed by Congress in this year were to have a profound effect on the future of the Carson City mint. These laws also affected the availability of the types and denominations of Carson City coins which have survived for today's numismatists.

The Act of 1873 changed many aspects of coinage law. It established that one dollar gold coins would be the new unit of value for the American monetary system. It authorized silver coinage only in dimes, quarters, half dollars and the new trade dollar. Thus, 1873 was the last year of production for the Liberty Seated silver dollar design which had been coined since 1840. The Act of 1873 also abolished free coinage (i.e., the lack of refining cost added to below par bullion to produce coinage) and effectively accomplished the demonetization of silver. Silver money was now legal tender only up to five dollars.

"No Arrows" Coins Made Rare By Melting

Another major change brought forth by the Act of 1873 was the increase in weight of silver coins. Almost 150,000 dimes, quarters and half dollars coined before April 1, 1873 were melted because they were lighter than the standard now allowed by the law. To distinguish the new, heavier coins, arrows were added to the obverse near the date. As a result of the melting of the 1873 "no arrows" issues, these coins are very rare today. The 1873-CC No Arrows dime is one of the rarest American coins, with a surviving population of only one piece. Only five 1873-CC No Arrows quarters are currently known to exist. The half dollar is reasonably obtainable in lower grades but extremely rare in higher grades. The silver dollar is very rare in all grades and is virtually unobtainable in grades approaching Mint State.

In May 1873, Frank Hetrich assumed the position of Superintendent of the Carson City mint. Superintendent Rice had resigned after some lightweight, debased coins dated 1872-CC and 1873-CC were discovered. When word leaked out about this, area residents lost confidence in their coins. This can be seen, today, by the edge marks and test marks on many coins from this period.

On October 19, 1873, Abe Curry died at the age of 58. In recognition of his passing, the mint closed for a day. The demand for coins grew to such great levels in 1873 that U.S. Mint Director Pollock actually drew up plans to expand the Carson City mint. However, no funds were appropriated for this purpose and the expansion never took place.

Coinage Increases At The Carson City Mint: 1874-1876

The Philadelphia mint was unable to meet the severe coin shortage that plagued the eastern states in 1873 and 1874. The western mints began to produce coins around the clock sending much of their production back east. Superintendent Hetrich doubled the number of tanks and furnaces from two to four and thus doubled the refining capacity of the facility from 7,000 ounces to 14,000 ounces daily. Nearly four million dollars in coins were struck in Carson City in 1874. Millions of dollars more were cast into silver and gold bars. This large increase in production helps to explain why the gold coins dated 1874 are so much more available than the other early date Carson City issues.

Hetrich resigned in August, 1874 and was replaced by James Crawford, a mill foreman from Dayton, Nevada. Crawford lasted for more than ten years as superintendent, the longest tenure of any of the Carson City superintendents. Late in 1874, Congress passed a bill denoting Philadelphia as the "parent" mint and all other mints as full-fledged--rather than branch-- mints.

Coinage increased by another two million dollars in 1875. A second small press was purchased by Crawford and installed. Because of the increased production which began in 1875, Carson City dimes, quarters and half dollars became much more obtainable beginning with that year. The mint soon became overworked. However, a recommendation that the facility be enlarged was once again shot down due to a lack of funds.

By the mid-1870's, Virginia City now had a population of more than 25,000 people. It was able to support 110 saloons, more than 50 dry goods stores, 20 laundries, four banks, six churches, public and private schools and an active railroad. A great fire in October, 1875 destroyed nearly three quarters of the city. It was rebuilt, but as the richness of the ore began to wane, Virginia City never again regained its former stature.

In 1875 and 1876, twenty cent pieces were struck at the Carson City mint. The public complained that this coin was too similar in size and design to the quarter and it was soon discontinued. Nearly all of the 10,000 1876-CC twenty cent pieces were melted. Approximately 16-18 exist today and this issue is among the most famous and highly prized of coins from the Carson City mint.

A third press arrived in Carson City in May, 1876. It was said that this third press produced the best quality coins ever struck at the mint.

Silver Dollar Regains Legal Tender Status

On February 28, 1878, the Bland-Allison Act was passed by Congress after intensive lobbying by the western silver mine owners. It forced the U.S. Treasury to purchase enormous amounts of domestic silver at artificially high prices. The bill also reinstated the silver dollar and restored its legal tender status. The Treasury Department was authorized to purchase two to four million dollars per month of silver for coinage into dollars. All trade dollar coinage was ordered stopped, with the exception of a small quantity struck each year as Proofs for collectors. The new Morgan dollar design was introduced as well.

In 1878 many internal developments took place within the Carson City mint itself. Recurrent bullion shortages plagued the mint throughout the year. Bullion depositors were required to receive payment in silver coin. Most of the mine owners chose to ship their bullion to San Francisco and draw bank checks on their deposits rather than be faced with the transport of excess coinage. Many of the heavy bagmarks seen today on the surviving Carson City coins of this era were incurred during the 300 mile trip from Carson City to San Francisco. In 1878, silver bullion was actually shipped back from San Francisco so that coinage at the Carson City mint could continue.

A new vault, constructed for the Carson City mint in 1879, was capable of holding one and a half million silver dollars. Previously, over half a million bagged silver dollars had been stacked in the halls of the mint due to a lack of storage space.

With apparent political motivation, Secretary of the Treasury John Sherman ordered the Carson City mint to stop the purchase of silver and to halt the coinage in that metal once the supply on hand was exhausted. By the end of March 1879, only gold coins were being minted. But the refining of gold and silver continued.

Mintage of dimes, quarters and half dollars ceased at the mint after 1878. In August 1879, silver was once again being coined but only in the form of silver dollars. By November 15 of that year, coinage was once again suspended entirely due to a lack of adequate silver bullion. The new mint administration publicly blamed the shortages on the miners owners who, it was said, wanted too high a price for their bullion.

Shortage of Bullion Shrinks Production

Debate to close the Carson City mint began anew. In 1879 and again in 1882, proposals were made attempting to shut this facility in favor of a new mint in the Mississippi Valley. The citizens of Carson City were baffled by such talk. Why close the mint, they thought, when it was so close to the actual sites of gold and silver production? They felt that if any of the mints should be closed it should be the one in New Orleans because of its great distance from any mines.

For the rest of the 19th century, the bullion deposits in the area were worked with varying degrees of success. For lack of adequate bullion, coinage did not resume until late in 1880, causing overall production at the mint to fall below one million dollars, the lowest figure since 1873. For the first time since the mint opened, no double eagles were minted in 1880 or in 1881. Coinage of other denominations resumed in early 1881 but stopped from April to October, once again due to a shortage of bullion.

In 1881, rumors of "sweating" (i.e., taking gold out of ingots by knocking them together and then collecting the dust) shook the mint. The Secret Service was sent to Carson City to investigate these charges. The people of Carson City, in a united effort to save their mint, did not cooperate with the agents. One of the agents was so frustrated that he wrote "any community where people seem determined to shield criminals is not a good place for a mint".

In 1882, mint officials received orders to double the previous year's production, which put a tremendous stress on the limited bullion reserves. The shortage of bullion was compounded by an accident in the Virginia City mines that flooded the deepest mine shafts and greatly slowed production.

By 1883, the silver interests in the western states were reeling from a backlash of anti-silver sentiment. Nevertheless, the mint operated at full capacity in 1883 and 1884.

Mint Closed by Cleveland; Production Peaks Under Harrison

Mint employees were greatly saddened by the election of Democrat (and staunch anti-silver man) Grover Cleveland as President in 1884. The new administration immediately replaced all key mint employees with Democrats and then closed the mint. A relatively small number of silver dollars and double eagles were struck before the mint was shut down on March 18, 1885. All the remaining bullion was shipped to Philadelphia. For the first time since it opened in 1870, the Carson City mint produced no coins from 1886 through 1888.

Though reopened in 1886 through the strong lobbying of the western silver interests, from 1886 to 1889 the mint served only as an assay office. During this period, over three million dollars in bullion was stored, while the mint awaited orders to resume coinage.

Benjamin Harrison, a Republican and silver supporter, was elected President in 1888. To no one's surprise, the mint's Democratic staff was ousted. Sam Wright, a judge and attorney, was named the new superintendent.

The decline in ore from the Comstock Lode had really begun in 1878. During the previous 19 years of production, almost $300 million worth of ore had been mined, including a peak of $38 million in 1876. Still, mining continued during the 1880's and the 1890's. By 1899, production would drop to a low of $172,000.

On June 12, 1889, the mint was notified that it could resume coin production on July 1. Since the coin presses had been sitting idle for several years, however, it took until September for the first coins to roll off the presses. During 1889, the mint struck a small quantity of silver dollars and double eagles.

From 1890 until the cessation of coinage in 1893, only silver dollars, half eagles, eagles and double eagles were produced at the Carson City mint. In April 1890, the Assay Commission meeting in Philadelphia declared that the purity and accuracy of the coins from Carson City exceeded those from the other mints. This good news was countered by an accusation that the mint had made a secret agreement with the Comstock mines. These claims were rejected, but only after comprehensive investigations.

On July 14, 1890, the Sherman Silver Purchase Act was signed into law. This obligated the Treasury to purchase four and a half million ounces of silver per month. Just as the mine owners had hoped, the price of silver rose dramatically. With the extra bullion authorized by the new law, the Carson City mint produced coins at its greatest rate in many years. The highest mintage figures ever recorded for half eagles and eagles at the mint were in 1891.

In March 1892, the Mining Stock Association of San Francisco asked Congress to investigate the Carson City mint. The association accused the mint of making false receipts for bullion deposits and taking in bullion past regular operating hours. Superintendent Wright admitted that since by law no individual could deposit more than 10,000 ounces, large shipments were logged in under false names but with checks being issued to the proper parties. Furthermore, said Wright, since Wells Fargo shipments often arrived after hours, the mint made accommodations to accept bullion after legal hours. The superintendent's explanation was evidently satisfactory.

In August 1892, Superintendent Wright died. Theodore Hofer, Chief Clerk at the Carson City mint, was named as his replacement.

Scandal Rocks Mint, Seals Its Coffin

While production reached full capacity that year, 1893 was to be the last year of operation for the Carson City mint. Grover Cleveland had been reelected as President in 1892 and production on the Comstock tapered off significantly. It was argued that, since not enough bullion was being produced, the San Francisco mint could easily accommodate all of the western mines' production. On June 1 1893, acting Mint Director Robert Preston gave the order suspending the production of coins at the Carson City mint. At the time, there was a surplus of eight million dollars in coins and one and a half million dollars in bullion within the mint's vaults.

From late 1893 through 1895, the mint was used only for accepting deposits of bullion, refining and assaying. As late as 1894, the Treasury Department requested from Superintendent Hofer a report on the facility's capacity for coining and refining. Hopes ran high that the mint would soon resume coin production. A disappointed Carson City soon heard word from Washington. Hofer was instructed to ask for the resignation from all but a few key employees by May 20, 1894.

In 1895, a scandal occurred that sealed the Mint's doom. On February 10 of that year, Hirsh Harris, the melter and refiner, reported to new superintendent Jewitt Adams that some ingots had come back from the melting room lighter than the weights and values which were stamped on them. An investigation revealed that $75,549.75 of gold was missing. From the viewpoint of Washington, the Carson City mint could no longer be trusted. By the 18th of April, all mint operations ceased. On April 20, the big engine in the machine room was coated with paraffin.

The mint staff found it hard to believe that, with all of the checking, weighing and issuing of necessary receipts at each step in the refining process, even one ounce of gold could be missing. The fact that 4,060.99 ounces had disappeared strongly suggested that an insider was responsible.

Andrew Mason, the superintendent of the New York assay office, was sent to Carson City to investigate the theft. He concluded that it had occurred sometime after the accounts were balanced in 1892. He then discovered that several gold bars had been sweated, after which copper and silver had been added to them to appear normal-sized. A nationwide search was led by the U.S. District Attorney, Charles A. Jones, for the culprits. He eventually arrested four ex-employees of the mint. Three were convicted and the other mysteriously died in his sleep before he could testify.

Despite this serious breach of security, the Treasury Department still required refining capacity in the region. So, processing of bullion at the Carson City mint began again in 1896. In 1897, Nevada's sole Congressman, Francis Newlands, argued in Congress that since the Philadelphia mint was unable to keep up with the demand for coinage, the Carson City mint should be authorized to strike coins once again. Detractors said that the mint was too far from major population centers and that it was too expensive to transport coins struck there to the eastern seaboard.

In an attempt to secure the passage of his proposal, Rep. Newlands added a rider to the Carson City mint's appropriations bill in 1899. This rider provided the Secretary of the Treasury with the power to designate the Carson City facility as either a full-fledged mint or an assay office. Shortly thereafter, the Secretary of the Treasury issued a statement that as of July 1, 1899 the Carson City mint would officially become an assay office.

The decreased production in the Comstock mines contributed to a steep decline in the economy of Nevada. It was not until the discovery of silver in Tonopah in 1900 that mining in the state had a resurgence. Substantial mineral deposits were soon discovered in other areas such as Goldfield and Rhyolite. Eventually, these and other mining towns were abandoned when their ore could no longer be worked for a profit. The mines around Virginia City, once the busiest in the world, are idle today. Virginia City is now a tourist attraction with many of its old buildings still standing.

The Carson City mint building remained an assay office until 1933, then was closed. A few years later, it became the Nevada State Museum. Additions have been made to the structure to expand the museum's capacity. The original mint building is open to visitors and contains interesting displays such as an original coining press and a nearly complete collection of both the gold and the silver coins struck at the mint from 1870 until 1893.

GRADING COMMENTARY

The Condition Census and in-grade rarity data in this book are based on my personal grading standards and may not reflect "modern" standards as dictated by PCGS and NGC. The reader should be aware of this and interpret this data accordingly.

When "Gold Coins of the Old West" was published in 1994, the grading services standards for Carson City gold coins tended to be somewhat conservative. These standards became progressively more and more loose through the latter part of the 1990's and remained so until the early part of 1999 when they became more akin to the standards seen in the early to mid-1990's. Unfortunately, many Carson City coins graded between 1995 and 1998 were done so on a more liberal standard and this is reflected in the PCGS and NGC population reports.

In my opinion, many coins graded About Uncirculated-50 and About Uncirculated-53 during this period are actually Extremely Fine. And a number of coins graded Mint State-60 to Mint State-62 are actually About Uncirculated. This belief is reflected in the Condition Census and in-grade rarity data in this book.

I purchase a considerable amount of Carson City gold coinage every year and I base my buying decisions on the eye appeal of a specific coin--not the grade ascribed to it by PCGS and NGC. The collector should do the same. In many instances, a coin graded About Uncirculated-50 will have better eye appeal than an example of the same date and denomination graded About Uncirculated-53 or even About Uncirculated-55. *Always buy the coin and not the holder.*

Any collector, dealer or investor contemplating the purchase of Carson City gold coins needs to become familiar with contemporary grading standards. This skill can not be taught in a book. The best way to become comfortable with grading Carson City gold coins (or any coins, for that matter) is to view as many pieces as possible.

The information in the Grading Guide that follows should be consulted by the new collector as he or she is viewing coins. If a collector or investor is not willing to take the time to learn grading skills, then I strongly advise him to find a reputable, knowledgeable dealer and establish a close relationship with that person.

GRADING GUIDE

Carson City gold coinage is very difficult to grade properly. Many of the issues from this mint (particularly those struck in the 1870's and the very early 1880's) are extremely tough to grade and even PCGS and NGC have a hard time with them.

It is essentially impossible to apply one rigorous set of standards to Carson City gold coins as a whole. The various issues differ from year to year and from denomination to denomination. While this may seem scary, this inconsistency is exactly what makes Carson City gold coinage so appealing to a certain type of collector.

Gold is a soft coinage metal. Therefore, strike does not play as much of a role in determining grade on gold coins as it does on, say, nickel coins. Most of the gold coins produced at the branch mints in the 19th century were poorly struck. Some Carson City issues rate among the worst struck coins ever made in this country.

The hardest Carson City gold coins to grade are the half eagles and the eagles made from 1870 until 1878. Many of these issues were struck from poorly aligned dies and it is not uncommon to see a coin on which the obverse appears one or two adjectival grades lower than the reverse, or vice versa. As an example, I have seen 1873-CC eagles with an obverse which technically graded Fine-12 and a reverse with a technical grade of Very Fine-30. Certain double eagles from the early 1870's lack detail on the hair of Liberty, even in mint or near mint grades.

On issues which typically show weak strikes, this factor must be compensated for. The collector should inspect how much luster is present and try to determine how the coin must have looked as it left the dies. On issues such as 1875-CC half eagles or 1873-CC eagles, it is very important to understand the striking characteristics when determining an accurate grade. If an issue is well known for having a very weak obverse but the reverse tends to be sharper, the overall grade of the coin should be based mainly on the reverse.

It is not fair to downgrade a Carson City gold coin simply because it was struck from an obverse or a reverse die which "looks worn." Once again, I cannot overemphasize how important it is for the collector to learn which issues come well struck and which come poorly struck. In the individual coin descriptions which appear later in this book, I have carefully mentioned the striking characteristics of each date. Read these carefully and use this information as a basis in deciding how you feel a coin should be graded.

The grading guide which follows should be applied only to those issues which show an average or above-average quality of strike.

Fine (Fine-12)

All of the letters in LIBERTY will be visible except for the upper corner of the L. The hair will show little detail and the jaw will be worn smooth. The eagle's feathers will show no more than one-quarter to one-third of the detail while the claws will show no detail at all. The lines in the shield will be merged. In addition to heavy wear, a Fine-12 coin will often show a number of heavy abrasions or mint-made planchet flaws. Such coins have often been cleaned.

Choice Fine (Fine-15)

A Fine-15 coin will show a bit more detail than a Fine-12, especially on the feathers. A coin graded Fine-15 will, in addition, have more eye appeal than a Fine-12. One should generally expect any gold coin graded Fine or lower to have been cleaned at one time.

Very Fine (Very Fine-20)

LIBERTY will be full and clear. On issues dated after 1878, some of the hair detail above the tiara will be visible. The rims and the denticles will usually show good detail. About 50 percent of the feather detail will be visible and the claws will show an outline. The vertical shield lines on certain issues will show around 50 percent of their detail. The pattern of wear on a Very Fine-20 coin may be even but many coins graded as such are abraded and not extremely appealing. Hairlines are often present from a past cleaning.

* **Very Fine-25:** A coin graded Very Fine-25 should have a touch more feather detail than a Very Fine-20. The major difference between the two grades is that a Very Fine-25 should have more overall appeal as well as slightly sharper overall detail.

* **Very Fine-30:** A coin graded Very Fine-30 will have more feather and hair detail than a Very Fine-25. The most appreciable difference between the two grades tends to be in the amount of luster present. A Very Fine-25 tends to show little if any luster while a Very Fine-30 may have a bit of luster in the protected areas.

Choice Very Fine (Very Fine-35)

LIBERTY will be noticeably sharper, as will the hair. The feather details will be sharp with the exception of certain issues which show diagnostic weakness on this area. Less wear will show on the tips of the wings and the shield lines will be sharper. The color and surfaces will usually be appreciably more pleasing than on a Very Fine-20 coin.

Extremely Fine (Extremely Fine-40)

The wear on a coin graded Extremely Fine-40 will be obvious but appreciably less than on a coin graded Very Fine. Most of the wear will be confined to the tip of the coronet, the hair above the ear of Liberty, and the wing tips. The shield and the claws will show much definition, except on those specific issues on which these details are always found weakly impressed. There will be traces of original Mint luster, especially in the protected areas (i.e., the fields closest to the devices and around the stars and the letters). A few abrasions or planchet flaws may be present.

Choice Extremely Fine (Extremely Fine-45)

The amount of wear will be somewhat less than on a coin graded Extremely Fine-40, especially on the cheek, below the eye of Liberty, and on the wing tips. Approximately one third of the original mint luster will be plainly visible except on those issues which are typically found with dull surfaces. The color and the surfaces will be more pleasing than those found on an Extremely Fine-40 coin.

About Uncirculated (About Uncirculated-50)

There will be a very small amount of wear visible to the naked eye and this will be concentrated on the tip of the coronet and, when applicable, the hair around LIBERTY and near the ear. On the reverse, wear will be concentrated on the wing tips and, when applicable, on the neck feathers and around the claws. Around half of the mint luster should be in evidence and the planchet will lack any severe, damaging flaws. Most Carson City gold coins grading About Uncirculated-50 will show numerous bagmarks or abrasions.

Choice About Uncirculated or better (About Uncirculated-55)

The only areas which show definite wear are the highest relief details. Most of the original mint luster will be present, both in the open and protected areas. The color should be original and the surfaces should be cleaner than on an About Uncirculated-50 coin. To many eyes, a coin which grades AU-55 (or AU-58) will appear to be fully Mint State.

Very Choice About Uncirculated (About Uncirculated-58)

A properly graded About Uncirculated-58 coin will often be more attractive to the naked eye than a coin graded Mint State-60, Mint State-61, or even Mint State-62. It should have nearly all of its mint luster, clean surfaces and appealing coloration. There will be minor wear or friction on the high spots; especially on the cheek, eagle's wing tips, coronet point and the rear of the hair bun.

Uncirculated

With the exception of a few issues such as the 1891-CC half eagle and eagle and certain double eagles, Carson City gold coins are not often found in Mint State grades. Since many collectors are drawn to coins which grade Uncirculated or thereabouts, it is important for the specialist in this area to have some conception of the grading standards for Mint State coins.

Mint State-60

The surfaces will be fully lustrous but may be slightly dulled on the high spots. Typically, the surfaces will show a number of abrasions or some fine hairlines. When available, Mint State-60 Carson City gold coins are generally not extremely appealing.

Mint State-61

There will be fewer marks than on a Mint State-60 coin and the color and over-all appearance will be slightly better. A coin graded Mint State-61 may show some hairlines from a gentle old cleaning but it will have no evidence of wear from circulation.

Mint State-62

The luster will be better on a Mint State-62 coin than on a lower-end Mint State coin. The surfaces will show some marks but will be reasonably clean with no densely abraded areas. The strike should be reasonably sharp and the overall level of eye appeal will usually be considerably better than a coin graded Mint State-60 or Mint State-61.

Mint State-63

The surfaces of a Mint State-63 gold coin are pleasing to the eye with minimal, well-scattered marks. The color is generally rich and original and the luster will be unbroken and above average for the issue. At this grade level, all Carson City gold coins--regardless of date or denomination--are rare.

Mint State-64

There are just a tiny handful of Carson City gold coins known to exist in Mint State-64 and higher grades. When such pieces are made available for sale (which is very infrequently, to say the least) they are notable for exceptional strikes, blazing luster, superb coloration, and uncommonly clean surfaces.

CARSON CITY HALF EAGLES:
AN INTRODUCTION AND OVERVIEW

Completing a collection of Carson City five dollar gold pieces or half eagles, regardless of grade, is among the more formidable tasks a gold coin specialist can endeavor to undertake. Consider the fact that only 45-55 examples of the key coin in this set--the 1870-CC--are thought to exist. This means that only 45 to 55 complete collections of Carson City half eagles can ever be assembled.

Much of the allure of collecting these coins (in addition to the romantic appeal of the "Old West") has to do with the fact that there are only 19 different dates. Unlike certain series where the run of dates seems endless and often numbing, this is a relatively short yet challenging project. In addition, there are no great rarities which are impossible to locate or are prohibitively expensive. The challenge of this set increases dramatically when the grades and eye appeal for each issue are given strong consideration.

For the collector or investor who is not familiar with Carson City half eagles, this series will come as a surprise. These are true "collector coins." They tend to hold their value in bear markets and show strong, steady appreciation over time. Carson City half eagles have multiple levels of demand. They are sought by general collectors, type collectors and specialists. Certain pieces may attract the attention of half eagle specialists, Carson City specialists or general collectors putting together seven mint sets of Liberty Head half eagles (the only gold denomination struck at all seven United States mints).

It is impossible to complete a set of Carson City half eagles in Mint State regardless of a collector's time or resources. Several of the dates are unknown in any Mint State grade. Currently, there is not a single Uncirculated 1872-CC or 1878-CC half eagle known to exist. Five other dates--the 1871-CC, 1873-CC, 1875-CC, 1876-CC and 1877-CC--are currently represented by just one or two Uncirculated examples. And six more dates--the 1870-CC, 1874-CC, 1879-CC, 1881-CC, 1883-CC and 1884-CC--have just two to four Uncirculated coins known.

The only Carson City half eagles relatively obtainable in Uncirculated are those struck in the 1890's. These range in scarcity from the 1892-CC with 50-75 coins known in Uncirculated to the 1891-CC with a population believed to be in the area of 400-500+. The 1891-CC half eagle is very popular as the only half eagle from this mint which can be purchased in Mint State by the collector of average means. (But, at the same time, this issue is surprisingly scarce in Mint State-63 and almost unknown in Mint State-65.)

Choice (Mint State-63 and Mint State-64) and Gem (Mint State-65) Carson City half eagles are scarce to very rare. I estimate that there are probably fewer than 10 pieces surviving in true Mint State-65. As of early 2001, only one Carson City half eagle has ever been graded higher than Mint State-65 by one of the major grading services.

There are probably fewer than three dozen choice Uncirculated Carson City pre-1890 half eagles known to exist. The vast majority of the choice and gem Carson City half eagles were struck during the 1890-1893 era.

Why are these coins so rare in Mint State? The obvious theory is that there were no coin collectors living in Nevada in the 19th century. No one saved these coins and the few Mint State pieces which exist today are here by chance. They may have been placed in a bank vault and forgotten for a century. Some found their way to European or South American banks where they were sent as payment for international debts. A few others may have been put in a drawer or a cabinet and subsequently lost by their original owners. And some were undoubtedly assay pieces sent to the Philadelphia Mint for inspection but never destroyed.

In examining the rarity of Carson City half eagles, several trends are noted. Survival figures correlate strongly to the original mintage figures for a specific issue and they also vary by the decade in which a coin was struck. In general, the rarest issues are those struck from 1870 to 1878. With the sole exception of the 1881, the half eagles produced from 1879 through 1884 are invariably less rare. And those coined from 1890 to 1893 are relatively common in comparison.

After careful analysis, it becomes apparent that one cannot simply deduce the number of surviving coins or the condition rarity of any Carson City gold coin solely from their original mintage figures. One must study auction records and private treaty sales and gather as much information as possible from prominent collectors and dealers as well as examine the population reports issued by PCGS and NGC. After careful study of the currently available information, certain trends clearly begin to emerge.

The older coins (i.e., those struck from 1870 to 1878) have survived roughly in proportion to their original mintage figures below. I estimate that between 2 percent to as little as one-half of 1 percent of each year's half eagle production has survived. In general, the older the coin, the lower the average surviving coin's grade and the lower number of high grade pieces which exist. This is common sense outcome, as the longer an issue is in circulation, the more likely it is that coins of that date will be worn or destroyed. Thus, the rarest Carson City half eagle is the 1870-CC (also the oldest) despite the fact that it has only the third lowest mintage.

The second rarest Carson City half eagle is the 1873-CC. This issue has an estimated surviving population of only 50-60 coins. My research indicates that this date is even more rare than was previously believed. The reasons for the rarity of the 1873-CC half eagle include its low mintage figure of 7,416 and its early date of issuance combined with the apparent fact that it was simply not saved.

One issue which I find very interesting is the 1878-CC. It has a relatively high mintage of 9,054 but is the third rarest Carson City half eagle with an estimated population of 60-70. The reason for the rarity and unusually low survival rate of this issue is not known.

Another interesting issue is the 1876-CC. I estimate 70-80 are known out of a low original mintage of 6,887 coins. Despite a significantly lower mintage than the 1878-CC, the 1876-CC is actually less rare. Conversely, the 1881-CC half eagle (with a mintage of 13,886) appears to be as rare as the 1876-CC.

The 1877-CC (with an original mintage of 8,680 coins) has a disproportionately high survival rate. Approximately 75-85 are known, making it as rare as the

1872-CC, which has an original mintage of 16,980 coins. There is no clear explanation as to why the 1877-CC half eagle is more common than its mintage suggests. It is interesting to note that its counterpart, the 1877-CC eagle, is found in higher grades (i.e., Extremely Fine and better) out of proportion to the other dates in the eagle series. This strongly suggests that there was a small hoard of higher grade 1877-CC half eagles and eagles in existence at one time.

The 1879-1884 Carson City half eagles are found in proportion roughly to their original mintage figures with the notable exceptions of the 1880-CC and the 1881-CC. The number of surviving 1880-CC half eagles is less than its original mintage of 51,017 suggests. In fact, the surviving population of this date most closely resembles the 1879-CC, which has a mintage nearly two-thirds smaller (17,281 coins). The 1881-CC has a surviving population of 70-80 coins, which is much smaller than one might project from its original mintage of 13,886.

What is unexpected about these two dates is that they actually have lower survival percentages than the issues from the 1870's. I cannot state with certainty why this is so, but a possible reason might be that some 1880-CC and 1881-CC half eagles were melted. This explanation becomes more plausible when one notes that there was a bullion shortage at the Carson City Mint in 1880-1881. (This is further confirmed by the fact that no double eagles were struck in Carson City during these two years due to a lack of available gold bullion). Another reason might be that the original mintage figures are incorrect and fewer 1880-CC and 1881-CC half eagles were produced than the current figures indicate.

The general trend that issues with higher mintage figures are more available today than those issues with lower original mintages applies to the 1890's as, but for one exception, the 1892-CC. With an original mintage of 82,968 coins, it is less commonly found in high grades than the lower mintage 1890-CC (53,800 struck) and 1893-CC (60,000 struck). Again, there is no satisfactory explanation for this anomaly.

In the early days of the western gold and silver rushes, paper money was viewed with suspicion and contempt. Gold coins quickly became the accepted medium of exchange. Thus, it is not surprising to learn that most surviving Carson City gold coins show heavy wear and excessive contact marks. These marks were often compounded when loose coins were thrown into bags and shipped by stagecoach to San Francisco or other distant cities. Gold is the softest coinage metal and coins struck in this metal tend to pick up heavy contact marks when they hit against each other. As a rule, half eagles have fewer marks than eagles and double eagles, because when these smaller coins hit against each other in bags they do not have the weight and surface area to make large bagmarks on each other (as do double eagles, in particular).

For the collector, locating attractive, higher grade Carson City gold coins without excessive surface marks is a tremendous challenge. Certain dates, especially those struck from 1870 to 1878, are inevitably found heavily worn and severely marked.

The rarest Carson City half eagle in Extremely Fine or higher grades is the 1878-CC. I estimate that only 16-20 such coins are currently known, of which only three or four grade About Uncirculated. Even though the 1870-CC is a rarer coin overall, with as many as 23-27 pieces remaining in Extremely Fine or higher grades. One can speculate that the number of 1870-CC half eagles that exist results from it being a first-year-of-issue coin which may have been saved (albeit in very small quantities) as a souvenir. The 1878-CC, on the other hand, lacked this novelty value and those that survived the melting pot tend to show considerable evidence of hard circulation.

Two other Carson City half eagles which are prohibitively rare in higher grades are the 1873-CC and the 1872-CC. Approximately 17-21 of the former are known in Extremely Fine or higher while the latter issue has a population estimated at 19-22 coins. The 1873-CC is extremely rare in About Uncirculated with just five or six known and two known in Mint State. The 1872-CC is even rarer, with only 6-8 About Uncirculateds and no Mint State examples known.

As one might well expect, dates with higher mintage figures are more available in most grades. The 1872-CC is less rare than certain other dates in the early 1870's because of its relatively high mintage. But its age makes it a very rare coin in About Uncirculated (with just six to eight known). The 1871-CC, while also an "older date," is a bit more available in higher grades (46-52 known in Extremely Fine or better including one or two Uncirculated pieces) since it has the second highest mintage figure of any date struck in the 1870's.

The 1874-CC is the second most available Carson City half eagle struck in the 1870's. Between 40-46 coins are known in Extremely Fine or better with twelve to fifteen of these grading About Uncirculated and three grading Mint State. I have an interesting theory to explain why this date is not only one of the two most common Carson City half eagles struck in the 1870's (aside from having the highest mintage) but also why a higher percentage of the survivors than one would assume are in high grades. In 1874, there was a coin shortage on the East Coast. Much of the Carson City coinage from 1874 was transported to the East for use in circulation there. As paper money was more readily accepted in this area of the country, it is possible that many of these coins did not see wide circulation. Perhaps some of them were even stored in banks and were never used. This also seems to be the case with 1874-CC eagles which have a similar level of availability in higher grades.

By 1879 and into the 1880's, the mintages of Carson City half eagles were higher and more were sent overseas to banks for debt payment. These coins saw less circulation than those struck in the 1870's and, thus, are found in higher grades today.

The 1881-CC is the rarest Carson City half eagle struck in the 1880's. But more examples have survived in high grades than its low mintage and overall rarity would suggest. I estimate that 33-39 pieces exist in Extremely Fine or better with possibly nine to twelve of these in About Uncirculated and another two or three in Mint State. The diminished use of gold in the 1880's gave this coin an unusual grade distribution of survivors.

The 1890's Carson City half eagles are by far the most plentiful of these issues. More than 50 percent of all the surviving Carson City half eagles--regardless of date--are dated from 1890 to 1893. Approximately 75 percent of all surviving Mint State Carson City half eagles date from the 1890's. Furthermore, about 90 percent of the remaining About Uncirculated Carson City half eagles date from the 1890's.

The relatively large survival of high grade Carson City half eagles from the 1890's stems from at least four causes: (1) the mintage figure for coins in this decade was much higher than in the previous two decades; (2) more of the coins were shipped overseas and thus escaped wholesale government meltings in the 1930's; (3) as paper money became more readily accepted in the western United States, these coins saw less and less circulation and (4): the decline of the western mining industry in the 1890's meant that fewer coins were needed in circulation.

Most of the early issues (particularly those dated 1870 through 1876) come weakly struck. This weakness is most noticeable in the central portion of the coin where the greatest amount of pressure is needed to raise the metal of the actual planchet. On the obverse, weakly struck coins will display flatness in the curls on the neck of Liberty as well as flatness on the top and the back of her hair. On the reverse, this weakness of strike is usually seen on the neck of the eagle, the central shield and on the talons of the eagle. This weakness is frequently misinterpreted as wear. Consequently, many early Carson City half eagles are often undergraded even by professional graders. Finding a sharply struck example of some dates can be challenging, and nearly impossible for other dates.

The 1870-CC is usually found weakly struck in the curls on Liberty's neck and in the neck feathers of the eagle. The 1871-CC half eagles are usually found with a better strike except for the shield on the reverse which often comes flat. The 1872-CC is nearly always very flat on the obverse as are 1873-CC's; this latter issue is also frequently weak on the eagle's neck. The 1874-CC shows a sharper obverse but the reverse comes weakly impressed, especially on the eagle's neck feathers. The 1875-CC is unquestionably the worst struck Carson City half eagle. Several varieties are known; some have a weak obverse and others have a weak reverse. The 1879-1893 issues do not suffer from such consistent problems of strike although it is not uncommon to see examples with some weakness at the centers of the obverse and the reverse.

The estimates of survival given in this book are based on current knowledge, as of 2001. As time passes, it is certain that more coins will surface from old or previously unknown collections, hoards and accumulations. This will in turn lead to more accurate survival estimates and Condition Census data. While most dates will show an increase in the number of coins believed to exist, others may actually show a decrease due to examples being lost by accident or ignorance.

When Walter Breen wrote his landmark monographs on United States gold coins in the 1960's, he believed that many Carson City coins were much, much rarer than we now know them to be. Multiple higher grade examples of even the rarest issues have surfaced in the past three decades. There are, without a doubt, several other very significant Carson City half eagles to be "discovered" in the years to come. I have attempted to address this situation by providing a probable high end and low end spread in my rarity estimates. This allows for the inclusion of currently unrecorded coins which I believe may exist.

My review of auction data, fixed price lists, dealer advertisements and available private treaty sale records provides an accurate idea as to the difficulty in amassing a complete collection of Carson City half eagles. For each of the 1870-1878 issues, typically between zero and four specimens became available each year. Often the only examples which can be purchased are in lower grades and may have minor to significant problems. As probability would have it, in some years a certain date may be unusually prevalent, or nearly impossible to find. As a rule of thumb, it is safe to say that the rarer the date and the higher the grade desired, the harder it will be to find a specific coin. Many high grade pieces are held by museums or are owned by collectors who have no intention of selling them.

It is certainly possible to put together a run of Extremely Fine to About Uncirculated Carson City half eagles dated from 1870 to 1884. Trying to complete this group in Uncirculated is, of course, virtually impossible and an About Uncirculated set is a great challenge as well. Obtaining nice Mint State examples of the 1890's issues, fortunately, is not that difficult or costly.

The budget-conscious collector should not feel excluded from this series. All Carson City half eagles (even the 1870-CC) can be found in nice Very Good to Very Fine grades. Although these coins do show substantial wear and are not as attractive as higher grade specimens, they are wonderfully evocative of the history of the Old West and the colorful characters who are the basis of its legends.

For the typical United States gold coin collector, obtaining one example of each date in grades ranging from choice Very Fine to Uncirculated is a realistic goal. This project can be completed in a year or two. Its estimated cost can be determined by obtaining a current numismatic pricing guide.

The connoisseur with a generous budget might be interested in putting together a set of Carson City half eagles grading Extremely Fine and better. For the 1870-1878 and 1881 issues, one should look for examples which grade Extremely Fine-40 or better and which have as few contact marks as possible. For the 1879, 1880 and 1882-1884 issues, the collector should look for pleasing, lustrous About Uncirculated-50 or better coins. For those issues struck in the 1890's, seek clean, lustrous Mint State-60 or better pieces. A collection such as this could be completed within a three to five year time frame.

There are a few advanced collectors who study die varieties. Such individuals seek to complete a collection which includes all of the known--and possibly some unknown--die varieties. To my knowledge, only a small number of individuals have a complete or nearly complete collection of Carson City half eagles by die variety.

Coin collectors of all budgets can enjoy the fun, romance and challenges of Carson City half eagles. To further assist collectors of all levels, the following pages give detailed information on each half eagle issue. Information on die characteristics, varieties and overall rarity as well as grade rarity are provided. Also, the current Condition Census listing of the finest known examples for each issue is listed for reference. The photographs of each half eagle are enlarged to twice their actual size for better clarity.

SECTION ONE

HALF EAGLES

I. LIBERTY HEAD, WITH MOTTO REVERSE (1870-1884, 1890-1893)

1870:	7,675	1881:	13,886
1871:	20,775	1882:	82,817
1872:	16,980	1883:	12,958
1873:	7,416	1884:	16,402
1874:	21,198	1890:	53,800
1875:	11,828	1891:	208,000
1876:	6,887	1892:	82,986
1877:	8,680	1893:	60,000
1878:	9,054		
1879:	17,281		
1880:	51,107		

Total Mintage...................... 709,617

1870-CC

MINTAGE: 7,675
RARITY RANKINGS:
   Overall Rarity: 1st of 19
   High Grade Rarity: 4th of 19

The 1870-CC is among the rarest half eagles from the Carson City mint. It is popular and well-known due to its status as the first coin of this denomination to be produced at this mint. It is also more available than its eagle and double eagle counterparts and the only one of the three occasionally seen in higher grades.

STRIKE: The strike tends not to be especially sharp. It is important, however, to note which Die State an 1870-CC half eagle is when discussing specific qualities of strike.

<u>Die State I:</u> A small number (including the coin illustrated above) show a very sharp strike with full hair detail on the obverse and sharp feathers on the neck of the eagle. This die state is very rare with probably no more than ten examples known. I believe it should sell for a strong premium over Die State II, given its far more desirable appearance.

<u>Die State II:</u> The majority of 1870-CC half eagles are very weak on the hair below and behind the ear of Liberty. This weakness corresponds to the reverse, where the feathers of the neck are totally indistinct and the top of the shield is quite blurry. Some of the Die State II coins show strong machine doubling especially on the letters UNIT in UNITED and on the denticles at the top of the reverse. Coins from this Die State should not be penalized when determining value as they represent the "typical" 1870-CC half eagle.

SURFACES: Nearly every known example has heavily abraded surfaces. This is typical of Carson City gold coins from this era, due to the fact that they circulated extensively. It is not uncommon to find an 1870-CC half eagle with detracting rim bruises as well. A few exist with relatively clean surfaces and these are very desirable.

LUSTER: Most 1870-CC half eagles are worn to the point that they do not display much mint luster. On the few high grade pieces that do exist, the luster is soft and frosty. The 1870-CC is actually above average in terms of quality when compared to other Carson City half eagles from the early 1870's.

COLORATION: High grade examples display a pleasing rich orange-gold hue while lower grade coins show a deep green-gold or faint coppery hue. It is hard to locate 1870-CC half eagles that have original coloration, as tends to be the case on all well-known, highly valued gold issues. The reason for this, in my opinion, is that coins like the 1870-CC half eagles have a great difference in value between grade levels. There is considerable financial motivation for a coin graded Extremely Fine-45 to "become" an About Uncirculated-50. Thus, a coin such as this is almost certain to be dipped or cleaned in an attempt to upgrade it and subsequently increase its value.

EYE APPEAL: It is extremely difficult to locate an 1870-CC half eagle with good eye appeal. Nearly every known example shows considerable weakness of strike and most are also heavily abraded. A few exist with sharp strikes, nice surfaces and good color and they always sell for levels well above those printed in current pricing guides.

DIE VARIETIES: There is one die variety known as well as two important die states.

Variety 1-A: On the obverse, the date is fairly high and slants downwards slightly to the right. The 1 is fairly close to the neck while the 0 is distant. There are light die file marks from the point of the coronet through the sixth star to the rim. On the reverse, the mintmark is high. The first C is higher than the second and nearly touches the arrow feather. The second C is close to the olive branch but does not touch it. All known examples show a raised die defect just below the S in the motto IN GOD WE TRUST. This same defect is seen on the reverse of some 1871-CC and 1873-CC half eagles, proving that this reverse was used from 1870 to 1873.

Die State I: The centers are mostly well impressed.

Die State II: Weakness of strike is noted at the central obverse and, especially, at the center of the reverse. On some coins, there will be no detail on the neck of the eagle.

RARITY:

Total Known: 50-60

BY GRADE:

VF*	EF	AU	MINT STATE
27-33	13-15	7-9	3

*NOTE: This includes a number of coins that grade below Very Fine. This is also true for most Carson City half eagles dated prior to 1880.

CONDITION CENSUS

1. Nevada Collection, ex: Old Mint Coin and Bullion (Joel Mitchell), 1996. Graded Mint State-61 by PCGS but at least a point or two better than this in my opinion. This coin was discovered in Carson City in early 1996. *The plate coin in this book.*

2. The Mint (Jay Parrino), ex: Bowers and Merena 10/99: 1170 ($69,000; as PCGS AU-58), Harry Bass collection, New England Rare Coin Auction 1979 ANA sale: 182. Graded Mint State-61 by PCGS.

3. Private collection, ex: Eastern dealer 1997, Charley Tuppen collection (referred to as "Southern dealer's collection" in the first edition of this book), Heritage 12/88: 1142 ($20,900). Graded Mint State-61 by NGC.

4. Private collection, ex: Bowers and Merena, Superior 2/92: 2688 (unsold), Dr. Richard Appel, Rarcoa Auction '79: 1248 ($7,250). Graded About Uncirculated-53 by PCGS in the early 1990's; this coin would grade at least About Uncirculated-55 by today's standards.

5. Midwestern collection 1998, ex: Lee Minshull, Liz Arlin, private collection. Graded About Uncirculated-58 by NGC.

Other nice About Uncirculated examples include the following:

- Chicago collection, ex: Doug Winter/Lee Minshull 6/97, Spectrum Numismatics. Graded About Uncirculated-55 by NGC.

- Northern California collection, ex: Winthrop Carner, Steve Ivy Numismatic Auctions 1982 ANA: 2675. I saw this coin at a Long Beach show in 1995 and graded it a strong About Uncirculated-53 to About Uncirculated-55 at the time.

- Bowers and Merena 11/00: 505 ($19,550), ex: Harry Bass collection, Rarcoa 1/69: 682. Graded About Uncirculated-53 by PCGS.

The 1870-CC is a rare and desirable first-year-of-issue. It is usually seen in very low grades and an accurately graded Extremely Fine-40 is quite rare. It is very rare in About Uncirculated although there are a few more known in the medium to higher AU grades than generally realized. In Mint State, there are just three pieces currently accounted for.

1871-CC

MINTAGE: 20,770
RARITY RANKINGS:
    Overall Rarity: 12th of 19
    High Grade Rarity: 9th of 19

The 1871-CC is a rare coin but it is considerably easier to locate than the other Carson City half eagles produced from 1870 to 1873.

STRIKE: The strike usually is much sharper than on the 1872-CC and 1873-CC half eagles (which are among the most poorly struck gold coins produced at the Carson City mint). On the obverse, there may be some weakness on the curls around the face and ear and at the top of Liberty's head. The reverse often shows minor weakness on the eagle's neck and wingtips. Well struck coins are definitely available to the patient collector. However, this can be a hard issue to grade as the amount of luster and the detail present may not be consistent.

SURFACES: This is an issue that was placed into circulation and used extensively in commerce. As a result, most 1871-CC half eagles have very heavily abraded surfaces. In addition, many have been cleaned. There are some known with choice surfaces and these are rare and desirable.

LUSTER: The quality of luster is above average. Some are frosty while others exhibit a soft semi-prooflike reflectiveness.

COLORATION: Uncleaned, original examples show appealing rich yellow-gold coloration and some have attractive coppery toning. It is very difficult to locate a higher grade 1871-CC half eagle with original coloration.

EYE APPEAL: The level of eye appeal for the 1871-CC half eagle is significantly better than for the other Carson City half eagles from the early years of this mint's production. However, coins that are well struck, lightly marked and natural in appearance are rare and worth a significant premium over a typical quality piece.

DIE VARIETIES: There are two die varieties known.

Variety 1-A: The date is positioned slightly closer to the bust than to the denticles. It is closely spaced and slants down to the right with the 71 very close at the top. On this variety, the reverse is the same as found on the 1870-CC half eagle. The quality of strike is similar to that described for the Die State I coins for 1870-CC with sharp feather detail on the eagle's neck.

Variety 1-B: The obverse is the same as on the other variety for this year. On the reverse, the mintmark is level and positioned more to the right than on the other variety. All known examples have a clashmark from the eagle's beak to the right wing and there is no raised die mark under the S in TRUST.

It is not known which of these two varieties are scarcer.

RARITY:
Total Known: 140-150

BY GRADE:

VF	EF	AU	MINT STATE
94-98	32-35	13-15	-2

CONDITION CENSUS:

1. Nevada collection 9/00, ex: Doug Winter, Spectrum Numismatics/Kevin Lipton 7/99, Jason Carter/Chris Napolitano, Kingswood 6/98: 676, private collection/unknown dealers(s), Heritage Rare Coin Galleries, Heritage 1997 ANA: 7686 (as PCGS MS-62; unsold), Brian Beardsley (Gulfcoast Rare Coins), Jeff Garrett (Mid American Rare Coin Galleries). Graded Mint State-63 by NGC.

2. Private collection, ex: Paramount Auction '80: 937 ($6,000), Rarcoa Auction '79: 1249 ($9,000). The Akers plate coin. Mint State-60 or thereabouts.

3. Nevada collection duplicate, ex: Doug Winter/Lee Minshull 11/96, Dr. Larry Cutler collection, Heritage 3/2/91: 5452. Graded About Uncirculated-58 by PCGS. *The plate coin in this book.*

4. (tie) Private collection, ex: Bowers and Merena 10/99: 1175 ($20,700), Harry Bass collection, Bowers and Ruddy Eliasberg sale (10/82): 525 ($1,210). Graded About Uncirculated-55 by PCGS.

• Southern California collection, ex: Doug Winter/Lee Minshull, Bowers and Merena 11/00: 510 ($12,650), Harry Bass collection, purchased from World Wide Coin Investments on October 20, 1972. Graded About Uncirculated-55 by PCGS.

5 (tie). Private collection, ex: Boston dealer, 6/97. Graded About Uncirculated-55 by NGC.

• Private collection, ex: Heritage Rare Coin Galleries, Superior 6/97: 1502 ($16,500), Robert Leece, Mike Brownlee. Graded About Uncirculated-55 by NGC.

• Bowers and Merena 8/98: 335 ($17,250). Graded About Uncirculated-55 by NGC.

• New York collector, ex: New World Rarities, 1996. Graded About Uncirculated-55 by NGC.

• Superior 3/00: 881 (unsold), ex: Monex. Graded About Uncirculated-58 by NGC.

The 1871-CC is the most available of the first four half eagles struck at the Carson City mint but it is still a scarce issue. It is typically seen in low grades and problem-free Extremely Fine-40 pieces are scarce. This is a very scarce coin in Extremely Fine-45 and a rarity in About Uncirculated. In Mint State, the 1871-CC half eagle is excessively rare with just one or two pieces currently known.

1872-CC

MINTAGE: 16,980
RARITY RANKINGS:
 Overall Rarity: 4th of 19 (tie)
 High Grade Rarity: 2nd of 19 (tie)

The 1872-CC is one of the scarcer half eagles from the Carson City mint. In higher grades, it is one of the rarest gold issues of any denomination from Carson City. It is one of just two Carson City half eagles (the other is the 1878-CC) that is, as of the publication of this book, unknown in any Uncirculated grade.

STRIKE: This is a poorly struck issue that typically shows much less detail than the 1870-CC and 1871-CC half eagles. Most are very weakly impressed on the top of Liberty's head and on the bun. The hair surrounding the face of Liberty is typically weak as well, especially the lock of hair below the ear. Surprisingly, the stars are often very sharp and may have full radial lines. On the reverse, the area that shows the most weakness is the center. This means that many have weak neck feathers on the eagle and the horizontal stripes in the shield are blurry as well.

Due to the aforementioned weakness of strike, this is a very hard issue to accurately grade. I have seen pieces that appeared Very Fine to Extremely Fine on the obverse and Choice About Uncirculated on the reverse. 1872-CC half eagles should be graded on the amount of luster that is present and the quality and appearance of the surfaces.

SURFACES: The surfaces on nearly every known example are extensively abraded. This is one of the most difficult half eagles from this (or any) mint to locate with clean fields. Most 1872-CC half eagles have clashmarks from the throat of Liberty between the beak and right wing of the eagle.

LUSTER: The luster is comparable to other issues from this era. It is usually soft and satiny. A few are known that are slightly reflective. It is very difficult to locate an 1872-CC half eagle that has undisturbed original mint luster as most have been cleaned at one time.

COLORATION: There are very few examples known that show original coloration. The few original coins that do exist have medium yellow-gold hues with some green-gold tinges.

EYE APPEAL: Only a small number of 1872-CC half eagles are known with any semblance of eye appeal. The typical example is well worn, heavily abraded and shows disturbed surfaces from having been repeatedly cleaned. Choice, original coins command a very strong premium.

DIE VARIETIES: There are two die varieties known.

Variety 1-A: The date is positioned midway in the field between the neck and the denticles. It slants downwards with the 1 noticeably higher than the 2. The mintmark is high and near the eagle. It is somewhat similar in appearance to the reverse seen on the 1870-CC half eagle and on the first variety of 1871-CC half eagle. It is appears to be the rarer of the two varieties.

Variety 1-B: On this variety, the mintmark is much lower with both of the letters even at their base. In addition, it is much closer to the VE in FIVE than on Reverse A. Many examples of this variety show minor doubling on some of the reverse lettering. A few have doubling on the B in LIBERTY.

RARITY:

Total Known: 70-80

BY GRADE:

VF	EF	AU	MINT STATE
51-58	13-14	6-8	0

CONDITION CENSUS:

1. Nevada Collection, ex: Doug Winter/Lee Minshull, 9/98, possibly ex: Stack's 5/89: 394. The sharpest struck example seen. Graded About Uncirculated-58 by PCGS. *The plate coin in this book.*

2. Private collection, ex: Bowers and Merena via private treaty sale (10/92), Long Island dealer, California dealer. Graded About Uncirculated-50 by PCGS but later removed from the slab by the owner.

3. Texas collection, ex: Austin Rare Coins, Casey Noxon, Carter Numismatics, Bowers and Merena 10/99: 1182 ($18,400; as PCGS AU-50), Harry Bass collection, Superior 2/73: 487 ($975). Graded About Uncirculated-55 by NGC.

4 (tie). Chicago collection 2/01, ex: Doug Winter, Doug Winter/Spectrum Numismatics, Stack's 10/00: 1745 ($10,925). Graded About Uncirculated-53 by NGC.

- Heritage 9/99: 6708 ($13,800), ex: Pennsylvania collection, 10/98, Doug Winter/Lee Minshull 9/98, Nevada Collection, Doug Winter/Lee Minshull 10/96, Dr. Larry Cutler collection. Graded About Uncirculated-53 by NGC. *The plate coin in "Gold Coins of the Old West, 1870-1893."*

- New Jersey collection 11/99, ex: Doug Winter/Lee Minshull, Eastern dealer, private collection, Superior 5/89: 1905 ($1,540). Graded About Uncirculated-53 by NGC.

• Bowers and Merena 10/99: 1181 ($14,950), ex: Harry Bass collection, Stack's Miles collection sale (10/68): 490. Graded About Uncirculated-53 by PCGS.

• Bowers and Merena 5/00: 507 ($14,950; as PCGS AU-50), ex: Harry Bass collection, Stack's 12/70: 229. Graded About Uncirculated-53 by PCGS.

• Colorado dealer; first seen at the 1998 ANA convention. Graded About Uncirculated-58 by NGC.

5 (tie). The following coins have all been graded About Uncirculated-50 by one of the two major services:

• Chicago collection, ex: Doug Winter/Lee Minshull, 11/97, Orange County collection, Doug Winter/Lee Minshull 11/96. Graded About Uncirculated-50 by PCGS.

• Private collection, ex: California dealer, Eastern dealer, Charley Tuppen collection. Graded About Uncirculated-50 by PCGS.

The 1872-CC half eagle is scarce in all grades. When it is available, it is generally found heavily worn and weakly struck. It is very scarce in Extremely Fine-40 and rare in properly graded Extremely Fine-45. In About Uncirculated grades, the 1872-CC is among the rarest Carson City half eagles with as few as four to six pieces currently known. At the present time, there are no Mint State coins accounted for.

1873-CC

MINTAGE: 7,416
RARITY RANKINGS:
    Overall Rarity: 2nd of 19
    High Grade Rarity: 2nd of 19 (tie)

There are only a handful of Liberty Head half eagles that can compare to the 1873-CC in terms of overall rarity and, in particular, rarity in high grades. Surprisingly, there are two Uncirculated pieces known; it is possible that these were saved as souvenirs from the annual Assay Commission meeting.

STRIKE: The quality of strike is among the poorest for any Carson City half eagle. Virtually all known examples are very flat at the top of the hair and on the bun of Liberty. The centers are often weakly detailed with weakness nearly always seen on the curls around the face and below the ear. On the reverse, the feathers on the neck of the eagle seldom show more than the slightest amount of detail and the horizontal lines in the shield are often very weak. The arrow feathers and the eagle's legs are often faintly impressed. The reverse milling from 7:00 to 10:00 is weaker than on the rest of the coin.

This is one of the hardest Carson City coins to grade because of its poor, irregular strike. As a result, most that are offered for sale are improperly graded.

SURFACES: It is extremely hard to find an 1873-CC half eagle with choice surfaces. In fact, even the few high grade examples that exist are generally seen with noticeable abrasions. It seems that this issue was readily employed in circulation and, as a result, survivors show signs of rough handling and/or excessive wear. A choice, relatively mark-free 1873-CC half eagle is worth a substantial premium above a typical example.

LUSTER: Very few 1873-CC half eagles are known that show original mint luster. On those that do, the luster tends to be frosty and better quality than one might expect from an issue that is otherwise not well produced.

COLORATION: There are not many 1873-CC half eagles that display original coloration. On the few original pieces known, the color is a medium to deep orange-gold and reddish hue.

EYE APPEAL: This is one of the more difficult 19th century United States gold coins to locate with good eye appeal. Most are poorly struck, well worn and have heavily abraded surfaces. Any example that has even acceptable eye appeal must be considered very rare and worth a strong premium over a typical quality 1873-CC half eagle.

DIE VARIETIES: There are three die varieties known.

Variety 1-A: On this obverse, the date numerals appear somewhat closely spaced with the 8 and the 7 having some distance between them. The date is fairly even with a slight slant down to the right. The reverse is the same as that seen on 1870-CC half eagles, with the mintmark small and compact and placed close to the eagle. The first C is higher than the second and there is a die defect under the S in TRUST in the banner. This variety always shows a weakly struck reverse, especially on the breast feathers of the eagle. It appears to be the most common of the three varieties known.

Variety 2-B: On this obverse, the date appears more widely spaced than on Variety 1-A and with considerable space between the 8 and the 7. The date slants down to the right. This obverse is usually seen with considerably better detail at the center than on Variety 1-A. The reverse has a slightly lower mintmark with the two C's being more or less level. This reverse was also used to strike the Variety 1-A 1872-CC half eagles. This is the best struck of the three varieties for this year but it is characterized by weakness on the reverse milling from 7:00 to 10:00.

Variety 2-A: This variety combines the obverse seen on the second variety of this year with the reverse from the first. Only one or two have been seen and it appears that it is very rare.

RARITY:
   Total Known: 55-65

BY GRADE:

VF	EF	AU	MINT STATE
38-44	10-13	5-6	2

CONDITION CENSUS:

1. Legend Numismatics/Chris Napolitano, ex: Goldberg 10/00: 915 ($48,300), The Mint (Jay Parrino), Bowers and Merena 10/99: 1188 ($66,125), Harry Bass collection, Stack's 1976 ANA: 2998. Graded Mint State-62 by PCGS.

2. Nevada collection (7/97), ex: Doug Winter, California dealer, Eastern dealer, Charley Tuppen collection. Graded Mint State-61 by PCGS. *The plate coin in this book.*

3 (tie). Private collection, ex: Bowers and Merena 10/99: 1189 ($23,000), Harry Bass collection, Rarcoa 4/72: 647. Graded About Uncirculated-55 by PCGS.

• Private collection via Tony Terranova, ex: Bowers and Merena 5/00: 511 ($32,200), Harry Bass collection, Stack's 12/78: 184 ($1,900), Harold Bareford collection, King Farouk collection. Graded About Uncirculated-55 by PCGS.

4. Private collection, ex: Lee Minshull, Heritage Rare Coin Galleries 1997. Graded About Uncirculated-55 by NGC.

5. Chicago collection, ex: Doug Winter, 8/97. Graded About Uncirculated-50 by NGC.

A small group of Extremely Fine-45 coins exist including those listed in the Condition Census of "Gold Coins of the Old West" and the following new pieces:

• Alaskan collector. Graded Extremely Fine-45 by PCGS.

• New Jersey collection 10/99, ex: Doug Winter/Lee Minshull, Heritage 4/99: 5920 ($7,762; as PCGS EF-40). Graded Extremely Fine-45 by PCGS.

• Bowers and Merena 10/99: 1190 ($9,775), ex: Harry Bass collection. Graded Extremely Fine-45 by PCGS.

• Bowers and Merena 11/00: 518 ($9,200), ex: Harry Bass collection, Stack's 12/70: 231.

Three other coins have been graded Extremely Fine-45 by PCGS as of March 2001.

The 1873-CC is the second rarest Carson City half eagle in terms of overall rarity and it is one of the rarest half eagles from this mint in high grades as well. When available, it is typically seen with considerable wear. A coin that grades Extremely Fine-40 is quite scarce while an accurately graded Extremely Fine-45 is rare. This issue is very rare in About Uncirculated with around a half dozen known. Surprisingly, there are currently two Mint State 1873-CC half eagles known to exist.

1874-CC

MINTAGE: 21,198
RARITY RANKINGS:
  Overall Rarity: 11th of 19
  High Grade Rarity: 10th of 19

The 1874-CC half eagle is slightly more available than the 1871-CC. This makes it the most available Carson City half eagle struck before 1879. It is, however, a much harder coin to obtain than any of the post-1878 issues with the exception of the 1881-CC.

STRIKE: The quality of strike found on the 1874-CC half eagle is a bit better than on the 1872-CC and the 1873-CC. While most show significant weakness, enough are known with a decent strike that the patient collector will be able to obtain an example that is well detailed. Nearly all 1874-CC half eagles are weak on the top of Liberty's head but most are well detailed at the obverse center. For some reason, many show significant weakness along the right side of the head and at the corresponding reverse. It is typical for an example to appear more worn on the obverse than the reverse, making this a hard coin to properly grade. On well struck coins, the reverse will appear quite well detailed, with the eagle's feathers showing nearly full definition. The neck feathers, however, are often weak as is the mintmark.

SURFACES: Most 1874-CC half eagles show heavily abraded surfaces. It is possible to locate an example that is not riddled with marks (as are most pre-1880 half eagles from this mint) but such coins are very scarce and worth a strong premium. Depending on the variety (see below), there will be a number of mint-made marks on the surfaces, including a raised die mark on the bridge of Liberty's nose, clashmarks and/or die scratches. These should not be confused with defects or impairments.

LUSTER: The luster on uncleaned, original pieces is soft and frosty. A few slightly reflective coins are known as well. Most 1874-CC half eagles are worn to the point that no luster remains. It is very unusual to find high grade survivors that have not been cleaned or dipped.

COLORATION: The original coloration is most often rich yellow-gold with faint coppery hues. Only a small handful of uncleaned pieces with full, natural color still exist.

EYE APPEAL: The overall eye appeal of the 1874-CC is much better than the 1870-CC to 1873-CC half eagles. However, it is still very difficult to find an example that combines a good strike with reasonably clean surfaces, original color and remaining luster. Any piece with good eye appeal routinely sells for a large premium over a typical quality piece.

DIE VARIETIES: There are at least six die varieties currently known. It is possible that other combinations of these varieties exist.

Variety 1-A: The date is large and it slants slightly downwards. There is a prominent raised die mark on the bridge of the nose and a thin die scratch through the I in LIBERTY. The mintmark is widely spaced and level. It is positioned over the V in FIVE. Most examples of this variety show a clashmark from the eagle's beak to its right wing.

Variety 1-B: On this variety, the mintmark is closely spaced and the second C is higher than the first. The placement of the mintmark is further to the right with the second C over the VE in FIVE. The mintmark is sometimes extremely faint on this variety.

Variety 1-C: On this variety, the two C's are level and centered below the eagle. The mintmark is more sharply impressed than on Reverse A or Reverse B and it appears to be slightly larger as well. There is a very obvious clashmark from the eagle's lower beak to the right wing. Many show four raised die scratches above the right wing.

Variety 2-D: The date is placed very slightly differently than on the other obverse. There is no raised die mark on the bridge of the nose as on the other obverse nor is there the die scratch through the I in LIBERTY. The reverse is a reuse of 1872-CC Reverse B but with two clashmarks from the eagle's beak to its right wing.

Variety 2-B, Variety 2-C: These varieties combine the obverse and reverse described above.

RARITY:
Total Known: 125-135

BY GRADE:

VF	EF	AU	MINT STATE
86-89	25-28	12-15	2-3

CONDITION CENSUS:

1. Private collection, ex: Bowers and Merena 6/91: 1512 ($29,700). Graded Mint State-62 by PCGS.

2. Nevada collection, ex: Doug Winter/Lee Minshull (11/96), Dr. Larry Cutler collection, Stack's 10/93: 995 ($20,900), Reed Hawn, Stack's 2/79: 498, Ellis Robison collection. Graded Mint State-62 by PCGS. *The plate coin in this book.*

3 (tie). The Mint (Jay Parrino), ex: Bowers and Merena 10/99: 1196 ($20,700), Harry Bass collection, Superior 2/73: 493. Graded About Uncirculated-58 by PCGS.

• Martin Paul/Casey Noxon, ex: Bowers and Merena 11/00: 522 ($13,800), Harry Bass collection, Stack's 12/70: 232. Graded About Uncirculated-58 by PCGS.

• Washington D.C. collection, ex: Doug Winter/Lee Minshull, Heritage 11/00: 7140 ($13,225), Nevada dealer, Bowers and Merena 1/99: 1419 ($20,700; as PCGS About Uncirculated-55). Graded About Uncirculated-58 by PCGS.

4 (tie). Chicago collection, ex: Doug Winter, Nevada collection duplicate. Graded About Uncirculated-55 by PCGS.

• Bowers and Merena 5/00: 513 ($9,775), ex: Harry Bass collection, Stack's 10/68: 496, R.L. Miles collection. Graded About Uncirculated-55 by PCGS.

• Dr. Nate Sonnheim collection, ex: Monex Rare Coins inventory, 6/98, Minnesota dealer, Minnesota collection, Doug Winter, North Carolina collector. Graded About Uncirculated-55 by PCGS.

• Mid American Rare Coin Galleries, ex: Bowers and Merena 10/99: 1197 ($10,350; as PCGS AU-53), Harry Bass collection, Paramount 5/66: 565. Graded About Uncirculated-55 by PCGS.

• New Jersey collection, ex: Doug Winter/Lee Minshull 6/99, Spectrum Numismatics. Graded About Uncirculated-55 by NGC.

• Private collection, ex: Doug Winter/Lee Minshull 8/99. Graded About Uncirculated-55 by NGC.

I am aware of approximately four or five examples which grade About Uncirculated-50 or slightly better. These include the following:

• Bowers and Merena 11/00: 523 ($8,050), ex: Harry Bass collection, purchased from Ed Shapiro on 12/28/71. Graded About Uncirculated-53 by PCGS.

• Heritage 9/99: 6712 ($6,900), ex: Pennsylvania Collection, Doug Winter/Lee Minshull inventory, 11/97, Orange County collection. Graded About Uncirculated-53 by NGC.

• Private collection, ex: Liz Arlin, Doug Winter, Wyoming collector, Bowers and Merena 1/88: 554. Graded About Uncirculated-50 by NGC.

• Private collection, ex: Texas dealer, Doug Winter/Lee Minshull inventory, 9/97. Graded About Uncirculated-50 by NGC.

A few other About Uncirculated-50 coins exist.

The 1874-CC half eagle is (along with the 1871-CC) one of only two "early date" issues from this mint that is reasonably easy to obtain in lower grades. When available, examples tend to be well worn. The 1874-CC becomes scarce in the higher Extremely Fine grades and it is rare in the lower range of About Uncirculated. In About Uncirculated-55 and above it is very rare and it is an extremely rare issue in Mint State.

1875-CC

MINTAGE: 11,828
RARITY RANKINGS:
    Overall Rarity: 8th of 19 (tie)
    High Grade Rarity: 5th of 19

For a number of years, the 1875-CC was regarded as a major rarity within the Carson City half eagle series; on a par with such issues as the 1872-CC and the 1873-CC. This changed when a number of examples, mostly in the Very Fine to Extremely Fine range, became available in the early to mid-1990's. The rarity of the 1875-CC half eagle in high grades remains undisputed.

STRIKE: This is one of the worst struck Carson City half eagles. For some unknown reason, quality control for both half eagles and eagles was very low in 1875 and, as a result, both are found with poor strikes. On the typical 1875-CC half eagle, the obverse is found with a very flat strike; usually quite a bit more so than the reverse. Liberty's hair and bun are often seen with almost no individual detail. Surprisingly, the stars and denticles are much better struck and many have full radial lines in the stars. The reverse is often very weak at the center with many having almost no detail on the neck feathers and on the horizontal lines in the shield. The claws are sometimes weak but many that are flat at the centers are surprisingly well defined on the claws as well as on the lettering and the denticles.

SURFACES: The vast majority of 1875-CC half eagles show heavily abraded surfaces. I have seen a number that have mint-made planchet problems and at least two or three with black grease stains in the fields. I have also seen a number that showed scratches in the fields and noticeable edge bumps.

LUSTER: The luster is above average and it is satiny in texture. A few show slightly reflective semi-prooflike fields. There are only a handful of 1875-CC half eagles that have not been cleaned or numismatically abused.

COLORATION: The natural coloration can range from a blend of greenish-gold and orange to a medium rose hue. There are very few left that have original color.

EYE APPEAL: The typical 1875-CC half eagle has below average eye appeal. This is primarily because so many are poorly struck. Any piece that is sharply detailed and has original color and luster is very rare and worth a strong premium over a typical quality example.

DIE VARIETIES: Two obverse and three reverse dies were used to strike 1875-CC half eagles. There are presently four die varieties known; other combinations of these dies could exist.

Variety 1-A. The date is centered and level. Most coins struck from this obverse show noticeable weakness on the hair of Liberty; especially on the bun. The reverse has a mintmark that is close and level. The second C is above the VE in FIVE. It was struck with a rusted die and die rust is visible around UNITED and the right side of the eagle. A large rust pit can be seen below ED in UNITED on the later die state.

Variety 1-B. The obverse is the same as on the previous variety. The reverse has a mintmark that is more widely spaced than on Reverse A and the second letter is much lower than the first. The second C is over the left side of the E in FIVE. This reverse appears to have been struck from a doubled die with this doubling most noticeable on FIVE D. In the later die state of Variety 1-B, this doubling fades. The overall quality of strike seen on Variety 1-B is fairly sharp, especially at the centers.

Variety 2-B. The date is higher than on the first variety and it is positioned off center towards the viewer's left. This variety generally shows a poorer quality of strike than Variety 1-B with weakness often seen at the center of the reverse; especially on the breast of the eagle and the horizontal lines in the shield.

Variety 2-C. On this variety, the mintmark is nearly level and it is positioned very high. The reverse differs from that seen on Variety 1-A as it lacks the aforementioned die rust and the pit below ED in UNITED. In addition, the mintmark is much further to the right with the second C above the middle of the E in FIVE. It is currently the rarest variety of the year with just a single coin known to exist.

RARITY:
    Total Known: 85-95

BY GRADE:

VF	EF	AU	MINT STATE
55-60	20-22	8-11	2

CONDITION CENSUS:

1. Chicago collection, ex: Doug Winter/Lee Minshull, 12/96, Dr. Larry Cutler collection via Winthrop Carner private treaty sale, 1992. Graded Mint State-63 by NGC.

2. Nevada collection, ex: Bob Leece/Larry Demerer, 6/97. Graded Mint State-61 by PCGS. *The plate coin in this book.*

3. Texas Numismatic Investments Incorporated (Casey Noxon), ex: Superior 10/00: 4631 ($14,375), The Mint (Jay Parrino), Bowers and Merena 10/99: 1201 ($23,000; as PCGS AU-55), Harry Bass collection, Paramount Auction '86: 1922 ($3,520). Graded About Uncirculated-58 by NGC.

4 (tie). Eastern dealer inventory, first seen 4/97. Graded About Uncirculated-55 by NGC.

- One coin has been graded About Uncirculated-55 by PCGS as of March 2001.

- Monex inventory, ex: Superior 3/00: 884 (unsold), Monex. Graded About Uncirculated-58 by NGC.

5. Alaska collection. Graded About Uncirculated-53 by PCGS and choice for the grade.

I am aware of the following coins that grade About Uncirculated-53 or thereabouts:

- Washington, D.C. collection, ex: Doug Winter. Graded About Uncirculated-53 by NGC.

- Private collection, ex: Texas dealer via Doug Winter/Lee Minshull, 11/97, Orange County collection. Graded About Uncirculated-53 by PCGS.

- Superior 2/99: 3234 ($9,200). Graded About Uncirculated-53 by PCGS.

- Superior Stamp and Coin/Mike Byers, ex: Heritage 1999 FUN: 8108 ($9,488), Spectrum Numismatics, Bowers and Merena 5/98: 1357 ($15,400), Massachusetts collection, Doug Winter/Lee Minshull, Heritage 2/95: 5863 ($6,050; as PCGS AU-50), Superior 9/93: 1908. Graded About Uncirculated-55 by NGC.

- Heritage 1/98: 7822 ($7,360). Graded About Uncirculated-53 by PCGS.

- Superior 1/96: 2362 ($7,700). Graded About Uncirculated-53 by PCGS.

The 1875-CC half eagle is nearly always seen in very low grades. This was clearly an issue that saw considerable circulation and most survivors grade Extremely Fine-40 or below. The 1875-CC becomes very scarce in Extremely Fine-45 and it is rare in the lower About Uncirculated grades. This is a very rare coin in the higher About Uncirculated grades and there are currently just two known in Mint State.

1876-CC

MINTAGE: 6,887
RARITY RANKINGS:
    Overall Rarity: 7th of 19
    High Grade Rarity: 6th of 19

The mintage figure for this date is lower than for any other half eagle from the Carson City mint. Despite this fact, the 1876-CC is not an especially well-known issue and it is generally not accorded a high degree of respect. Still, it is a very scarce coin in all grades.

STRIKE: This is a much better struck issue than the 1875-CC. On the obverse, the detail is generally good although it is not uncommon to find examples with weakness on the bun and at the top of Liberty's hair. The stars and the denticles are nearly complete while the hair is sharp with the exception of the curl below the ear. The reverse is a bit less sharp with weakness often found on the neck of the eagle, the inner portion of the tip of the left wing and the top of the legs and claws. Every 1876-CC half eagle that I have ever seen shows distinctly bevelled edges on both the obverse and the reverse.

SURFACES: The surfaces are usually heavily abraded with deep, detracting marks in the fields and on the devices. There are a number that have mint-made planchet flaws. I have seen four or five 1876-CC half eagles with small black streaks in the planchet. Every known example has a small raised die lump on the neck of Liberty, just below the jaw. Interestingly, similar die lumps can be found on 1876 Philadelphia and San Francisco quarter eagles.

LUSTER: The luster is typically frosty and a few high grade pieces are known with semi-prooflike fields. The luster tends to be of a higher quality than on the earlier half eagles from this mint. Many 1876-CC half eagles have been cleaned and locating an example that has original luster is extremely challenging.

COLORATION: The coloration seen on original, uncleaned 1876-CC half eagles can be outstanding. Many have very attractive rich yellow-gold coloration and this can be accentuated by rose and coppery-orange splashes. As more and more 19th century gold coins are cleaned or dipped, locating an example with natural coloration has become increasingly difficult.

EYE APPEAL: The 1876-CC tends to be among the best looking Carson City half eagles from the 1870's. It generally shows an above-average strike and there are a small number of extremely pleasing coins available. One of these, a superb gem discussed in the Condition Census section below, is the single finest Carson City half eagle of any date that I have seen or am aware of.

DIE VARIETIES: Only a single variety is known.

Variety 1-A: The date is level and somewhat low in the field. The mintmark is close and level. The edge of the arrow feather rests midway between the first and the second C. Many show light machine doubling on FIVE D. But this is not as pronounced as on some of the half eagles struck at the Carson City mint earlier in the 1870's.

RARITY:
Total Known: 80-90

BY GRADE:

VF	EF	AU	MINT STATE
48-54	20-23	10-11	2

CONDITION CENSUS:

1. Private collection, ex: Superior 5/91: 1390, Superior 5/90: 5598 ($121,000), David Akers' session of Auction '89: 1395, Andy Lustig, Joe Kuehnert, Melnick 11/83 sale, Bowers and Ruddy Eliasberg (10/82): 540, John Clapp, Chapman Brothers (1893). Graded Mint State-65 by PCGS; graded Mint State-64 and Mint State-65 by both services at various times. The listings for a Mint State-64 and a Mint State-65 in the NGC "Census Report" are both for this coin. It remains the finest Carson City gold coin of any denomination that I have ever seen.

2. Northern California collection, ex: Bowers and Merena 10/99: 1207 ($26,450), Harry Bass collection, Rowe & Brownlee 8/4/70. Graded About Uncirculated-58 by PCGS.

3. Nevada collection, ex: Heritage 10/94: 6776 ($8,580). Graded About Uncirculated-58 by PCGS. *The plate coin in this book.*

4 (tie). Tahoe collection, ex: Doug Winter/Lee Minshull (11/96), Dr. Larry Cutler collection, Doug Winter, Heritage 10/94: 6775 ($6,820). Graded About Uncirculated-55 by PCGS.

 • Tennessee collection via The Mint (Jay Parrino), ex: Bowers and Merena 5/00: 517 ($14,950), Harry Bass collection, Stack's 5/70: 934, Gaston DiBello collection. Graded About Uncirculated-55 by PCGS.

5 (tie).   Texas collection, ex: Austin Rare Coins, Casey Noxon, Lee Minshull, 7/98. Graded About Uncirculated-58 by NGC.

 • Gillio 2/00: 41 ($12,660). Graded About Uncirculated-58 by NGC.

Three to five pieces grade About Uncirculated-53. These are as follows:

 • Delaware Valley Rare Coins inventory, 6/00. Graded About Uncirculated-53 by PCGS. Possibly the same coin as the next.

• Heritage 1/00: 5492 ($9,200). About Uncirculated-53 or better.

• Chicago collection, ex: Doug Winter/Lee Minshull 11/95, Winthrop Carner, North Carolina collection. Graded About Uncirculated-53 by PCGS.

• Private collection, ex: Eastern dealer 9/97, Charley Tuppen collection. Graded About Uncirculated-53 by PCGS; earlier graded the same by NGC.

• Private collection, ex: Doug Winter/Lee Minshull, 11/97. Graded About Uncirculated-53 by PCGS.

NOTE: As of March 2001, PCGS shows two additional coins graded About Uncirculated-55 which are probably not the same as the pair of coins listed as #4 above; I am not aware of their location or pedigree. They may actually be resubmissions of one (or more) of the coins listed above.

The 1876-CC has the lowest mintage figure of any Carson City half eagle. It is a scarce coin in all grades and the majority of survivors fall in the Very Fine-Extremely Fine range. There are fewer than a dozen About Uncirculated pieces known, as well as two pieces that grade Mint State.

1877-CC

MINTAGE: 8,680
RARITY RANKINGS:
Overall Rarity: 8th of 19 (tie)
High Grade Rarity: 7th of 19

While comparable in rarity to such dates as the 1872-CC, 1875-CC and 1876-CC, this is an issue that is curiously overlooked. It is very hard to find in any grade and in high grades it is very rare.

STRIKE: The quality of strike seen on the typical example is not really sharp but it is still better than that seen on most of the 1873-76 Carson City half eagles. On the obverse, the top of Liberty's hair, the hair bun, and the curls around the face and ear are often weak. The borders are a bit sharper. The stars often show much of their radial line definition while the denticles are fairly sharp and well separated. The reverse is nearly always quite weak on the neck of the eagle, the top of the shield, and the arrow feather. Some examples have weakness at the denticles; most often in the area of 9:00 to 1:00.

SURFACES: Like nearly all of the Carson City half eagles from the 1870's, the 1877-CC is invariably found with very heavily abraded surfaces. These coins saw heavy use in local commerce and were handled very roughly between the time that they were struck and when they were released into circulation. A good number are hairlined or unnaturally bright from numismatic abuse.

LUSTER: Because most 1877-CC half eagles are well worn, this issue is not often seen with much original mint luster. High grade pieces show good frosty luster with a slightly subdued satiny texture in the fields.

COLORATION: The natural coloration for the 1877-CC half eagle is greenish-gold with rose or medium orange-gold overtones. Not many that survive that retain their original coloration and such pieces command a strong premium over the typical cleaned or dipped coin.

EYE APPEAL: This is another issue that is very hard to find with good eye appeal. Many 1877-CC half eagles are weakly struck, show severe surface impairments, and have been cleaned. However, I have seen some reasonably attractive examples in the Extremely Fine-40 to About Uncirculated-50 range and would anticipate that the patient collector should be able to find a satisfactory piece given enough time.

DIE VARIETIES: Two die varieties are known.

Variety 1-A. The same obverse die was used to strike all 1877-CC half eagles. The date is placed somewhat low in the field and it slants slightly downwards. On this first variety, the mintmark is fairly compact and it is placed high in the field. The second C is much lower than the first and it is placed wholly above the E in FIVE.

Variety 1-B. On this variety, the mintmark is placed higher than on Reverse A. The letters are level and the second C is placed above the right edge of the V and the left edge of the E in FIVE.

It is not known which of these two varieties is scarcer.

RARITY:
Total Known: 85-95

BY GRADE:

VF	EF	AU	MINT STATE
55-59	18-22	11-13	1

CONDITION CENSUS:

1. Monex / Bob Leece, ex: Bowers and Merena 10/99: 1212 ($46,000; as PCGS MS-60), Harry Bass collection, Mike Brownlee 10/7/72. Graded Mint State-62 by PCGS.

2. Private collection, ex: Eastern dealer, Charley Tuppen collection, possibly ex: Stack's 6/89: 522. Graded About Uncirculated-58 by NGC.

3. Nevada collection, ex: Winthrop Carner via private treaty in 1995, earlier in a North Carolina collection. Graded About Uncirculated-58 by PCGS. *The plate coin in this book.*

4 (tie). Chicago collection, ex: Doug Winter, Heritage Rare Coin Galleries, Heritage 6/94: 1115 (unsold). Graded About Uncirculated-55 by NGC.

• Midwestern collection, ex: unknown dealer, Lee Minshull, Heritage Rare Coin Galleries 8/97. Graded About Uncirculated-55 by PCGS.

5 (tie). Private collection, ex: Doug Winter, Nevada collection. Graded About Uncirculated-53 by PCGS.

• New Jersey collection, ex: Doug Winter/Lee Minshull 1/00, Monex Rare Coins. Graded About Uncirculated-55 by NGC.

NOTE: NGC, as of January 2001, lists a second About Uncirculated-58 coin; I am not certain if this is a resubmission of coin #2 above or if it is another example.

PCGS has graded two other coins About Uncirculated-55 as of March 2001 and NGC had graded one other About Uncirculated-55 as of January 2001; I am unaware of the location and pedigree of these.

The 1877-CC half eagle is a scarce issue in all grades. When available, the typical coin grades Very Fine to low-end Extremely Fine. This date becomes very scarce in Extremely Fine-45 and it is rare in the lower About Uncirculated grades. In the higher AU grades, the 1877-CC is extremely rare and it is currently unique in Mint State.

1878-CC

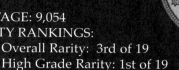

MINTAGE: 9,054
RARITY RANKINGS:
    Overall Rarity: 3rd of 19
    High Grade Rarity: 1st of 19

The 1878-CC is one of the rarest Carson City half eagles. It is also the rarest half eagle from this mint in higher grades and one of two issues (along with the 1872-CC) that is currently unknown in Mint State.

STRIKE: This is not a well struck issue. Most 1878-CC half eagles show an overall softness which can easily be confused with wear. The obverse is nearly always at least a full grade lower in appearance than the reverse. On the obverse, the hair near the ear and around the face of Liberty is very weak as is the top of the hair and the bun. The stars are sharper than one might imagine but the denticles are weak and sometimes appear fuzzy and indistinct. The reverse shows a sharper impression but always has noticeable weakness on the neck of the eagle. The denticles are often weak and may also have a fuzzy appearance.

SURFACES: The surfaces on most 1878-CC half eagles are heavily abraded. These marks are often situated in very obvious places (such as the face of Liberty or the obverse fields) and tend to be deep. I have seen a number of 1878-CC half eagles that had mint-made problems such as laminations or grease stains as well. This is one of the hardest Carson City half eagles to find with smooth, even surfaces.

LUSTER: The 1878-CC has poor quality luster, partly because the way that this issue was prepared and partly because most show so much wear that they have little or no remaining mint luster. On the few high grade coins that exist, the luster is soft and slightly satiny in its texture. I would estimate that as many as 90% of the surviving 1878-CC half eagles have been cleaned at one time.

COLORATION: The natural coloration seen on this issue is medium gold or green-gold. Some show medium to deep rose undertones. As mentioned above, since so many 1878-CC half eagles have been cleaned, it is extremely hard to locate one that has original coloration.

EYE APPEAL: This is an issue that is extremely difficult to find with good eye appeal. Most 1878-CC half eagles are heavily worn and have been cleaned. In addition, many are not well struck and have mint-made planchet problems. I can not recall having seen more than a half dozen examples that, in my opinion, had good overall eye appeal.

DIE VARIETIES: There is just one die variety known.

Variety 1-A. The date is placed somewhat low in the field and it slants downwards from left to right. The mintmark is even and somewhat compact. The edge of the arrow feather is located over the right side of the first C.

RARITY:
Total Known: 60-70

BY GRADE:

VF	EF	AU	MINT STATE
44-50	13-15	3-5	0

CONDITION CENSUS:

1. Private collection via Colorado dealer, ex: Heritage 9/99: 6715 ($24,150; as PCGS AU-55), Pennsylvania collection, Doug Winter/Lee Minshull, 11/97, Orange County collection, Doug Winter/Lee Minshull (10/96), Dr. Larry Cutler collection, Winthrop Carner, Superior 9/93: 1911 ($24,200; as PCGS AU-50). Graded About Uncirculated-58 by PCGS. *The plate coin in the first edition of this book.*

2 (tie). Private collection, ex: Eastern dealer, Charley Tuppen collection. Graded About Uncirculated-55 by NGC.

• The Mint (Jay Parrino) inventory, 2000, possibly ex: Bowers and Merena 10/99: 1216 ($17,250; as PCGS AU-50), Harry Bass collection, from Paramount via private sale 2/68. Graded About Uncirculated-58 by NGC.

• Texas collection, ex: Austin Rare Coins, Casey Noxon. Graded About Uncirculated-55 by NGC.

3. Nevada collection. Graded About Uncirculated-55 by PCGS. *The plate coin in this book.*

4. Private collection. Graded About Uncirculated-53 by PCGS.

5 (tie) Washington D.C. collection, ex: Doug Winter. Graded About Uncirculated-53 by NGC.

NGC had graded another coin About Uncirculated-53 as of January 2001.

As of March 2001, PCGS had graded five examples in About Uncirculated-50 while NGC had recorded five in this grade as of January 2001. These include the following:

• Heritage 1996 ANA: 8352 ($15,950). Graded About Uncirculated-50 by PCGS.

• Stack's 11/94: 1456 ($11,000). Graded About Uncirculated-50 by NGC.

• Heritage 1994 ANA: 7458 ($14,300). Graded About Uncirculated-50 by NGC.

The 1878-CC is among the rarest half eagles from this mint. It is usually seen in Fine to Very Fine grades and an accurately graded Extremely Fine-40 is about as nice an example as is generally available to the collector. This date is very scarce in Extremely Fine-45 and it is a rarity in About Uncirculated. I am aware of no more than three to five that grade About Uncirculated and none of these, in my opinion, grade higher than About Uncirculated-55.

1879-CC

MINTAGE: 17,281
RARITY RANKINGS:
    Overall Rarity: 13th of 19
    High Grade Rarity: 13th of 19

The 1879-CC is the first Carson City half eagle that is relatively easy to obtain, especially in lower grades. While it is not hard to locate in lower grades, it is very scarce in the higher circulated grades and extremely rare in full Mint State.

STRIKE: Most 1879-CC half eagles show a good overall quality of strike. The obverse is generally quite sharp, although the typical example shows some weakness on the top of Liberty's head, the bun and some of the curls around the face. On some, there may be minor weakness on the denticles. Most show a prominent mint-made die scratch through the bottom right serif of the E in LIBERTY. The reverse is usually the sharper of the two sides. It is not uncommon for the reverse of an 1879-CC half eagle to have extremely sharp detail on the neck and legs of the eagle.

SURFACES: This issue appears to have been well circulated. As a result, most are very heavily abraded with a somewhat "scuffy" appearance. A few higher grade pieces are known that have relatively clean surfaces and these command a strong premium among specialists.

LUSTER: The luster on this issue is above average in relation to other Carson City half eagles from this decade. It is frosty in texture with a soft, warm appearance.

COLORATION: The natural coloration is a rich yellow-gold with greenish overtones. A number of 1879-CC half eagles are known that have very dark, somewhat dirty hues. These pieces are from a small hoard that entered the market in the early to mid-1990's.

EYE APPEAL: The collector is more likely to find an appealing 1879-CC half eagle than any other issue from the 1870's. It is definitely possible to locate an original example with a good strike, acceptable surfaces and nice overall appearance. However, high end coins are becoming harder to locate as more and more are cleaned or dipped.

DIE VARIETIES: There are two die varieties known.

Variety 1-A. The date is well spaced between the base of the neck and the denticles. There is no die scratch noted through the bottom right serif of the E in LIBERTY. On late die states of this variety, there is noticeable doubling of the mintmark.

Variety 2-A. The date is very slightly higher and positioned differently than on Variety 1-A. This variety is immediately identifiable by a die scratch through the bottom right serif of the E in LIBERTY.

RARITY:

Total Known: 200-250

BY GRADE:

VF	EF	AU	MINT STATE
103-140	60-72	25-35	2-3

CONDITION CENSUS:

1. Colorado collection, ex: Heritage 9/99: 6715 ($17,250), Pennsylvania Collection, 8/98, Doug Winter/Lee Minshull, Superior 5/89: 1913 ($4,400). Graded Mint State-61 by NGC.

2. Nevada collection, ex: West Coast dealer, 10/97. Graded Mint State-61 by PCGS. *The plate coin in this book.*

3 (tie). Eastern dealer, ex: Bowers and Merena 11/98: 2316 ($11,500). Graded Mint State-60 by NGC.

- Superior Stamp and Coin inventory, ex: Bowers and Merena 10/99: 1219 ($11,500; as PCGS AU-55), Harry Bass collection, Bowers and Merena Norweb collection sale (10/87), Part One: 902; from J.C. Morganthau 10/11/35. Graded Mint State-60 by NGC.

4. Chicago collection, ex: Doug Winter/Lee Minshull 9/94, Paul Nugget, David Akers. Graded About Uncirculated-58 by PCGS.

5 (tie). California collection 7/00, ex: Doug Winter/Lee Minshull, Kingswood 6/00: 618 (unsold), Doug Winter/Lee Minshull, Bowers and Merena 10/99: 1218 ($8,050; as PCGS AU-55), Harry Bass collection, Paramount 1969 ANA: 2001. Graded About Uncirculated-58 by PCGS.

- Bowers and Merena 1/01: 522, ex: Heritage 2/99: 6310 ($10,350). Graded About Uncirculated-58 by PCGS.

- Heritage 6/98: 6372 ($13,225). Graded About Uncirculated-58 by NGC.

The following coins just miss the Condition Census but are still worthy of mention:

- Oregon collection, ex: Doug Winter, Nevada collection duplicate, North Carolina collection, Doug Winter/Winthrop Carner, Bowers and Merena 9/93: 1085 ($4,620). Graded About Uncirculated-58 by PCGS.

• Private collection, ex: Western dealer, Eastern dealer, Charley Tuppen collection. Graded About Uncirculated-58 by PCGS.

• Heritage 6/96: 7347 ($4,730). Graded About Uncirculated-58 by NGC.

• Private collection, ex: Blanchard & Co., Doug Winter/Lee Minshull, 10/96, Dr. Larry Cutler collection. Graded About Uncirculated-58 by NGC.

• Washington D.C. collection, ex: Doug Winter. Graded About Uncirculated-58 by NGC.

The 1879-CC is the most obtainable Carson City half eagle from the 1870's. It is relatively easy to locate in lower grades and is not even that hard to obtain in the lower range of About Uncirculated. This date becomes rare in the higher About Uncirculated grades and it is extremely rare in Mint State. I am aware of just two or three Uncirculated 1879-CC half eagles and none of these grade higher than Mint State-61.

1880-CC

MINTAGE: 51,107
RARITY RANKINGS:
  Overall Rarity: 14th of 19
  High Grade Rarity: 14th of 19

The mintage figure for this date is significantly greater than for any of the ten prior half eagles from the Carson City mint. The 1880-CC is scarcer in overall rarity than its mintage would suggest but a surprisingly high number of survivors are known in higher grades.

STRIKE: The quality of strike is similar to that found on the 1879-CC half eagle. Many 1880-CC half eagles show a very sharp strike. There may be some weakness on the hairbun and the curls around the face of Liberty, but still the 1880-CC tends to be among the best struck Carson City half eagles from this decade.

SURFACES: The vast majority of 1880-CC half eagles have extensively abraded surfaces. These marks are often deep and situated in noticeable areas, such as on the cheek of Liberty or in the fields close to the face. A number of examples have copper spots. These are not considered detracting unless they are severe or poorly situated. Most 1880-CC half eagles have raised mint-made obverse die marks (see "Die Varieties," below, for more information) which should not be confused with abrasions or damage.

LUSTER: The luster on this issue varies. Many higher grade examples have frosty luster while a few are known with semi-prooflike reflectiveness. Original, uncleaned pieces are easier to locate than many other pre-1890 half eagles from this mint, but are getting more difficult with each passing year.

COLORATION: The natural coloration seen on 1880-CC half eagles is most often a medium yellow-gold with strong green-gold undertones. There are some known that show attractive deep natural coloration and these trade at a premium among knowledgeable specialists.

EYE APPEAL: The level of eye appeal seen on the typical 1880-CC half eagle is better than on any Carson City half eagle struck prior to 1890 with the possible exception of the 1882-CC. Many are very well struck and show a good amount of luster. Still, locating clean examples with original coloration is not as easy as a few years ago.

DIE VARIETIES: There are three die varieties currently known. I would not be surprised if one or two others existed.

Variety 1-A: The date is placed slightly below midway between the neck and the denticles below. There are raised mint-made die marks above and below the eye of Liberty, near the mouth and on the neck. The mintmark is small, compact and placed close to the eagle. The second C is directly over the right serif of the V in FIVE.

Variety 1-B: The obverse is the same as on Variety 1-A. The mintmark is slightly lower than on Reverse A. The second C in the mintmark is directly over the space between V and E and the point of the arrow feather is over the end of the first C. This variety is most easily identifiable by a raised circular die mark just below the tip of the eagle's right wing.

Variety 2-C: The date position is very similar on this variety to that seen on Obverse 1. Liberty appears to be "crying" due to the presence of a series or raised die marks that appear as "tears" streaming from the eye of Liberty. The mintmark is lower than on the other two reverses and positioned over the left and right serifs of the V in FIVE.

RARITY:

Total Known: 275-325+

BY GRADE:

VF	EF	AU	MINT STATE
132-142	88-116	49-59	6-8

CONDITION CENSUS:

1 (tie). Nevada collection, ex: Doug Winter/Lee Minshull, 10/96, Dr. Larry Cutler collection. Graded Mint State-62 by PCGS. *The plate coin in this book.*

• Texas Numismatic Investments (Casey Noxon), ex: Bowers and Merena 5/00: 527 ($13,800), Harry Bass collection, Bowers and Merena 10/87: 905 ($1,980), Norweb collection, Kosoff 4/56: 2173. Graded Mint State-62 by PCGS.

• Midwestern collection. Graded Mint State-62 by NGC.

2 (tie). Private collection, ex: New York dealer, Charley Tuppen collection. Graded Mint State-61 by NGC.

• Private collection via Blanchard & Co. 12/99, ex: Doug Winter/Lee Minshull 4/99, Heritage Rare Coin Galleries inventory, 7/98, Bob Leece. Graded Mint State-61 by NGC.

• Bowers and Merena 3/01: 147 ($9,200), ex: unknown dealer(s), Lee Minshull 2/00. Graded Mint State-61 by NGC.

• New Jersey collection, ex: Doug Winter/Lee Minshull 5/00, ex: Heritage Rare Coin Galleries, Bowers and Merena 10/99: 1222 ($8,050; as PCGS AU-58), Harry Bass collection, Superior 2/75: 1212, Dr. Charles Ruby collection. Graded Mint State-61 by NGC.

• Texas collection, ex: Austin Rare Coins, Casey Noxon. Graded Mint State-61 by NGC.

3 (tie). At least four or five more certified Uncirculated coins are known to exist. These are as follows:

• Private collection 12/99, ex: Doug Winter/Lee Minshull, Spectrum Numismatics 7/99, David Carr. Graded Mint State-61 by PCGS.

• Chicago collection, ex: Doug Winter/Lee Minshull, 11/97. Graded Mint State-60 by NGC.

• Upstate New York collection. Graded Mint State-60 by PCGS.

• Private collection, ex: Heritage 9/99: 6719 ($7,763; as PCGS MS-60), Pennsylvania collection, Doug Winter/Lee Minshull, 11/97, Orange County collection. Graded Mint State-61 by PCGS.

The 1880-CC is the second most available Carson City half eagle struck before 1890. It is a relatively easy issue to obtain in the lower circulated grades and can be obtained in the lower end of the About Uncirculated range without much difficulty. Choice About Uncirculated examples are relatively scarce and the 1880-CC half eagle is a rare coin in Uncirculated. I have never seen a piece better than Mint State-62 and only one at that level.

1881-CC

MINTAGE: 13,886
RARITY RANKINGS:
    Overall Rarity: 4th of 19 (tie)
    High Grade Rarity: 8th of 19

The 1881-CC is the rarest Carson City half eagle from the 1880's. It also compares favorably to many of the lower mintage, higher priced issues from the 1870's, especially in terms of its overall rarity.

STRIKE: The quality of strike seen on the 1881-CC half eagle is not as sharp as that found on the 1880-CC or the 1882-CC. Liberty's hair surrounding the face and brow is often very weak. In addition, the hair at the top of the head shows weakness and some of the stars are flat at the centers. On the reverse, the wings are often softly struck as are the feathers on the neck of the eagle.

SURFACES: For some reason, this date is not usually seen with deep, detracting marks as on the 1879-CC and 1880-CC half eagles. However, the typical 1881-CC tends to have other problems. This was not a well-produced issue and many are found with mint-made impairments. I have seen pieces that had noticeable depressions on the surfaces as well as ones with extensive grease stains.

LUSTER: The quality of luster is below average. Many higher grade 1881-CC half eagles are dull and grainy in appearance. On the few attractive, original high grade pieces that are known, the luster is frosty and slightly satiny.

COLORATION: The natural coloration is medium green-gold. On some original specimens, there is rather extensive coppery toning. There are probably fewer than a dozen 1881-CC half eagles known that are totally original and do not show bright, unnatural coloration due to repeated cleanings and dippings.

EYE APPEAL: It is extremely difficult to locate an 1881-CC half eagle with good eye appeal. Many show a poor strike and this is often compounded by the mint-made problems discussed above. In addition, most have been cleaned at one time.

DIE VARIETIES: Only one die variety is known.

Variety 1-A: The date is large and well centered. All known examples have a long, diagonal die scratch which runs through the top of ER in LIBERTY. There are also die scratches just in front of Liberty's eye and a vertical irregular die defect just below the ear of Liberty. Beginning with this year, the mintmark has a much different size and shape than on previous half eagles from this mint. The 1881-CC has a tall, narrow mintmark that is placed over the V in FIVE with the second C slightly higher than the first.

RARITY:

Total Known: 70-80

BY GRADE:

VF	EF	AU	MINT STATE
47-51	22-24	9-12	2-3

CONDITION CENSUS:

1. Chicago collection, ex: Doug Winter/Lee Minshull (11/96), Dr. Larry Cutler collection, Winthrop Carner, Bowers and Ruddy 9/81: 1582, Stack's 10/79: 201. Graded Mint State-63 by NGC.

2. Nevada collection (7/97), ex: Eastern dealer, Charley Tuppen collection, possibly also ex: Heritage Rare Coin Galleries, James Cohen. Graded Mint State-61 by PCGS.

3. Private collection, ex: Winthrop Carner (1/95), Dr. Larry Cutler collection, Heritage 1994 ANA: 5764 ($7,700). Graded About Uncirculated-58 by PCGS. *The plate coin in this book.*

4. Tahoe collection, ex: Doug Winter (9/97), Nevada collection. Graded About Uncirculated-55 by PCGS. Very choice for the grade.

5 (tie). A group of approximately three to five pieces grade About Uncirculated-55 but are not as choice as coin #4. These include the following:

• Eastern dealer, ex: Bowers and Merena 10/99: 1233 ($8,050; as PCGS AU-55), Harry Bass collection, Paramount 2/13/68. Graded About Uncirculated-58 by NGC.

• Bowers and Merena Norweb I (10/87): 908.

• Chicago collection duplicate, ex: Doug Winter (1995). Graded About Uncirculated-55 by NGC.

• New Jersey collection, ex: Doug Winter 5/00, New York dealer, Heritage 9/99: 6721 ($9,200; as PCGS AU-55), Pennsylvania collection, Doug Winter/Lee Minshull, 2/98. Graded About Uncirculated-58 by NGC.

• National Gold Exchange inventory, 3/98. Graded About Uncirculated-55 by NGC.

The 1881-CC half eagle is a scarce and underrated issue. When available, the typical example grades Very Fine to low end Extremely Fine. This is a very scarce coin in Extremely Fine-45 and a very rare issue in About Uncirculated with no more than a dozen known. In Mint State, the 1881-CC is extremely rare with just two or three currently known to exist.

1882-CC

MINTAGE: 82,817
RARITY RANKINGS:
    Overall Rarity: 15th of 19 (tie)
    High Grade Rarity: 15th of 19

In 1882, the mintage figure for Carson City half eagles increased to its highest level since the mint opened in 1870. The 1882-CC is the most available pre-1890 half eagle from this mint in terms of its overall rarity and its availability in high grades.

STRIKE: The quality of strike on most 1882-CC half eagles is above average. Most are slightly weak in the centers but have nearly full detail on the hair of Liberty, the feathers of the eagle and the denticles. All 1882-CC half eagles show a number of interesting diagnostic characteristics. On the obverse, a thin diagonal die scratch runs through the IB in LIBERTY. Another die scratch runs through the eye of Liberty. On many, there is also a clashmark below the neck of Liberty, a die scratch above the 82 in the date and a thin reverse clashmark that connects the eagle's beak to its right wing.

SURFACES: The majority of 1882-CC half eagles show heavily marked surfaces. However, it is easier to locate a relatively mark-free example of this date than nearly any other Carson City half eagle struck during the 1880's. Some are known with mint-made copper spots or other types of discoloration in the planchet.

LUSTER: The luster is most often satiny with a slightly grainy appearance in the fields. The quality of luster is better than on most Carson City half eagles. It is difficult to locate a piece with original, undisturbed mint luster.

COLORATION: The natural coloration is light to medium orange-gold with a few pieces showing a green-gold hue. Coins with full original coloration are very scarce.

EYE APPEAL: The 1882-CC is the only pre-1890 Carson City half eagle that can be found with good eye appeal on more than an extremely infrequent basis. I have seen at least four or five that had "thin" areas on the obverse edge in the area of 3:00 to 5:00 and at 9:00 to 11:00. These do not significantly affect the value of a coin and are, in my opinion, the result of improperly prepared planchets.

DIE VARIETIES: Only one variety is known.

Variety 1-A: The date is placed centrally and is level. The mintmark is tall and rather widely spaced. It is positioned above the V in FIVE.

RARITY:

Total Known: 350-400+

BY GRADE:

VF	EF	AU	MINT STATE
110-120	170-195	60-70	10-15

CONDITION CENSUS:

1 (tie). Private collection, ex: National Gold Exchange, 8/98. Graded Mint State-62 by NGC.

• Heritage 1/00: 7787 (unsold). Graded Mint State-62 by NGC.

• One more example has been graded Mint State-62 by NGC as of January 2001. I have not seen it.

• New Jersey collection, ex: Doug Winter/Lee Minshull, Monex, Superior 3/00: 894 (unsold). Identifiable by obverse rim voids at 11:00 and 5:00, as struck. Graded Mint State-62 by PCGS.

• Goldberg 9/99: 1773 (unsold). Graded Mint State-62 by PCGS.

• One other example has been graded Mint State-62 by PCGS as of March 2001.

2 (tie). Six have been graded Mint State-61 by NGC as of January 2001 and five have been graded as such by PCGS, as of March 2001. The specific coins I am aware of are as follows:

• Bowers and Merena 8/98: 337 ($7,188), ex: Bob Leece. Graded Mint State-61 by NGC.

• Private collection, 4/98, ex: Blanchard & Co., Doug Winter/Lee Minshull. Graded Mint State-61 by NGC.

• Chicago collection, ex: Doug Winter/Lee Minshull, Heritage 9/99: 6723 ($5,520), Pennsylvania collection 9/97, Eastern dealer, Charley Tuppen collection, Winthrop Carner. Graded Mint State-61 by PCGS.

• Private collection, 9/97, ex: Doug Winter/Lee Minshull. Graded Mint State-61 by NGC.

• Private collection, ex: Winthrop Carner, late 1994. Graded Mint State-61 by NGC.

• Nevada collection. Graded Mint State-61 by PCGS. *The plate coin in this book.*

• Private collection, ex: Heritage Rare Coin Galleries 10/99. Graded Mint State-61 by PCGS.

• Private collection, ex: Heritage Rare Coin Galleries 1/95. Graded Mint State-61 by NGC.

• A coin graded Mint State-61 by PCGS was advertised in a November 1997 issue of Coin World by Delaware Valley Rare Coins.

3 (tie). I am aware of the following coins that grade Mint State-60:

• Oregon collection, ex: Doug Winter/Lee Minshull, Winthrop Carner, Florida dealer, North Carolina collector. Graded Mint State-60 by PCGS.

• Long Island collection, ex: Doug Winter (1992), Stack's 3/90: 1043. Once graded Mint State-60 by PCGS; now unencapsulated.

• Two examples have been graded Mint State-60 by NGC as of January 2001.

The 1882-CC half eagle is the most available pre-1890 Carson City half eagle. It is reasonably common in lower circulated grades and while slightly scarce in the higher About Uncirculated grades, it can be located with relatively little effort. This date is very scarce in the lower Mint State grades and it becomes very rare in Mint State-62. I have never seen a piece that graded higher than Mint State-62 and only one or two at that level.

1883-CC

MINTAGE: 12,958
RARITY RANKINGS:
    Overall Rarity: 9th of 19 (tie)
    High Grade Rarity: 12th of 19

The mintage for this date is significantly lower than for the 1882-CC half eagle and, as a result, this is a much scarcer coin. In my opinion, the 1883-CC half eagle is considerably rarer than generally acknowledged, especially in higher grades.

STRIKE: Most 1883-CC half eagles are found with a good strike. On the obverse, the hair above the eye and ear of Liberty is typically somewhat weak. The upper part of the hair and the bun tend to be well defined and the stars are fully detailed including their radial lines. The denticles are sometimes weak and, oddly, are not as sharp overall to the naked eye as on the reverse. The quality of strike on the reverse is very good with the wings and talons sharp.

SURFACES: Nearly every known example shows heavily abraded surfaces as a result of heavy commercial use. For some reason, the obverse fields are often riddled with clusters of deep, detracting marks.

LUSTER: The type of luster most often seen is satiny with a somewhat grainy texture. The typical 1883-CC half eagle is worn to the point that little mint luster is seen on the surfaces. On many higher grade pieces, the luster has been disturbed by cleaning.

COLORATION: The natural coloration for this issue is medium coppery-orange and greenish-gold. Very few 1883-CC half eagles exist with original coloration.

EYE APPEAL: This issue closely rivals the 1881-CC as the most difficult Carson City half eagle from the 1880's to locate with good eye appeal. Despite the fact that many examples are well struck, the typical 1883-CC half eagle is heavily abraded and has impaired luster. Choice, high end pieces with good eye appeal are rare.

DIE VARIETIES: There is just one variety known. A second variety (with a tall mintmark) was reported by Walter Breen but remains unverified.

Variety 1-A: The date is large and positioned evenly between the base of the neck and the denticles. The mintmark is small and round. As it is totally unlike any other Carson City half eagle from this decade, we can presume that it is a left-over, unused die from the 1870's.

RARITY:

Total Known: 100-125

BY GRADE:

VF	EF	AU	MINT STATE
39-49	35-44	23-28	3-4

CONDITION CENSUS:

1. Private collection, ex: Bowers and Merena 1/94: 1413 ($15,950), New Jersey dealer, Superior 2/92: 2699 ($9,818; as PCGS MS-60). Graded Mint State-61 by PCGS.

2. Washington, D.C. collection, ex: Doug Winter/Lee Minshull, 3/96. Graded Mint State-61 by NGC.

3. Superior 3/00: 895 (unsold), ex: Monex, Stack's 3/98: 1562 ($16,500), Bowers and Merena 1/86: 292. Graded Mint State-61 by PCGS.

4 (tie). A group of approximately six or seven examples grade About Uncirculated-58. These include the following:

• Private collection, ex: Doug Winter, Jason Carter/Chris Napolitano, Bowers and Merena 10/99: 1241 ($8,625; as PCGS AU-55), Harry Bass collection, Stack's 2/72: 752. Graded About Uncirculated-58 by NGC.

• Private collection, ex: Country Lane Rarities (Bill Von Elm), Doug Winter/Lee Minshull 2/00, Spectrum Numismatics. Graded About Uncirculated-58 by PCGS.

• Bowers and Merena 5/00: 537 ($7,475), ex: Harry Bass collection. Graded About Uncirculated-58 by PCGS.

• Chicago collection, ex: Doug Winter/Lee Minshull, 5/95. Graded About Uncirculated-58 by NGC.

• Private collection, ex: Doug Winter/Lee Minshull 12/97, Orange County collection. Graded About Uncirculated-58 by NGC.

• Nevada collection, ex: Winthrop Carner, North Carolina collection, Bowers and Merena 9/93: 1094. Graded About Uncirculated-58 by PCGS. *The plate coin in this book.*

• Private collection, ex: Doug Winter/Lee Minshull 8/99, Carter Numismatics. Graded About Uncirculated-58 by NGC.

• Private collection, ex: Eastern dealer, Heritage 1999 FUN: 5119 ($10,350; as NGC AU-55). Graded About Uncirculated-58 by PCGS.

NGC has graded twelve other examples About Uncirculated-58 as of January 2001 while PCGS has recorded four others in this grade as of March 2001. These numbers are inflated by resubmissions.

The 1883-CC half eagle is a scarce and undervalued issue that is most often seen in Very Fine and Extremely Fine grades. It is very scarce in the lower About Uncirculated grades and quite rare in the higher range of this grade. In Mint State, the 1883-CC is very rare and no Choice Uncirculated examples are currently known.

1884-CC

MINTAGE: 16,402
RARITY RANKINGS:
  Overall Rarity: 9th of 19 (tie)
  High Grade Rarity: 11th of 19

The 1884-CC half eagle is similar in terms of its overall and high grade rarity to the 1883-CC. It is another issue that is underrated in comparison to the better known low mintage issues from the 1870's.

STRIKE: The strike is not as sharp as on the other Carson City half eagles from the 1880's. The obverse is nearly always weak on the tip of the coronet, the curls near the ear and eye of Liberty and on the curl beneath the ear. In addition, the stars are often flat at the centers. On the reverse, the neck feathers are often weak. Many are also weak on the eagle's upper legs and on the horizontal lines in the shield. The reverse border is occasionally incomplete from 10:00 to 2:00.

SURFACES: Nearly every known 1884-CC half eagle is characterized by heavily abraded surfaces. These marks are often very detracting as they tend to be deep and poorly situated. I have seen a fair number of pieces that had copper spots or planchet streaks as well.

LUSTER: High grade 1884-CC half eagles show excellent luster with a cross between mint frost and a satiny texture. The quality of luster seen on original, high grade pieces is excellent.

COLORATION: The natural coloration ranges from rich yellow-gold to russet-orange. There are not many 1884-CC half eagles left with completely original coloration and such pieces trade at strong premiums over typical quality coins.

EYE APPEAL: This is an extremely hard date to find with above-average eye appeal. Even though sharply struck examples can be found from time to time, many have very heavily abraded surfaces and are likely to have been cleaned at one time.

DIE VARIETIES: There is only one die variety known.

Variety 1-A: The date is very large and it slants slightly downwards from left to right. There is thin die scratch through the RTY in LIBERTY which can be seen even on low grade coins. The mintmark is tall and widely spaced. The first C is positioned above the left side of the V in FIVE while the second C is over the left side of the E in FIVE.

RARITY:

Total Known: 100-125

BY GRADE:

VF	EF	AU	MINT STATE
40-48	35-47	22-25	3-5

CONDITION CENSUS:

1. Unknown private collection, ex: Bowers and Ruddy 9/81: 1584, Stack's 10/79: 205. Mint State-60+. Possibly the same coin #2.

2. Chicago collection, ex: Doug Winter/Lee Minshull, Heritage 9/99: 6728 ($12,650), Pennsylvania collection, Eastern dealer, Charley Tuppen collection. Graded Mint State-61 by PCGS.

3. Lee Minshull 1/00, ex: Monex inventory, first seen 7/98. Graded Mint State-62 by PCGS.

4. Private collection, ex: Bowers and Merena 9/93: 1100 ($8,250). About Uncirculated-58 or better. There is a good chance that this coin would be graded Uncirculated if it were sent to one of the grading services today.

5. Northern California collection, ex: Doug Winter, Heritage 2/01: 6944 ($6,038; as NGC AU-58), Florida collection 1/00, Doug Winter, Chicago collection, Doug Winter, Paul Nugget 8/94. Graded About Uncirculated-58 by PCGS.

Other About Uncirculated-58 examples include the following:

• Eastern dealer, ex: Bowers and Merena 10/99: 1246 ($4,140; as PCGS AU-55), Harry Bass collection, Stack's 10/71: 1033. Graded About Uncirculated-58 by NGC.

• California collection, ex: Doug Winter/Lee Minshull, Heritage Rare Coin Galleries. Graded About Uncirculated-58 by NGC.

• Nevada collection. Graded About Uncirculated-58 by PCGS. *The plate coin in this book.*

• Bowers and Merena 11/92: 1115 ($5,060). Graded About Uncirculated-55 but About Uncirculated-58 by today's standards.

• Private collection, ex: Doug Winter/Lee Minshull, 2/98. Graded About Uncirculated-58 by PCGS.

• Oregon Collection, ex: Bowers and Merena 1/99: 1421 ($7,475). Graded About Uncirculated-58 by NGC.

• Heritage 1/00: 7790 (unsold). Graded About Uncirculated-58 by NGC.

• NGC has graded four other coins About Uncirculated-58 as of January 2001. This figure is inflated by resubmissions.

The 1884-CC half eagle is similar in rarity to the 1883-CC. It is most often seen in Very Fine and Extremely Fine grades. It is very scarce in the lower About Uncirculated grades and most examples in this range are marginal, at best. High end About Uncirculated half eagles are quite rare and this is a very rare coin in Mint State.

1890-CC

MINTAGE: 53,800
RARITY RANKINGS:
    Overall Rarity: 17th of 19 (tie)
    High Grade Rarity: 18th of 19

After a six year hiatus, production of half eagles resumed at the Carson City mint. Beginning with this issue, the half eagles from this mint are far more available than those from the 1870-1884 era; especially in higher grades.

When my book "Gold Coins of the Old West" was released in 1994, this date was considered rare to very rare in the higher Mint State grades. It is still very rare in Mint State-65 and above, but a hoard of between twenty and thirty nice Uncirculated pieces entered the market in the fall of 1996. This included a number of coins in the Mint State-62 to Mint State-64 range.

STRIKE: Many 1890-CC half eagles show a very good quality of strike. On the obverse, the curls near the ear and brow may have some weakness, but it is possible to locate an example that has complete definition on the hair. On the reverse, many are slightly weak on the neck and breast of the eagle.

SURFACES: The typical 1890-CC half eagle has numerous abrasions in the fields. There are some clean, high end pieces known that show minimal marks and these are, of course, very desirable. It is not uncommon for an 1890-CC half eagle to have light copper spotting or areas of mint-made discoloration.

LUSTER: The luster is as good as on any half eagle produced at the Carson City mint. This makes the 1890-CC a favorite among collectors seeking one truly first-rate Carson City half eagle for their collection. The luster is generally very frosty with a slightly grainy appearance in the fields. I have seen a small number that are semi-prooflike on the obverse.

COLORATION: The coloration ranges from rich yellow-gold to deep green-gold and even rose. It is easier to find an 1890-CC with original color than any of the issues from the 1870's or the 1880's but it is becoming difficult as more are dipped or cleaned.

EYE APPEAL: This is not a difficult issue to find with good eye appeal as there are a relatively sizable number of sharp, lustrous coins known in the Mint State-60 to Mint State-62 range. If a collector is patient, he should be able to obtain a truly pleasing 1890-CC half eagle without great effort.

DIE VARIETIES: Only one die variety is currently known. It is probable that one or two other positional varieties exist and await discovery.

Variety 1-A: The date is large and spaced evenly between the base of the neck and the denticles. The mintmark is tall, closely spaced and placed rather high. On late die states, there is a reverse crack that runs through the lettering.

RARITY:

Total Known: 400-500+

BY GRADE:

VF	EF	AU	MINT STATE
40-50	60-80	175-200	110-135

CONDITION CENSUS:

1. Private collection, ex: Jason Carter/Chris Napolitano 6/98, Alhambra Coins (Mal Varner), Larry Hanks, private collection(s), Mid American Rare Coin Galleries (Jeff Garrett), Florida dealer, unknown collection(s). Graded Mint State-66 by PCGS.

2. A coin graded Mint State-65 by PCGS. This may be the piece that was first sold as Lot 525 in the Bowers and Merena 9/89 sale.

3 (tie). An example graded Mint State-65 by NGC. This coin was available for sale during the early part of 1997.

• Private collection via New York dealer, Doug Winter/Lee Minshull, Heritage 5/00: 7689 ($14,375). Graded Mint State-65 by NGC.

4 (tie) Twenty-one pieces had been graded Mint State-64 by PCGS as of March 2001 and thirteen by NGC as of January 2001. This number is significantly inflated by resubmissions.

The 1890-CC is tied for the third most common Carson City half eagle. It is seldom found in grades lower than Extremely Fine-40 and it is relatively common in all About Uncirculated grades. It is not a really scarce coin in the lower Mint State grades but it becomes difficult to locate in properly graded Mint State-62 and it is rare in Mint State-63. Gems are extremely rare.

1891-CC

MINTAGE: 208,000
RARITY RANKINGS:
    Overall Rarity: 19th of 19
    High Grade Rarity: 19th of 19

This is easily the most available half eagle from the Carson City mint. Its original mintage figure of 208,000 is more than two times as great as the next most common Carson City half eagles (the 1892-CC with 82,968 and the 1882-CC with 82,817). It is the only Carson City half eagle plentiful in the lower Mint State grades, making it very popular as a type issue.

STRIKE: The 1891-CC is one of the better struck Carson City half eagles. Most have some weakness on the curls around the face and ear but show very good overall detail on the obverse. The reverse is generally well struck with minor, localized weakness sometimes found on the eagle's right leg.

SURFACES: Many 1891-CC half eagles were shipped to banks or exported. They were probably sent loose in bags and, as a result, they show heavy marks from contact with other coins. It is not uncommon for an example to have mint-made spotting. It is sometimes possible to locate a piece relatively free of marks but the vast majority of survivors have below average quality surfaces.

LUSTER: The luster tends to be better than on all but a handful of gold coins produced at the Carson City mint. It is usually frosty in texture but a few semi-prooflike examples are known. I have even seen a small number of truly impressive, fully reflective 1891-CC half eagles and these typically command strong premiums among collectors.

COLORATION: The natural coloration ranges from deep coppery-orange to rose-gold and greenish gold. Many 1891-CC half eagles have a "ring" of deeper color at the borders which is probably the result of having been stored in rolls while in overseas banks for the past 50-100 years. This is one of the few half eagles from this mint that can still be found with original color on a fairly regular basis. This will change as more and more 1891-CC half eagles are cleaned or dipped.

EYE APPEAL: The level of eye appeal is among the highest for any Carson City half eagle. Most are seen with sharp strikes and very good luster as well as pleasing color. Locating a high end Mint State coin with clean surfaces is, however, extremely difficult.

DIE VARIETIES: I am aware of two die varieties but I have not studied this issue as carefully as the other half eagles from this mint and would not doubt there were a number of other varieties.

Variety 1-A: The date is placed somewhat low in the field and is positioned a bit more to the right than on Variety 2-A. The mintmark is somewhat squat and closely spaced.

Variety 2-A: The date is more central than on Variety 1-A. The reverse is identical.

RARITY:

Total Known: 1250-1500+

BY GRADE:

VF	EF	AU	MINT STATE
55-105	115-165	680-780	400-450+

CONDITION CENSUS:

1. National Gold Exchange inventory, fall 1998. Graded Mint State-65 by NGC. Same coin as the next?

2 (tie). Private collection, ex: Heritage Rare Coin Galleries 3/96. Graded Mint State-65 by PCGS.

• Private collection, ex: Heritage Rare Coin Galleries, Bowers and Merena 10/99: 1257 ($16,500; as "MS-62"), Harry Bass collection. Graded Mint State-65 by PCGS.

• U.S. Coins (Kenny Duncan) inventory, first seen 1/01. Graded Mint State-65 by NGC.

3 (tie). Approximately fifteen to eighteen examples are known which grade Mint State-64.

• As of March 2001, PCGS had graded twenty-six in Mint State-64 while NGC had graded twenty-six as of January 2001. This is a very dramatic increase from the start of 1998, when PCGS had graded ten in Mint State-64 while NGC had graded eight. These figures include a number of resubmissions and crossovers but are also reflective of a slackening of grading standards during this period.

The 1891-CC is far and away the most common Carson City half eagle. It is almost never seen in grades below Extremely Fine and it is plentiful in all About Uncirculated grades. Lower end Uncirculated 1891-CC half eagles can be obtained with great ease and this issue is only moderately scarce in Mint State-63. In properly graded Mint State-64, the 1891-CC half eagle is very scarce and gems remain extremely rare.

1892-CC

MINTAGE: 82,968
RARITY RANKINGS:
    Overall Rarity: 15th of 19 (tie)
    High Grade Rarity: 17th of 19

The 1892-CC remains the scarcest Carson City half eagle from this decade in terms of its overall rarity. The number of Uncirculated 1892-CC half eagles currently known has approximately doubled since "Gold Coins of the Old West" was released in 1994. This is the result of a hoard of approximately two dozen Uncirculated pieces entering the market in the mid-1990's.

STRIKE: The 1892-CC half eagle is not as well struck an issue as the 1891-CC. The curls around the face are often weak and there is often softness on the hairbun of Liberty as well. The reverse tends to be better struck but weakness on the eagle's right leg is not uncommon.

SURFACES: Many examples are heavily abraded but not to the extent seen on other dates from this decade. The patient collector should be able to locate an 1892-CC half eagle with relatively mark-free surfaces. Coppery toning spots are sometimes seen, but not to the extent as on 1891-CC half eagles.

LUSTER: This date is found with above average luster. Uncleaned, original pieces have a frosty texture with a slightly subdued appearance. Coins with blazing or "flashy" luster are very seldom seen but a few high end pieces with great luster exist.

COLORATION: The natural coloration ranges from a rich orange-gold shade to a more subdued rose-green. Many have a ring of deeper toning around the obverse and reverse borders. It is still not difficult to locate an 1892-CC half eagle that has original color but this is likely to change as more and more pieces are dipped or cleaned.

EYE APPEAL: It is not easy to find an 1892-CC half eagle with above average eye appeal. In my experience, the few coins that are well struck seem to have many bagmarks while those with nice color have detracting copper spots. If the collector sees a really appealing example, he should purchase it as a better piece may prove hard to procure.

DIE VARIETIES: Only one die variety is known but there are at least three distinct die states.

Variety 1-A: The date is placed high in the field and positioned a bit to the left. The mintmark is medium sized and widely spaced with the first C above the left side of the V in FIVE and the second above the left side of the E in FIVE.

Die State I: The mintmark is normal and the scroll under the word WE in the motto is intact.

Die State II: The mintmark is normal and the scroll is broken.

Die State III: The mintmark shows noticeable machine doubling and there is doubling noted on the E in FIVE as well. The scroll under WE is totally missing due to die polishing. On the latest pieces struck, there is a die crack that develops from the D in the value to the second A in AMERICA.

RARITY:

Total Known: 350-450+

BY GRADE:

VF	EF	AU	MINT STATE
50-75	100-125	150-175	50-75

CONDITION CENSUS:

1. Private collection, ex: Delaware Valley Rare Coins, Mark Chrans, National Gold Exchange inventory 11/97, unknown dealer or dealers, Superior 9/97: 2949 ($30,800), Superior 1/90: 4674 ($33,000), Superior Auction '89: 902 ($23,100), Pacific Auctions (Ron Gillio) 2/89: 953, Stack's 10/88: 97, Les Fox/Amazing Gold Rarities, Bowers and Ruddy Eliasberg 10/82: 580 ($4,400). Graded Mint State-66 by NGC; earlier graded Mint State-65 by PCGS.

2. Private collection, ex: Heritage Rare Coin Galleries 2/97. Graded Mint State-64 by NGC.

3 (tie). A half dozen or so pieces are known which grade Mint State-63.

• As of March 2001, PCGS had graded eight in Mint State-63 and three had been graded as such by NGC as of January 2001. I have personally seen four different slabbed examples in Mint State-63 holders. One is a PCGS Mint State-63 in a Nevada collection.

The 1892-CC half eagle is a relatively common coin by the standards of this series. It is not as hard to find in Uncirculated as it used to be due to the appearance of a small hoard in the mid-1990's. It is still somewhat scarce in the lower Mint State grades and it is quite scarce in Mint State-62. In Mint State-63 or better, this is a very rare coin and gems are extremely rare.

1893-CC

MINTAGE: 60,000
RARITY RANKINGS:
    Overall Rarity: 17th of 19
    High Grade Rarity: 16th of 19

Its status as the final year of issue for Carson City half eagles makes the 1893-CC a popular coin. This is among the more common Carson City half eagles.

STRIKE: This issue is usually seen with a sharp strike. On some, there will be minor weakness on the curls around the face but most are quite well detailed at the centers and the borders.

SURFACES: As with nearly all issues from this mint, the 1893-CC half eagle is often seen with very heavily abraded surfaces. This typically affects the luster and minimizes the overall eye appeal. Some show mint-made copper spots but not as extensively as on the 1891-CC or 1892-CC half eagles.

LUSTER: The luster is among the best of any half eagles from the Carson City mint. It typically has a rich, frosty texture. Some have a slightly grainy appearance, as struck, and a few marginally prooflike examples exist.

COLORATION: There is a broad range of coloration found on 1893-CC half eagles. This includes rich green-gold, orange-gold and rose. Many have a distinctive appearance with a strong band of color at the periphery contrasted by lighter shades at the centers. This look is seen on coins that have been located in Europe or other overseas sources, probably the result of having been stacked in rolls and subsequently developing toning at the edges.

EYE APPEAL: There are some extremely attractive 1893-CC half eagles available to collectors but many are found with heavily abraded surfaces.

DIE VARIETIES: Two die varieties are currently known. It is possible that at least one other exists.

Variety 1-A: The date is placed centrally. The mintmark is placed high with the first C distinctly lower than the second. Early die states show doubling on the second C.

Variety 2-A: On this variety, the date is lower and placed more towards the viewer's left. The reverse is the same as on Variety 1-A. This variety appears to be scarcer than the first.

RARITY:
Total Known: 375-475

BY GRADE:

VF	EF	AU	MINT STATE
60-80	90-100	125-215	60-80

CONDITION CENSUS:

1 (tie). Nevada collection, ex: Superior 3/00: 903 (unsold), Brian Hendelson, Bowers and Merena 10/99: 1261 ($14,950; as PCGS MS-64), Harry Bass collection, Julian Leidman 8/12/69. Graded Mint State-65 by NGC.

2 (tie). Lee Minshull inventory 10/99. Graded Mint State-64 by PCGS.

• Three others have been graded Mint State-64 by PCGS as of March 2001.

3 (tie). Seven have been graded Mint State-64 by NGC as of January 2001. I have personally seen three of these.

4 (tie). At least ten pieces exist in Mint State-63. This includes three graded as such by PCGS as of March 2001 and fifteen graded as such by NGC as of January 2001. These numbers are significantly inflated by resubmissions.

The 1893-CC half eagle is common in all circulated grades and it is relatively easy to obtain in the lowest Mint State grades. It becomes scarce in Mint State-62, rare in Mint State-63 and very rare in any grade higher than this. I have only seen one Gem example.

RARITY SUMMARY: CARSON CITY HALF EAGLES

DATE	GRADES				
	VF	EF	AU	MINT STATE	TOTAL
1870-CC	27-33	13-15	7-9	3	50-60
1871-CC	94-98	32-35	13-15	1-2	140-150
1872-CC	51-58	13-14	6-8	0	70-80
1873-CC	38-44	10-13	5-6	2	55-65
1874-CC	86-89	25-28	12-15	3	125-135
1875-CC	55-60	20-22	8-11	2	85-95
1876-CC	48-54	20-23	10-11	2	80-90
1877-CC	55-59	18-22	11-13	1	85-95
1878-CC	44-50	13-15	3-5	0	60-70
1879-CC	103-140	60-72	25-35	2-3	200-250
1880-CC	132-142	88-116	49-59	6-8	275-325+
1881-CC	47-51	22-24	9-12	2-3	70-80
1882-CC	110-120	170-195	60-70	10-15	350-400+
1883-CC	39-49	35-44	23-28	3-4	100-125
1884-CC	40-48	35-47	22-25	3-5	105-125
1890-CC	40-50	60-80	165-190	110-135	375-475
1891-CC	55-105	115-165	680-780	400-450+	1250-1500+
1892-CC	50-75	100-125	150-175	50-75	350-450
1893-CC	60-80	90-100	125-215	60-80	375-475

II. CARSON CITY HALF EAGLES: OVERALL RARITY

RANKING	DATE	TOTAL KNOWN
1.	1870-CC	50-60
2.	1873-CC	55-65
3.	1878-CC	60-70
4.	1872-CC	70-80
4 (tie).	1881-CC	70-80
6.	1876-CC	80-90
7.	1875-CC	85-95
7 (tie).	1877-CC	85-95
9.	1883-CC	100-125
9 (tie).	1884-CC	100-125
11.	1874-CC	125-135
12.	1871-CC	140-150
13.	1879-CC	200-250
14.	1880-CC	275-325
15.	1882-CC	350-400
15 (tie).	1892-CC	350-450
17.	1890-CC	375-475
17 (tie).	1893-CC	375-475
19.	1891-CC	1250-1500+

III. CARSON CITY HALF EAGLES: HIGH GRADE RARITY

RANKING	DATE	TOTAL KNOWN
1.	1878-CC	3-5
2.	1872-CC	6-8
2 (tie)	1873-CC	6-8
4.	1870-CC	10-12
5.	1875-CC	10-13
6.	1876-CC	12-13
7.	1877-CC	12-14
8.	1881-CC	11-15
9.	1871-CC	14-17
10.	1874-CC	14-18
11.	1884-CC	25-30
12.	1883-CC	26-32
13.	1879-CC	27-38
14.	1880-CC	55-62
15.	1882-CC	70-85
16.	1893-CC	185-295
17.	1892-CC	200-250
18.	1890-CC	275-325
19.	1891-CC	1080-1230+

CARSON CITY EAGLES:
AN INTRODUCTION AND OVERVIEW

Of the three gold denominations struck by the Carson City mint, the ten-dollar gold piece or eagle series is the most difficult to collect. Carson City gold coins were struck for use in circulation. During the western gold and silver rushes, paper money was suspect. Thus, gold and silver coins were the accepted method of payment and saw very active commercial use. It is not surprising to find that those Carson City gold coins that did survive show extensive wear and heavily marked surfaces from their years in circulation.

The 1870-CC eagle is of comparable rarity to its more celebrated and far more expensive counterpart, the 1870-CC double eagle. The completion of a Carson City eagle set is a very formidable task. Since only 35-45 1870-CC eagles are estimated to exist, only this number of complete sets of Carson City eagles can be formed. In comparison, 50-60 Carson City half eagles and 35-45 Carson City double eagles sets can be formed.

As with the half eagle and double eagle series, completion of a set of the Carson City eagles is difficult but certainly realistic. There are only 19 dates in this series. Unlike the Philadelphia eagle series, the Carson City coinage is short yet, simultaneously, formidable. There are no impossibly rare or prohibitively expensive coins that would make finishing a set impossible. Thus, it is a reasonable expectation to finish a Carson City eagle set, given enough time, money, and patience.

If a collector desires more of a challenge, he need only set his sights on higher grade coins. The Carson City eagles are generally rarer in higher grades (in this case About Uncirculated-50 or above) than their half eagle and double eagle counterparts.

While Carson City eagles have never been touted as an investment vehicle, they have, in fact, shown excellent price appreciation over the past few decades. Values rose steadily in the past decade despite a large price drop in the levels for common, "generic" coins. The western migration of the American people, along with a related increase of interest in western history and art, caused Carson City coinage to be in demand among an increasing number of avid, well-heeled collectors and investors. The romance of the Old West along with the rarity of the Carson City eagles has made this a very popular series. These coins are also in demand by general collectors and type collectors.

Regardless of one's time and resources, a complete set of Carson City eagles in Uncirculated grades will almost certainly never be assembled. Seven or eight of the 19 dates are currently unknown in full Mint State and there are many more dates in the eagle series that do not exist in Mint State than there are in the half eagle or double eagle series.

A partial Uncirculated set is just as daunting. The two most common issues from the 1870's, the 1871-CC and the 1874-CC, are exceedingly rare in Uncirculated. A half dozen or fewer Mint State 1880-CC, 1882-CC, 1883-CC, 1884-CC and 1893-CC eagles are known and nearly all of them are either in tightly-held collections or are no better than Mint State-60. Even the second most obtainable Carson City eagle in

Uncirculated, the 1890-CC, is a reasonably rare coin and the only issue that can be located in Uncirculated with any degree of regularity is the 1891-CC.

Choice Mint State (MS-63 and MS-64) Carson City eagles are very rare with probably no more than two dozen of all dates combined in existence. Gem Mint State (MS-65) Carson City eagles are essentially unobtainable. From the entire decade of the 1870's, only one MS-64 Carson City eagle (an 1874-CC) is known. Choice examples from the 1880's are currently unknown. The majority of the choice and gem pieces available are from the 1890's, specifically from 1891.

As with the other gold coin denominations from this mint, the rarity of the Carson City eagles in high grades is attributable to the total absence of coin collectors in Nevada at the time they were struck. The few Mint State pieces that do exist have survived either by good luck or sheer coincidence. They may have been hidden in a bank vault for many years (as were some very high grade Carson City eagles purchased at the beginning of the 20th century by John Clapp, Sr. and later sold by his son to Louis Eliasberg, Sr. in 1942) or sent to European or South American banks as foreign trade payments. The coins overseas or found by collectors before the Depression were spared the cruel fate of being melted in the 1930's. Other surviving Uncirculated pieces may have been assay coins that were shipped to Philadelphia and never destroyed after being weighed and examined.

A careful look at the Carson City eagle series reveals some very interesting trends. Survival statistics depend, to some extent, on the original quantity minted and vary according to the era in which they were struck. In general (the sole exception being the 1882-CC), the rarest coins in the series are those minted from 1870 through 1879. The 1882-CC is about as rare as the most available date from the 1870's, the 1874-CC. The Carson City eagles produced in 1880, 1883-84 and 1893 are the next rarest. The 1881-CC is the most common date from the 1880's. The 1890 and the 1892 issues are considerably more difficult to locate than the 1891-CC which is by far the most readily available Carson City eagle.

The coins minted during the heyday of the Comstock Lode (1870-1879) have survived roughly--although not strictly--in proportion to their original mintage figures. I estimate that between two percent and as little as one half of one percent of each year's original production of eagles has survived. In general, the older the coin, the lower the average surviving grade and the fewer the high grade specimens that are known. This is intuitive reasoning as much as anything. The longer a coin remains in circulation, the more likely it is to become heavily worn or destroyed. Thus, the rarest Carson City eagle (the 1870-CC) is the oldest, despite the fact that this issue has only the sixth lowest mintage figure in the series.

The 1879-CC is the next rarest coin in the series and it has the lowest mintage figure of any Carson City gold coin, with just 1,762 pieces produced. I estimate that around 40 to 50 of these have survived. This makes it only a bit less rare than the more famous and far more expensive 1870-CC double eagle. Given the fact that it has such a low mintage, the 1879-CC eagle is actually a bit more available than one might assume. This issue has an estimated survival population of between 2.5% and 3% which is far and away the highest survival percentage of any pre-1890 Carson City eagle. This strongly suggests that there was once a hoard of this date.

The third rarest Carson City eagle is the 1878-CC. This date has the second lowest mintage figure--3,244 coins. I estimate that between 45 and 55 pieces exist. The survival percentage of this issue is higher than average and its rarity is primarily attributable to its very small original mintage. Interestingly, all of the 1877-1879 Carson City eagles have higher survival percentages than the rest of the coins in this series. This suggests that the hoard of 1879-CC eagles that was described above may have also included pieces dated 1877-CC and 1878-CC.

The 1872-CC is just a bit more available than the 1878-CC with an estimated 60-70 pieces known. This date has the fifth lowest mintage figure of all Carson City eagles with 4,600 pieces struck. However, as the 1872-CC is one of the earliest dates in this series, it had more time to acquire wear in circulation and/or to be destroyed. This has made the 1872-CC eagle rare both in terms of total numbers known and the average grade of the surviving population.

The 1873-CC and the 1877-CC eagles are similar to the 1872-CC in terms of the total numbers known. Each of these has an estimated surviving population of 55-65 coins. The mintage figures for these issues is fairly similar with 4,543 for the former and 3,332 for the latter. The comparable mintage figures for these two dates and the fact that they were struck just four years apart probably best explains why they are so similar in terms of their overall rarity.

A relatively high proportion of the surviving 1877-CC eagles grade Extremely Fine or higher. Of the 55-65 pieces believed to exist in all grades, twenty-five to thirty-one of these grade Extremely Fine or above. This is a disproportionately high percentage of high grade pieces when compared to the other dates from the 1870's. Interestingly, the same scenario is true in regards to the 1877-CC half eagle. This strongly suggests that, at one time, a small hoard of 1877-CC half eagles and eagles included coins in the Extremely Fine to About Uncirculated grade range.

The 1875-CC has one of the lowest survival rates of the 1870's dates and a much lower survival rate than the 1876-1879 issues. There has never been an explanation but my research has uncovered a fact that may provide an answer. It seems possible that a quantity of newly minted 1875-CC eagles were damaged while stored in banks, shops or saloons during the great fire that ravaged Virginia City, Nevada in October, 1875.

The second most available Carson City eagle from the 1870's is the 1871-CC. Of the 8,805 that were originally struck, approximately 90-100 survive. With the exception of the 1874-CC, the 1871-CC has the highest mintage figure of any of the 1870's Carson City eagles. However, its rarity is maintained by its status as a very early date and consequently its high rate of heavily worn and/or destroyed coins.

The most common Carson City eagle from the 1870's is the 1874-CC. Its mintage figure of 16,767 is more than double that of any other Carson City eagle struck during that decade. Much of this production was sent to Eastern states to meet a severe coin shortage. Despite its comparatively high mintage figure, the 1874-CC actually has one of the lowest survival rates of any Carson City eagle from this decade. This explains why this issue is still scarce. It should also be noted that the 1874-CC half eagle also has a low survival percentage. It seems likely that a similar fate befell both of these issues, destroying an abnormally high percentage of the original mintage.

The 1882-CC is the only post-1880 Carson City mint that can be termed as scarce in any grade. An estimated 125-150 survive from its original mintage of 6,764. It has a relatively high survival percentage since it is a later date and, possibly, because a small hoard existed at one time.

The 1883-CC, 1884-CC, and 1893-CC eagles are of similar original mintage and estimated survival figures. The mintages for these three issues were, 12,000, 9,925 and 14,000 respectively. I estimate that between 125 and 215 of each issue have survived. The 1880-CC, due to the discovery of a hoard in the mid-1990's is now more available than these three dates. The 1881-CC is the most common Carson City eagle struck prior to 1890. There are 400+ coins surviving from the original mintage figure of 24,015. This comparably high mintage figure accurately predicts that this date would be the most available from the 1880's.

The 1890-CC and the 1892-CC eagles are relatively close in rarity. The former has an estimated 350-450 known while the latter has approximately 400-500. These figures are interesting as the mintage figures for these two (17,500 for the 1890-CC and 40,000 for the 1892-CC) are so dissimilar. I noted in the overview on Carson City half eagles that fewer high grade 1892-CC half eagles have survived than of the other high mintage dates of the 1890's. The same is true with 1892-CC eagles. I can not offer an exact reason for this curious anomaly. It does seem likely that many of the 1892-CC half eagles and eagles, at some time, underwent a similar destructive fate. Perhaps a large quantity of coins was not released and was later melted.

The 1891-CC eagle is by far the most common date of this series, as clearly suggested by its large mintage of 103,732 coins.

It remains very curious that more higher grade Carson City eagles, especially from the 1870's, did not survive. Every eagle struck during this decade is now very rare in About Uncirculated and either unknown or excessively rare in Mint State. Why is this so, especially when quantities of eagles from Philadelphia and San Francisco from the late 1870's and throughout the 1880's are readily found in these higher grades?

One of the most likely reasons is the fact that, in the 1870's, ten dollars was so much money that only a tiny handful of people could even think of saving an eagle as a collectible item. But, conversely, there were some very wealthy people in the West at that time. Some of these newly made millionaires appreciated art and were collectors in their own right. So why didn't even a single one of these people decide to keep a newly-minted Carson City eagle from each year as a momento? It is even more surprising that no one bothered to save a new 1870-CC eagle as a first-year-of-issue souvenir, especially when one considers that a number of 1870-CC silver dollars were saved in this fashion.

The few Mint State Carson City eagles which do exist are almost invariably less choice than comparable Carson City half eagles. There is a sensible explanation for this. Eagles are larger than half eagles and they weigh more. When they come into contact with each other during transfer and storage, they cause larger marks. These coins were thrown loose into bags after they were struck and little care was given to them. This is precisely why they are so rare in high Mint State grades. And, Carson City double eagles are even more difficult to find in high grades since they are the heaviest of the three gold denominations produced at the Carson City mint.

For the collector, locating attractive Carson City eagles in higher grades (i.e., Extremely Fine and better) is very challenging. The typical coin, especially for the 1870-1879 dates, grades Very Fine or so and is characterized by excessive bag-marks and poor overall eye appeal.

The rarest Carson City eagle in Extremely Fine or higher is the 1873-CC with an estimated population of 12-15 coins. I estimate that only 13-15 1870-CC and 1872-CC eagles are known in Extremely Fine or higher, making these the second rarest Carson City eagles in this grade range. The 1875-CC and the 1878-CC have esti-mated populations of 16-21 and 17-21 coins, respectively, in Extremely Fine or high-er grades. The extreme condition rarity of these issues is a combination of their sta-tus as early dates and their very low original mintage figures.

The next rarity tier for higher grade Carson City eagles is led by the 1879-CC with an estimated 20-25 coins known in Extremely Fine or higher grades. Even though this issue is the second rarest Carson City eagle in terms of its overall rar-ity, it is more obtainable in higher grades than generally believed. While this date does not appear for sale very often, when it does come up for sale, the average piece is likely to be in a higher grade than such dates as the 1870-CC, 1872-CC, 1873-CC and 1875-CC.

As one would expect, as mintage figures increase for these coins and the dates of issuance become more recent, the rarity of higher grade pieces diminishes. The two highest mintage dates of the 1870's are the 1871-CC and the 1874-CC and these are, not surprisingly, the two most available Carson City eagles of this era in high-er grades. I estimate that there are between 37 and 43 1871-CC eagles known in Extremely Fine and above and between 54 and 71 of the 1874-CC.

Despite its very low mintage, the 1877-CC is more common in Extremely Fine than other Carson City eagles of this era. There are an estimated 18-22 known in Extremely Fine. However, this date is truly rare in About Uncirculated, and com-pares favorably to issues such as the 1872-CC, 1873-CC, 1875-CC, 1876-CC and 1878-CC in this very high grade range.

Like the similarly dated half eagle, the 1874-CC eagle is the most available issue from the 1870's both in terms of overall rarity and availability in high grade. In the overview on half eagles earlier in this book, I proposed a hypothesis which explains this. The 1874-CC does have the highest mintage figure of any Carson City half eagle from the 1870's. But being an early date, one would guess that it would be less available in higher grades than it actually is. I feel that many 1874-CC eagles were shipped to the east coast to meet a need for circulating coins. It is conceivable that a decent-sized group of 1874-CC eagles stayed in an eastern bank where they sat for many years and were later melted.

The 1882-CC eagle is a rare coin but it, too, is a bit less rare in high grades than one might assume. I estimate that 85-97 are known in Extremely Fine or above with approximately three dozen in About Uncirculated and just one or two in Uncirculated. For some reason, this date has an odd distribution of specimens known. One would expect there to be more lower grade and fewer higher grade 1882-CC eagles than there actually are.

The 1880-CC, 1883-CC, 1884-CC, and 1893-CC are fairly similar in terms of their high grade rarity. The 1880-CC is the most available of these issues in About

Uncirculated while the 1880-CC and the 1893-CC are the most often seen in Uncirculated. Taken as a group, all of these issues are reasonably available in Extremely Fine, scarce to very scarce in About Uncirculated and very rare in Uncirculated.

The 1881-CC is the most common Carson City eagle struck prior to 1890. The number of Uncirculated pieces has swelled in recent years, due to the discovery of a moderate-sized hoard in the late 1990's.

The 1892-CC is an underrated coin. This is due to its higher mintage and its late date of issuance. The 1892-CC is almost comparable to the 1881-CC in terms of the number believed to exist in About Uncirculated to Uncirculated but it is priced considerably lower.

The existing Carson City eagles from the 1880's and the 1890's are found in considerably higher grades than those struck in the 1870's. This may be the result of the diminishing use of gold coins as the 19th century drew to a close and also because the older coins were in circulation for ten to twenty years longer. By the 1880's, mintages of Carson City eagles had increased and a greater percentage of these coins were sent overseas to banks for debt payment. The existence of such a large number of 1891-CC eagles in higher grades is clear evidence that the coins of this era served a much different function than did the coins produced two decades earlier. These coins exist in higher grades today mainly because they were sent overseas and avoided the melting pot. There is no telling how many Carson City eagles from the 1870's and the 1880's were melted in the 1930's.

I estimate that more than 50% of all remaining Carson City eagles, regardless of date, are from the 1890's. This implies that these four issues have more surviving specimens than the other fifteen years combined. Approximately 90% of all existing Carson City eagles are from the 1890's. Furthermore, I estimate that around 75% of all the existing About Uncirculated Carson City eagles are from this four year period. The 1891-CC eagle is more plentiful than the other three dates from the 1890's combined. Approximately 90% of all the Uncirculated Carson City eagles extant are from this one date. In fact, the only other date available with even the slightest degree of regularity is the 1890-CC, of which maybe five dozen are known.

Many of the early issues are weakly struck. This weakness of strike is most noticeable in the central portions of the coin, where the most pressure is needed to raise the metal of the planchet to give definition to the design. On the obverse, these softly struck coins often display considerable flatness on the neck of Liberty and brow as well as on the top and the rear of her hair. On the reverse, the weakness of strike is usually obvious on the neck feathers of the eagle, the central portion of the shield and the talons. This weakness of strike is often erroneously described as wear. Because of this, Carson City eagles from the 1870's are often incorrectly graded; even by professional graders.

The 1870-CC is often found with weakness of strike on Liberty's neck and the eagle's neck feathers. The 1871-CC is typically found with a reasonably sharp strike. The 1872-CC is usually seen with a very soft obverse and the 1873-CC is another issue that is often found flatly detailed. The 1874-CC shows a better overall strike. The 1875-CC, like its similarly dated half eagle counterpart, is probably the worst struck date in the entire series. The 1876-CC eagle is often weak at the centers while the 1877-CC tends to be found with a better quality of strike. The 1878-CC and the 1879-CC are both frequently seen with noticeable weakness at the centers. The issues from 1880 to 1893 are generally better struck although it is not uncommon to find pieces with some weakness at the centers.

The survival estimates given in this book are based on current knowledge as of 2001. As time passes, it is inevitable that more coins will surface from previously unknown collections, hoards or accumulations, which will lead to even more accurate survival estimates and Condition Census listings. In some cases, future revisions may show fewer examples of a particular issue than currently estimated. In addition, today's grading standards will change the grades of some coins currently assumed to be a certain grade. Depending on the coin, the grades of certain pieces could lower or rise, considerably affecting the Condition Census.

My review of auctions, price lists and known private treaty sales should provide the reader with some idea of how difficult it is to complete a collection of Carson City eagles. The rare 1870-1879 issues tend, on average, to reach the market at the rate of 0-3 pieces per year. For the rarest dates, it is not uncommon for a year or two to pass without a single decent quality coin being available. And oftentimes the only coins available are rejects from someone's collection; pieces that are well-worn, extensively abraded and visually unappealing. Carson City eagles, like all rare coins, may experience both droughts and gluts of specimens. In some years, a rare date may come onto the market as many as seven or eight different times while in other years, this same date may be completely unavailable. As a rule, obviously, the rarer the date, the less frequently available it is. A good percentage of the Condition Census or above-average Carson City eagles are tightly held by private individuals, families or institutions, essentially not for sale at any price.

A nice quality Carson City eagle collection will probably take a minimum of one to three years to complete. This is a series that requires a fairly substantial budget but it can be completed by someone of slightly above-average means if this person is patient and willing to purchase Very Fine examples of the truly rare dates, Extremely Fine examples of the scarce dates and About Uncirculated examples of the more common dates.

The collector with a large budget is probably going to be more inclined to purchase Extremely Fine examples of the rare dates, About Uncirculated examples of the scarce dates and Uncirculated examples of the common dates.

The true connoisseur with a nearly unlimited budget and a great deal of patience can put together a set which contains About Uncirculated examples of the rare issues, Choice About Uncirculated to Uncirculated examples of the scarce issues, and Choice Uncirculated examples of the common issues.

To aid all levels of collectors, the following pages give much more specific information about each of the Carson City eagles. The photographs of each coin that follow are enlarged one and one-half times their actual size to enhance the clarity of the details.

SECTION TWO

EAGLES

I. LIBERTY HEAD, WITH MOTTO REVERSE (1870-1884, 1890-1893)

1870:	5,908	1881:	24,015
1871:	8,085	1882:	6,764
1872:	4,600	1883:	12,000
1873:	4,543	1884:	9,925
1874:	16,767	1890:	17,500
1875:	7,715	1891:	103,732
1876:	4,696	1892:	40,000
1877:	3,332	1893:	14,000
1878:	3,244		
1879:	1,762		
1880:	11,190		

Total Mintage..................... 299,798

1870-CC

MINTAGE: 5,908
RARITY RANKINGS:
    Overall Rarity: 1st of 19
    High Grade Rarity: 1st of 19

Six Carson City eagles have lower mintage figures than the 1870-CC, but this is still clearly the rarest eagle from this mint. It is also the rarest Carson City eagle in terms of high grade rarity. At one time, in fact, I regarded this as the single rarest gold coin from this mint; eclipsing even the more famous (and considerably more expensive) 1870-CC double eagle. This coin's indisputable rarity and its status as the first gold issue struck at the Carson City mint should make it one of the most desirable 19th century United States gold coins. Yet this is a curiously overlooked and, in my opinion, undervalued issue.

STRIKE: The quality of strike is better than one might expect and it is certainly superior to that seen on 1870-CC half eagles and double eagles. Many 1870-CC eagles are slightly weak on the curls over the ear of Liberty and below BERT in LIBERTY. The remainder of the hair is quite sharp and many of the stars tend to have partial or full radial line detail. The reverse has a good overall strike with some weakness on the neck of the eagle and the inner portions of the wings.

SURFACES: I have seen just a small number of 1870-CC eagles that did not show numerous abrasions on the surfaces. On many, these marks are poorly situated and they severely impair the visual appeal of the coin. Any piece with minimal detracting bagmarks is very rare and desirable.

LUSTER: There are only a handful known that show any original mint luster. On some, this luster is very slightly reflective while on others it is more satiny in its texture.

COLORATION: The natural coloration is medium to deep yellow-gold with coppery overtones. Most 1870-CC eagles have been cleaned or dipped and only a few are known with original color.

EYE APPEAL: These are among the most difficult gold coins from the Carson City mint to find with decent eye appeal. The typical survivor, while relatively well struck, is heavily worn and abundantly abraded. Any piece with good eye appeal is very rare and is eagerly sought by serious collectors.

DIE VARIETIES: There are two varieties known.

Variety 1-A: The date is placed slightly low in the field and slants downwards from left to right. The mintmark is small and round. It is positioned close to the eagle. Some show mild doubling on the reverse letters.

Variety 1-B: The mintmark is high and close to the eagle but is positioned slightly more to the right than on Variety 1-B. It can be quickly distinguished from Variety 1-A by having the first C much higher than the second. It appears that this variety is slightly rarer.

RARITY:

Total Known: 35-45

BY GRADE:

VF*	EF	AU	MINT STATE
22-30	9-11	4	0

***NOTE**: Includes a number of coins that grade below Very Fine. This is also true for any Carson City eagle dated before 1880.

CONDITION CENSUS

1. Orange County collection via Doug Winter, ex: Heritage 6/00: 7603 (withdrawn prior to sale; there graded AU-55 by NGC), Heritage Rare Coin Galleries, 2/00. Discovered in Europe in 1999. Graded About Uncirculated-55 by PCGS.

2. (tie) Dr. Nathan Sohnheim collection, ex: Doug Winter/Dean Schmidt 1/99, Midwestern dealer. Graded About Uncirculated-50 by PCGS.

• Nevada collection ex: Doug Winter 4/00, Spectrum Numismatics. Graded About Uncirculated-50 by PCGS.

• Austin Rare Coins inventory 5/00 via Casey Noxon/Jeff Garrett. Graded About Uncirculated-50 by NGC.

3. (tie) Approximately four or five examples are known to exist that grade Extremely Fine-45 or thereabouts. These include the following:

• Kevin Lipton, ex: Bowers and Merena 11/00: 696 ($19,550), ex: Harry Bass collection, Joe Flynn. Sharpness of About Uncirculated-50 or better but with a small reverse gouge below the eagle's throat.

• Jack Copeland (Royalty Coins), ex: Heritage 1/01: 8285 ($21,850), Heritage 11/00: 7189 (unsold), private collection via Lee Minshull 6/00, Heritage Rare Coin Galleries, Heritage 1999 ANA: 8117 (unsold). Graded About Uncirculated-50 by NGC.

• Chicago collection, ex: Doug Winter, Superior 6/97: 1540 ($29,700). Graded Extremely Fine-45 by PCGS.

• Alaska collection. Graded Extremely Fine-45 by PCGS.

• Private collection 1/01, ex: Spectrum Numismatics. Graded Extremely Fine-45 by NGC.

• Michigan collection, ex: Bowers and Merena Norweb II (3/88): 2197 ($10,450), Morganthau 12/10/35. Extremely Fine-45; possibly later graded as such by NGC.

• Private collection, ex: RARCOA Auction '79: 1307 ($7,750). Extremely Fine-45.

In addition to these pieces, there are others which grade Extremely Fine-40. These include the following:

• Tony Terranova, ex: Goldberg 6/00: 1525. Graded Extremely Fine-40 by PCGS.

• Bowers and Merena 5/99: 2425 ($19,550) ex: New Jersey collection, 11/98, Dr. Richard Appel. Graded Extremely Fine-40 by NGC.

• Northern California collection, ex: Doug Winter, Nevada collection, Winthrop Carner, Stack's 9/95: 698 ($16,500), Stack's 4/87: 1104, Stack's 10/71: 1069. Graded Extremely Fine-40 by PCGS. *The plate coin in this book.*

• Tahoe collection, ex: Heritage 10/95: 6353 ($22,000), Warren Miller collection. Graded Extremely Fine-40 by PCGS.

• Orange County collection duplicate, ex: Doug Winter/Lee Minshull, Dr. Larry Cutler. Graded Extremely Fine-40 by NGC. *The plate coin in "Gold Coins of the Old West."*

• Private collection, ex: Eastern dealer, Charley Tuppen collection, possibly ex: Bowers and Merena 11/92: 1120 ($10,450). Graded Extremely Fine-40 by NGC.

• Tennessee collection, ex: The Mint (Jay Parrino) Bowers and Merena 10/99: 1520 ($25,300), Harry Bass collection, Rarcoa 8/24/73. Graded Extremely Fine-40 by PCGS.

• Washington D.C. collection, ex: Doug Winter 1998. Graded Extremely Fine-40 by NGC.

The 1870-CC eagle is the second rarest Carson City gold coin, trailing only the well-known double eagle of this year. It is most often seen very well worn. It is very rare in properly graded Extremely Fine-40 and extremely rare in the higher range of this grade. There are currently only four known in About Uncirculated and none in Uncirculated.

1871-CC

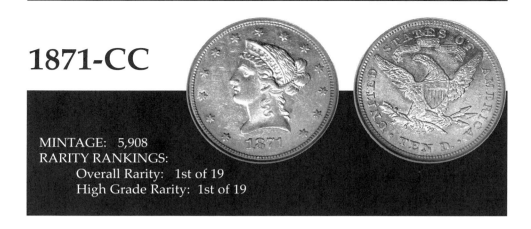

MINTAGE: 5,908
RARITY RANKINGS:
    Overall Rarity: 1st of 19
    High Grade Rarity: 1st of 19

This date is a bit more available than one might expect and it is actually the second most common Carson City eagle from the 1870's, trailing only the 1874-CC. It is a very rare coin, however, in higher grades.

STRIKE: The 1871-CC eagle is generally seen with a better quality of strike than the other Carson City eagles from the early part of the 1870's. The obverse is generally not as well struck as the reverse and often shows weakness on the curls surrounding the face and ear of Liberty. In addition, the hair is typically weak at its top, as is the bun. The reverse shows some weakness on the neck feathers but it is almost always quite a bit sharper than the obverse.

SURFACES: Almost every piece that I have seen is very heavily abraded. This is obviously an issue that was placed into circulation and most were used extensively in commerce. There are a few that show reasonably clean surfaces and these are rare.

LUSTER: Most 1871-CC eagles are worn to the point that they show little--if any--original mint luster. Those with natural luster display a blend of satiny frost and slight reflectiveness. There are a small number that are almost fully prooflike but these tend to show extremely heavy bagmarks.

COLORATION: The natural coloration is a deep green-gold or orange-gold hue with a somewhat "dirty" or smudgy appearance. Very few 1871-CC eagles have survived with completely original coloration.

EYE APPEAL: There are actually a fair number of reasonably attractive Extremely Fine examples of this date. Higher grade coins with good eye appeal are very hard to locate and most About Uncirculated pieces are extensively abraded or have been cleaned.

DIE VARIETIES: Two die varieties are known. Breen's claims that varieties exist with a normal reverse and a doubled reverse are incorrect as this doubling is actually light machine doubling as seen on some examples.

Variety 1-A: The date is straight and level. The reverse is a reuse of that found on the first variety of the 1870-CC eagle with the mintmark positioned well to the left of the arrowfeathers. Many examples of this variety show light to heavy machine doubling on the letters. On late states, there is a mint-made depression on the ER in LIBERTY which extends to the lower part of Liberty's hair.

Variety 2-A: The date is placed slightly lower and slants down from left to right. The reverse is the same as on Variety 1-A and it often has no doubling. This variety appears to be considerably scarcer than the first.

RARITY:

Total Known: 90-100

BY GRADE:

VF	EF	AU	MINT STATE
53-57	26-29	10-12	1-2

CONDITION CENSUS

1. Private collection, ex: Heritage 1995 Midwinter ANA Sale: 5959 ($44,000). Graded Mint State-62 by NGC. Found in Europe.

2. West Coast dealer, ex: Eastern dealer 8/97, Charley Tuppen collection, Heritage Numismatic Auctions 10/95: 6358 ($30,800; as PCGS AU-55), Warren Miller collection via Delaware Valley Rare Coins in May, 1991. Graded Mint State-60 by NGC.

3. Northern California collection 8/99, ex: Doug Winter 5/99, Nevada Collection 6/98, Doug Winter/Lee Minshull. Graded About Uncirculated-58 by NGC. *The plate coin in this book.*

4 (tie). Chicago collection, ex: Doug Winter/Lee Minshull 8/97. Graded About Uncirculated-55 by NGC.

- Spectrum Numismatics, ex: Jason Carter/CNL, 10/98, Spectrum Numismatics, J.J. Teaparty, New Jersey dealer inventory, first seen by me at the 11/97 Baltimore coin show. Graded About Uncirculated-58 by NGC.

- Heritage 2/00: 6763 ($14,950), ex: Heritage Rare Coin Galleries, 6/99. Graded About Uncirculated-55 by NGC.

- Orange County collection, obtained 3/97. Graded About Uncirculated-55 by PCGS.

- Private collection 7/00, ex: Doug Winter/Spectrum Numismatics, Tony Terranova, Goldberg 6/00: 1528 as PCGS AU-50). Graded About Uncirculated-55 by NGC

5 (tie). The following coins grade About Uncirculated-53 or thereabouts:

• Washington D.C. collection, ex: Doug Winter 5/00. Graded About Uncirculated-53 by NGC.

• Superior 2/98: 3484 ($15,950), ex: Charley Tuppen collection. A duplicate example from this collection, first seen at the 1996 ANA convention. Graded About Uncirculated-53 by NGC.

• New Jersey collection, 12/98, ex: Doug Winter/Lee Minshull, 7/98, Nevada collector. Graded About Uncirculated-53 by NGC.

• Oregon collection. Graded About Uncirculated-53 by NGC.

Other slabbed About Uncirculated-53 coins exist, including two graded as such by PCGS as of March 2001.

The 1871-CC is the second most available Carson City eagle from the 1870's but it is still a scarce coin in all grades. It is most often seen in Fine to Very Fine and accurately graded Extremely Fine pieces are rare. There are fewer than a dozen known in About Uncirculated and most are in the lower range of this grade. Only one unquestionably Mint State 1871-CC eagle is currently known to exist.

1872-CC

MINTAGE: 5,908
RARITY RANKINGS:
    Overall Rarity: 1st of 19
    High Grade Rarity: 1st of 19

The 1872-CC is one of the rarest Carson City eagles, both in terms of overall and high grade rarity. This date is not as underrated as it was when the first version of this book was published in 1994, but its true rarity still remains unknown to most non-specialists.

STRIKE: Beginning with this date, the quality of strike found on Carson City eagles becomes worse than the fairly good quality seen on the 1870-CC and 1871-CC issues. The 1872-CC is nearly always seen with soft, blurry details on the obverse. The curls over the eye are frequently very soft, as is the curl beneath the ear and the hair bun. Many of the stars show flatness at the centers as well. The reverse typically appears much sharper than the obverse. The shield, lower neck feathers and the right leg are often somewhat weak.

SURFACES: As on all Carson City eagles from this era, the surfaces on most 1872-CC eagles are usually seen with noticeable abrasions. For some reason, these marks seem less obtrusive than on the 1870-CC and 1871-CC issues. I have seen at least a few 1872-CC's that had mint-made grease stains or areas of discoloration in the fields.

LUSTER: With the typical grade range for this date running from Fine to Very Fine, few 1872-CC eagles have more than a hint of original mint luster. The few pieces with luster show a soft, frosty texture.

COLORATION: There are probably not more than a dozen 1872-CC eagles that have natural coloration. The hues seen on these range from rich yellow-gold to a deeper green-gold shade. This coloration tends to be very attractive, making these coins especially desirable.

EYE APPEAL: The level of eye appeal for the 1872-CC eagle is generally below average. Most are weakly struck, heavily abraded, and show considerable wear. This is a hard coin to grade, due to the fact that the obverse is typically five to ten points lower in sharpness than the reverse.

DIE VARIETIES: Two die varieties are known.

Variety 1-A: The date is somewhat large and low and it appears to be fairly even to the naked eye. The reverse is a reuse of Reverse A from 1870. It can be identified by the small, even mintmark positioned well to the left of the arrowfeathers.

Variety 1-B: The obverse is the same as on Variety 1-A. The reverse is a reuse of Reverse B from 1870. The mintmark is positioned closer to the arrowfeathers and the first C is higher than the second.

Die State I: The reverse is normal with some very slight recutting noted on the lettering.

Die State II: This die state shows doubling on the reverse with this doubling most noticeable on the STA in STATES and the eagle's left wing tip.

RARITY:
    Total Known: 60-70

BY GRADE:

VF	EF	AU	MINT STATE
47-55	9-10	4-5	0

CONDITION CENSUS

1 (tie). Private collection, ex: Heritage Numismatic Auctions 10/95: 6362 ($44,000), Warren Miller collection, Winthrop Carner. Supposedly earlier in a Brazilian collection. Graded About Uncirculated-55 by PCGS.

• Nevada collection via Doug Winter, ex: Bowers and Merena 11/00: 702 ($34,500), Harry Bass collection, purchased from John J. Ford, Jr. on April 7, 1975. Graded About Uncirculated-55 by PCGS.

2. Chicago collection, ex: Doug Winter/Lee Minshull, Larry Cutler collection, Bowers and Merena Stetson sale (5/93): 2064 ($16,500). Graded About Uncirculated-55 by NGC.

3. Orange County collection, ex: Eastern dealer, Charley Tuppen collection. Graded About Uncirculated-53 by PCGS.

4 (tie). Northern California collection, ex: Teletrade 10/99. Graded About Uncirculated-50 by PCGS.

• Colorado dealer, ex: Bowers and Merena 2000 ANA: 2392 (unsold). Graded About Uncirculated-50 by PCGS.

5. Private collection, ex: Superior 1/96: 2454 ($12,650; as "Extremely Fine-40"). Graded About Uncirculated-50 by NGC.

Note: There is a coin listed as having been graded About Uncirculated-53 by NGC as of January 2001; it is possibly the same as #3, above. NGC also lists two other About Uncirculated-50 coins as of January 2001.

The 1872-CC is among the rarest of Carson City eagles. Most survivors are very well worn and a properly graded Extremely Fine-40 is about the best example one will generally find. This date is very rare in About Uncirculated grades and it is currently unknown above About Uncirculated-55.

1873-CC

MINTAGE: 5,908
RARITY RANKINGS:
 Overall Rarity: 1st of 19
 High Grade Rarity: 1st of 19

The 1873-CC has a mintage similar to the 1872-CC eagle. These two dates are also similar in terms of their overall and high grade rarity. Like the 1872-CC, the 1873-CC is an extremely hard coin to locate above Very Fine-35.

STRIKE: The quality of strike is akin to that seen on the 1872-CC eagle. Typically, the obverse is less well detailed than the reverse and an 1873-CC eagle may have Very Fine detail on the obverse with Extremely Fine detail on the reverse. The weakest areas on the obverse are the hair and the face and ear of Liberty, the top of the hair and most of the bun. The reverse shows better overall detail but will often be weak on the neck feathers and right leg feathers.

SURFACES: Most 1873-CC eagles are very heavily abraded. These marks are usually deep and poorly situated--i.e., on the face of Liberty or directly in front of Liberty's profile. For some reason, a number of well worn pieces are actually fairly clean; meaning that it is easier to locate a clean, choice Fine to Very Fine coin than an acceptable Extremely Fine. Only a small number have original surfaces with most having been cleaned at least once.

LUSTER: Nearly every known 1873-CC eagle is worn to the point that little of the original mint luster remains. Those that do have luster are usually frosty with a slightly reflective appearance.

COLORATION: Some lower grade pieces possess natural coloration but most of the 1873-CC eagles that grade Extremely Fine-40 or above have been cleaned. The original hues seen range from rich yellow-gold to deep green-gold. A higher grade piece with totally original color is very rare and worth a strong premium.

EYE APPEAL: As hard as this date is to find in higher grades, it is even harder to locate with good eye appeal. Most 1873-CC eagles are not well struck, have an unbalanced appearance between the obverse and reverse and are heavily bag-marked.

DIE VARIETIES: There are three die varieties known. One of these has an important Die State that has previously been described as a separate variety.

Variety 1-A: Closed 3 as on all. The date is normal with no signs of repunching. The reverse is a reuse of Reverse A from 1870 and 1871 with the mintmark high and positioned entirely to the left of the arrowfeathers.

Variety 2-A: Closed 3 as on all. The date shows repunching at the bottom of the 1 and the 8. The reverse is the same as on the last variety with no signs of doubling. (This is properly designated as Die State I).

Die State II: The reverse shows light to moderate strike doubling on the lettering.

Variety 2-B: Closed 3 as on all. The obverse is the same as the last but may show slightly less doubling on the 18. The reverse is new. The mintmark is lower and placed far more to the right with the second C entirely beneath the arrow feather. There is a thin die scratch in the O in the motto IN GOD WE TRUST which causes this letter to resemble a Q. There is usually distinct doubling on the letters of TEN D.

RARITY:
    Total Known: 55-65

BY GRADE:

VF	EF	AU	MINT STATE
43-48	8-10	4-5	0

CONDITION CENSUS

1. Northern California collection, ex: Carter Numismatics, Bowers and Merena 10/99: 1538 ($32,200; as PCGS AU-53), Harry Bass collection, Superior 2/73: 707 ($2,200). Graded About Uncirculated-58 by NGC.

2 (tie). Private collection, ex: Eastern dealer, Charley Tuppen collection. Graded About Uncirculated-53 by NGC.

   • Private collection via The Mint (Jay Parrino), ex: Bowers and Merena 5/00: 681 ($33,350), ex: Harry Bass collection, Abner Kreisberg via private treaty on 3/1/68. Graded About Uncirculated-53 by PCGS.

3. Chicago collection, ex: Doug Winter/Lee Minshull, 12/94, Florida dealer. Graded About Uncirculated-50 by PCGS.

4 (tie). Orange County collection 5/99, ex: Doug Winter, Nevada collection, Doug Winter, Heritage Numismatic Auctions 10/95: 6366 ($13,750), Warren Miller collection. Graded About Uncirculated-50 by PCGS. *The plate coin in this book.*

   • Northern California collection duplicate, 7/99, ex: Doug Winter/Lee Minshull. Graded About Uncirculated-50 by PCGS.

• Heritage 4/01: 7838. Graded About Uncirculated-53 by NGC.

• Monex inventory 3/00, ex: Spectrum Numismatics. Graded About Uncirculated-53 by NGC.

5. Heritage Rare Coin Galleries, 1/99. Graded About Uncirculated-50 by NGC. Probably the same as one of the coins listed below.

Coins that grade Extremely Fine-45 include the following:

• Alaska collection. Graded Extremely Fine-45 by PCGS.

• Private collection, ex: David Carrothers (Grand Gold Exchange, Reno, NV), Doug Winter/Lee Minshull, Dr. Larry Cutler collection, Doug Winter, National Gold Exchange, found in Europe in 1994. Graded Extremely Fine-45 by NGC. The plate coin in *"Gold Coins of the Old West."*

• Bowers and Merena 10/99: 1539 ($12,650), ex: Harry Bass collection, William Donner 2/68. Graded Extremely Fine-45 by PCGS.

• Heritage 1999 ANA: 8121 ($9,487). Graded Extremely Fine-45 by PCGS.

• Heritage 4/99: 5919 ($9,487). Graded Extremely Fine-45 by NGC.

Other encapsulated Extremely Fine-45 pieces exist.

The 1873-CC eagle is a rare coin in all grades. Most show considerable wear and any that grades Extremely Fine-40 represents unusual quality. There are probably no more than a half dozen known in About Uncirculated and no 1873-CC eagle is currently known or rumored in any Mint State grade.

1874-CC

MINTAGE: 5,908
RARITY RANKINGS:
    Overall Rarity: 1st of 19
    High Grade Rarity: 1st of 19

There were nearly as many eagles struck at the Carson City mint in 1874 as there were in the three previous years combined. The 1874-CC is the most available Carson City eagle from the 1870's and it is the only issue from this decade that can be found in high grades (About Uncirculated-50 and above) without extreme difficulty. Approximately twenty to thirty pieces, most of which graded Very Fine to Extremely Fine, came onto the market in the mid-1990's from a hoard.

STRIKE: The strike is a bit sharper than on the 1872-CC and 1873-CC eagles but it still is below average. The obverse is slightly convex in appearance and it is usually much weaker than the reverse. To the collector not familiar with this issue, it may appear five to fifteen numerical points less in terms of sharpness. The central obverse is often weak and some have very soft curls around the face. The tip of the coronet and the back of the hair bun are often weak as well. The reverse tends to be sharper but the neck feathers, leg feathers and the right claw may show significant weakness. On some 1874-CC eagles, the mintmark is quite weak as well.

SURFACES: As on nearly every Carson City gold issue from the 1870's, the surfaces on the typical 1874-CC eagle are very heavily abraded. On most, the obverse fields show deep, detracting marks while the reverse is slightly cleaner.

LUSTER: The luster on the 1874-CC is better than on other Carson City eagles from this era. The texture is frosty and on some of the high grade pieces known to exist, it is comparable to a Philadelphia eagle of this date.

COLORATION: More 1874-CC eagles are found with original coloration than other Carson City eagles from the early 1870's. However, most have been cleaned or dipped. The natural coloration is often somewhat dark with deep green-gold and yellow-gold hues. Some of the higher grade pieces have rich coppery-orange overtones.

EYE APPEAL: The typical 1874-CC eagle has below average eye appeal due to poor strikes, uneven balance between the obverse and the reverse, and excessive bagmarks. But more relatively attractive 1874-CC eagles exist than any other Carson City eagle prior to 1880 and the date collector should be able to find an acceptable piece without an exhausting search.

DIE VARIETIES: Only one variety is currently known. Given the fact that the previous four eagles from this mint have more than one variety (with significantly smaller mintages) it is possible that at least one other exists.

Variety 1-A: The date is medium sized and well spaced between the neck and the denticles. The reverse is a reuse of 1873-CC Reverse B. This can be confirmed by the presence of the die scratch through the O in GOD.

RARITY:
Total Known: 150-175

BY GRADE:

VF	EF	AU	MINT STATE
96-104	42-57	10-12	2

CONDITION CENSUS

1. Private collection, ex: Heritage Numismatic Auctions 10/95: 6374 (unsold), Bob Leece. Graded Mint State-64 by NGC. This coin did not sell at the Miller auction but was later sold via private treaty to its present owner. The finest Carson City eagle of any date that I have ever seen.

2. Nevada collection via Doug Winter, ex: Bowers and Merena 11/00: 712 ($66,700), Harry Bass collection, Bowers and Ruddy Eliasberg collection (10/82): 746 ($17,600), Clapp, Chapman Brothers 1/1900. Graded Mint State-63 by PCGS.

3. Orange County collection 6/99, ex: Doug Winter, Nevada collection, Doug Winter, Heritage Numismatic Auctions 10/95: 6373 ($6,875; as PCGS AU-53). Graded About Uncirculated-58 by NGC. *The plate coin in this book.*

4 (tie). Chicago collection, ex: Doug Winter, Nevada collection duplicate. Graded About Uncirculated-55 by NGC.

• Heritage 11/00: 7190 (unsold), ex: Heritage Rare Coin Galleries inventory, 10/00. Graded About Uncirculated-55 by PCGS.

• National Gold Exchange inventory, obtained at the 1997 ANA convention via private treaty. Graded About Uncirculated-55 by PCGS.

• There is one other piece graded About Uncirculated-55 by PCGS as of March 2001.

• Northern California collection, ex: Doug Winter/Lee Minshull, Superior Coin Co., 2/99, Superior 2/99: 3352 (unsold). Graded About Uncirculated-55 by NGC.

• Jason Carter inventory, 2000. Graded About Uncirculated-55 by NGC. Probably one of the following.

• There are two other pieces graded About Uncirculated-55 by NGC as of January 2001.

5 (tie). Approximately three or four pieces exist which grade About Uncirculated-53. These include the following:

• Bowers and Merena 10/99: 1547 ($10,350), ex: Harry Bass collection, Stack's 5/19/71. Graded About Uncirculated-53 by PCGS.

• Alaska collector, ex: Doug Winter/Lee Minshull, 2/95. Graded About Uncirculated-53 by NGC.

• Private collection, ex: Paul Nugget 7/00, Doug Winter, Orange County collection duplicate. Graded About Uncirculated-53 by PCGS.

• Private collection via Minnesota dealer, ex: Dean Schmidt 7/00. Graded About Uncirculated-53 by PCGS.

As of January 2001, NGC had graded three other examples in About Uncirculated-53.

The 1874-CC eagle is a reasonably easy issue to locate in grades up to and including Extremely Fine-40. Attractive Extremely Fine-45's are scarce while About Uncirculated examples are quite rare. There are currently two 1874-CC eagles known in Uncirculated and both are choice.

1875-CC

MINTAGE: 5,908
RARITY RANKINGS:
Overall Rarity: 1st of 19
High Grade Rarity: 1st of 19

A few more high grade 1875-CC eagles are known than when the book *"Gold Coins of the Old West"* was released in 1994. However, this date remains one of the rarest Carson City eagles.

STRIKE: The 1875-CC is the most poorly struck eagle from the Carson City mint. I have seen examples on which the obverse appeared to be twenty to twenty- five numerical points lower than the reverse (i.e., the obverse had the sharpness of Very Fine-20 to Very Fine-25 while the reverse had the sharpness of Extremely Fine-40 to Extremely Fine-45). The entire obverse appears very flat. It is weakest on the curls around the face and ear as well as on the top of the hair, the coronet point and the top of the bun. The rim has a bevelled appearance--not unlike that seen on certain Dahlonega half eagles--suggesting some sort of technical difficulties at the mint. The reverse is better detailed but the neck feathers, the left leg of the eagle, and the olive branch usually show some amount of weakness. It is important to learn the characteristics of strike for this issue as it is very hard to properly grade.

SURFACES: The surfaces on nearly all 1875-CC eagles are very heavily abraded. I have seen a number that had prominent and extremely detracting marks present; often on the face or neck and frequently very deep into the planchet. I have seen a handful that have not been cleaned or dipped.

LUSTER: The luster is below average and it has a soft, slightly fuzzy appearance. Most 1875-CC eagles are worn to the point that no luster remains and many of the surviving coins that grade Extremely Fine-40 or above have impaired luster from repeated cleanings.

COLORATION: The natural coloration ranges from a medium to deep green-gold hue. Not many 1875-CC eagles retain their original color.

EYE APPEAL: This is one of the hardest Carson City gold coins to locate with good eye appeal, because so many are poorly struck and have such a completely different appearance on the obverse than on the reverse. Any 1875-CC eagle with even average quality eye appeal is rare and attractive, lightly marked pieces with natural color trade for a very strong premium among knowledgeable specialists.

DIE VARIETIES: One die variety is known. Another, mentioned by Breen, could exist but I have not seen it.

Variety 1-A: The date is slightly high in the field and it slants downwards from left to right. There is a lump on the right arm of the Y in LIBERTY which serves as a good hallmark of authenticity. The reverse is very similar to that seen on the 1874-CC eagle but the mintmark is slightly higher and the second C is almost totally to the right of the arrowfeather. The first C is higher than the second and it is always more weakly impressed.

Variety "1-B": Breen reports that this variety has a mintmark that is placed lower in the field than on Reverse A and which is more sharply impressed. I have never seen an example of this variety.

RARITY:

Total Known: 65-75

BY GRADE:

VF	EF	AU	MINT STATE
47-54	12-14	6-7	0

CONDITION CENSUS

1 (tie). Private collection, ex: Doug Winter/Lee Minshull 5/99, Nevada Collection 7/98, Doug Winter/Spectrum Numismatics, Kansas dealer, private collection, Superior 2/94: 2455 ($26,400; as PCGS AU-53). Graded About Uncirculated-55 by PCGS. *The plate coin in this book.*

• Private collection via The Mint (Jay Parrino), ex: Bowers and Merena 5/00: 687 ($28,750), Harry Bass collection, Paramount 8/67: 2132. Graded About Uncirculated-55 by PCGS. Either this or the next coin was later graded Mint State-60 by NGC.

• Eastern dealer, ex: Bowers and Merena 11/00: 716 ($31,050), Harry Bass collection, Pullen and Hanks via private treaty, 8/75. Graded About Uncirculated-55 by PCGS.

2 (tie). Chicago collection 1/95, ex: Doug Winter/Lee Minshull, Florida dealer. Graded About Uncirculated-53 by PCGS.

• Bowers and Merena 10/99: 1552 ($21,850; as PCGS AU-50), ex: Harry Bass collection. Graded About Uncirculated-55 by PCGS.

3. Orange County collection, ex: Doug Winter/Lee Minshull, Dr. Larry Cutler collection, Mid American Rare Coin Auctions 5/92: 396 ($12,000). Graded About Uncirculated-53 by PCGS.

4 (tie). Northern California collection, ex: Eastern dealer, Charley Tuppen collection. Graded About Uncirculated-53 by PCGS.

• Heritage 11/00: 7191 ($24,000), ex: Heritage Rare Coin Galleries inventory, 8/00. Graded About Uncirculated-53 by PCGS.

• Spectrum Numismatics, ex: MGS/NSI (Gary Adkins) inventory, first seen 3/01. Graded About Uncirculated-55 by PCGS.

• NGC lists two coins graded About Uncirculated-53 as of January 2001. Their location and pedigree are unknown.

5 (tie). Bowers and Merena 2000 ANA: 2400 (unsold). Graded About Uncirculated-50 by PCGS.

• Southern California collection 8/00, ex: Doug Winter, Heritage Rare Coin Galleries, Heritage 8/00: 7833 (unsold), Country Lane Rarities, private collection. Graded About Uncirculated-50 by PCGS.

As of January 2001, the NGC "Census Report" lists a graded coin Mint State-63. I have no information about it but if this coin exists it is clearly the finest known.

The 1875-CC eagle is a very scarce coin although it is somewhat more available in low grades than generally realized. Accurately graded Extremely Fine-40 pieces are about the best quality that is usually seen and this is a rare coin in Extremely Fine-45. Only a half dozen or so About Uncirculated pieces exist and no Uncirculated 1875-CC eagles are currently known of which I am aware.

1876-CC

MINTAGE: 4,696
RARITY RANKINGS:
  Overall Rarity: 8th of 19
  High Grade Rarity: 5th of 19

The 1876-CC is one of the rarest Carson City eagles. Like its half eagle counterpart, this is a coin appreciated only by students of Carson City gold coinage. Specialists are well aware of the rarity of this date; especially in the higher grades.

STRIKE: Beginning with the 1876-CC, the quality of strike seen on Carson City eagles improves over the poor level seen on the 1872 through 1875 issues. Most 1876-CC eagles have a slightly flat appearance at the centers. The hair around the face of Liberty is weak as is the top of the hair and the upper part of the bun. The reverse is always soft on the neck feathers and the inner feathers around the left wing. On many pieces, the mintmark is faint and might be overlooked at first glimpse.

SURFACES: I have not seen more than a handful of 1876-CC eagles without a large number of marks on the surfaces. These are usually obtrusive and deep and, more often than not, appear in the obverse fields. For some reason, this date is more likely to show serious edge bruises than other Carson City eagles from the 1870's. On unencapsulated pieces, collectors should look out for signs of edge filing where such bruises have been removed.

LUSTER: This issue does not have good luster. The few examples high grade enough to have more than a small amount of original luster are frosty with a slightly satiny texture. Many have been cleaned or dipped.

COLORATION: The original coloration is often a deep coppery-orange or green-gold. An original 1876-CC eagle tends to have deeper coloration than other Carson City issues of this era.

EYE APPEAL: Not many 1876-CC eagles have good eye appeal. Most are softly struck at the centers, have severe abrasions and/or rim marks, and have been cleaned. Attractive, original examples trade for a strong premium over typical quality pieces.

DIE VARIETIES: A single variety is known.

Variety 1-A: The date is medium sized and slightly low in the field. The 6 in the date is closed with the top loop of this digit touching the lower loop. The mintmark is small and widely spaced with the first C a bit higher than the second, and is placed high. The second C nearly touches the bottom of the arrow feather.

RARITY:

Total Known: 70-80

BY GRADE:

VF	EF	AU	MINT STATE
47-52	17-20	6-8	0

CONDITION CENSUS

1. Private collection, ex: Eastern dealer 7/97, Charley Tuppen collection, Heritage Numismatic Auctions 10/95: 6382 ($26,400), Warren Miller collection, Bowers and Merena Stetson sale (5/93): 2071 ($29,700). Once graded About Uncirculated-58 by PCGS; apparently removed from its holder and now unencapsulated.

2. Private collection, ex: Winthrop Carner, Heritage 10/94: 6953 ($22,000). About Uncirculated-55 or better.

3 (tie). Orange County collection 5/99, ex: Doug Winter, Nevada collection 6/97, Doug Winter/Delaware Valley Rare Coins, New England dealer. Graded About Uncirculated-58 by PCGS. *The plate coin in this book.*

• Private collection 2/99, ex: Heritage Rare Coin Galleries. Graded About Uncirculated-58 by NGC.

• NGC lists two other coins graded About Uncirculated-58 as of January 2001. I have not seen these.

4 (tie). Tennessee collection via The Mint (Jay Parrino), ex: Bowers and Merena 5/00: 688 ($28,750), Harry Bass collection, Julian Leidman via private treaty sale, 11/21/69. Graded About Uncirculated-55 by PCGS.

• Private collection, ex: Bowers and Merena 11/00: 719 ($23,500), Harry Bass collection, Stack's 1976 ANA: 3100. Graded About Uncirculated-55 by PCGS.

5 (tie). Private collection, ex: Charley Tuppen collection duplicate. Graded About Uncirculated-53 by NGC.

• Bowers and Merena 3/01: 198 (unsold). Graded About Uncirculated-53 by PCGS.

• Private collection, ex: Eastern dealer 1998. Graded About Uncirculated-53 by PCGS.

• One other coin has been graded About Uncirculated-53 by PCGS as of March 2001.

Coins that grade About Uncirculated-50 include the following:

- Superior 1/31-2/1/94: 2580 ($11,550). Graded About Uncirculated-50 by PCGS.

- TIA/Robert Hughes, ex: Casey Noxon, 8/00. Graded About Uncirculated-50 by PCGS.

- PCGS had graded five other examples About Uncirculated-50 as of March 2001. This number is inflated by resubmissions.

The 1876-CC eagle is scarce in all grades and most of the known examples are in the Fine to Very Fine range. It is very hard to locate in the lower Extremely Fine grades and rare in the higher range of this grade. In About Uncirculated this is a very rare issue and there are no Mint State 1876-CC eagles currently known.

1877-CC

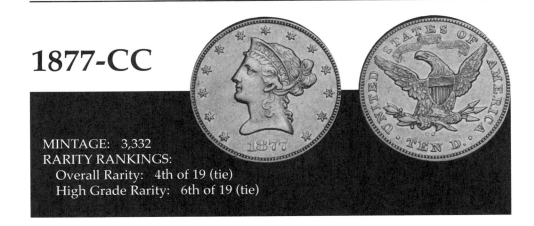

MINTAGE: 3,332
RARITY RANKINGS:
  Overall Rarity: 4th of 19 (tie)
  High Grade Rarity: 6th of 19 (tie)

In my book *"Gold Coins of the Old West,"* I stated that the 1877-CC eagle "...is found with greater frequency than any other of the issues from the 1870's." Given the fact that virtually no high quality examples of this date have been on the market since the mid-1990's, I must either admit making a mistake or conclude that the few nice 1877-CC eagles that do exist are tightly held in private collections and have not come up for sale in many years.

STRIKE: The 1877-CC eagle is somewhat better struck than the Carson City eagles from the earlier part of the 1870's. The obverse center is nearly always weak but the curls around the face show better detail than one might expect. On the reverse, there is sometimes weakness on the neck feathers and the inner feather on the right wing. There is often a clashmark above the left wing of the eagle.

SURFACES: On most examples, the surfaces are very heavily abraded. One must remember that these low mintage Carson City eagles from the 1870's were actively used in daily commerce and were handled roughly. Furthermore, there were no coin collectors in the Carson City area in the 19th century, meaning that the few high grade coins that exist from this time have survived by accident or circumstance.

LUSTER: The luster is average quality and exhibits a frosty, very slightly reflective texture. Not many 1877-CC eagles show much luster and no more than a handful that have original, undisturbed surfaces.

COLORATION: The natural coloration for this issue is a rich green-gold hue. As on most Carson City eagles from the 1870's, few have not been cleaned, dipped or otherwise mishandled.

EYE APPEAL: The level of eye appeal is generally below average. The surfaces are often so heavily abraded that a coin with the sharpness of, say, Extremely Fine-45 might be net graded down to Extremely Fine-40 on account of these marks. An 1877-CC eagle with good eye appeal is very rare and in strong demand among specialists.

DIE VARIETIES: There are two die varieties known.

Variety 1-A: On this variety, the date is closer to the denticles than it is to the base of Liberty's neck. The mintmark is small, rather widely spaced and positioned entirely to the left of the bottom arrow feather.

Variety 2-A: On this variety, the date is slightly higher. The base of the 77 shows light to moderate repunching. The reverse is the same as on the previous variety although on this there is sometimes light machine doubling on the word STATES.

RARITY:
Total Known: 55-65

BY GRADE:

VF	EF	AU	MINT STATE
30-34	18-22	6-8	1

CONDITION CENSUS

1. Private collection, ex: Paramount 2/74: 689. Mint State-60 or better. Unseen by me but reliably described by David Akers as being "choice."

2 (tie). Private collection, ex: Heritage 10/95: 6386 ($27,500), Bowers and Merena 3/92: 2095 ($12,100), Pine Tree 5/76: 409. Graded About Uncirculated-55 by PCGS.

• Northern California collection via Doug Winter, ex: Bowers and Merena 5/00: 690 ($41,400), Harry Bass collection, Stack's via private treaty sale 10/7/70. Graded About Uncirculated-55 by PCGS.

3. Chicago collection, ex: Doug Winter. Graded About Uncirculated-55 by NGC.

4 (tie). Orange County collection via Doug Winter, ex: Superior 6/98: 2300 ($12,650), National Gold Exchange inventory, 7/97. Graded About Uncirculated-53 by PCGS.

• New Jersey collection, ex: Doug Winter/Lee Minshull, Superior 2/01: 4641 ($10,925). Graded About Uncirculated-53 by PCGS.

• Nevada collection 6/00 via Nevada dealer, ex: Eastern dealer inventory, 1/00. Graded About Uncirculated-53 by PCGS.

• PCGS had graded one other coin About Uncirculated-53 as of March 2001.

5 (tie). Eastern dealer inventory, 7/97, ex: Charley Tuppen collection. Graded About Uncirculated-50 by NGC.

- As of January 2001, NGC had graded two additional examples About Uncirculated-50.

- As of March 2001, PCGS had graded two coins in About Uncirculated-50.

The 1877-CC is a rare coin in any grade. When available, the typical specimen grades Very Fine. This date is sometimes seen in Extremely Fine-40 but attractive Extremely Fine-45 pieces are very difficult to locate. There are only a few known in About Uncirculated and the 1877-CC eagle may not exist in Mint State.

1878-CC

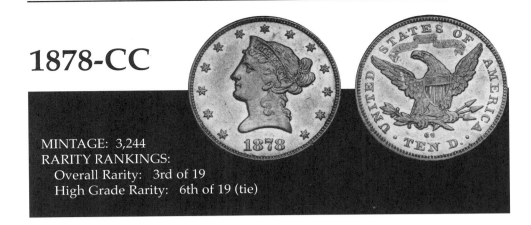

MINTAGE: 3,244
RARITY RANKINGS:
Overall Rarity: 3rd of 19
High Grade Rarity: 6th of 19 (tie)

Only one Carson City gold coin--the 1879-CC eagle--has a lower original mintage figure than the 1878-CC. This date is among the rarest Carson City eagles in terms of its overall rarity. In high grades, it is comparable to other very rare issues such as the 1872-CC, 1873-CC, 1875-CC, and the 1876-CC.

STRIKE: The quality of strike seen on 1878-CC eagles varies. Most are somewhat weakly impressed at the centers with notable flatness on the curls around the face of Liberty and the corresponding reverse. Others are sharper at the centers with some of the aforementioned weakness but with better detail on the curls. The stars are often flat at the centers and it is not uncommon for a high grade 1878-CC eagle to be very soft on the neck feathers of the eagle. All genuine pieces have three important diagnostic criteria. On the obverse there is a small raised bar below the bottom of the curl that extends beneath the ear of Liberty. On the reverse there is a clashmark running from the neck of the eagle into its right wing and another more extensive clashmark from the left wing into the neck.

SURFACES: Almost every 1878-CC eagle that I have seen is very heavily abraded. These abrasions tend to be deep and detracting. A number have rim bumps and any unencapsulated piece should be checked for signs of rim filing.

LUSTER: This is an issue that does not have especially good luster. On the small handful of high grade pieces known, the luster is soft and satiny in texture. The majority of 1878-CC eagles have been cleaned or dipped.

COLORATION: The natural coloration is an attractive dark coppery-orange or medium to deep green-gold. Some show extensive mint-made copper spots or have small areas of discoloration in the planchet. There are more 1878-CC eagles with natural color than other dates of this era but this could change as more and more are dipped or cleaned.

EYE APPEAL: The 1878-CC eagle is not often seen with good eye appeal. Most are either weakly struck or have numerous deep abrasions on the surfaces. Examples that are relatively well defined at the centers, minimally abraded, and have their natural coloration are worth a substantial premium over a typical piece.

DIE VARIETIES: There is just a single variety known.

Variety 1-A: The date is placed low in the field. The mintmark is tall and it is shaped differently than on any of the previous eagles from this mint. The second C is placed midway below the bottom arrow feather.

RARITY:
Total Known: 45-55

BY GRADE:

VF	EF	AU	MINT STATE
28-34	10-12	7-9	0

CONDITION CENSUS

1. Private collection, ex: Bowers and Merena 10/99: 1565 ($27,600), Harry Bass collection, Heritage 10/95: 6391 ($25,300), Warren Miller collection. This coin and the next were discovered by New York dealer Ed Shapiro in Europe ca. 1976. Graded About Uncirculated-55 by PCGS.

2. Northern California collection, ex: Doug Winter, Nevada collection, Winthrop Carner, Midwestern collection, Bowers and Merena 11/92: 1128 ($20,350), Texas collection, Bowers and Merena 3/92: 2097 ($12,100). Graded About Uncirculated-58 by NGC. *The plate coin in this book.*

3 (tie). Orange County collection via Doug Winter, ex: Superior 2/97: 3161 ($14,850; as PCGS AU-50). Graded About Uncirculated-55 by PCGS.

• Doug Winter 1/01, ex: Mike Storeim. Graded About Uncirculated-55 by PCGS.

4 (tie). Private collection, ex: Eastern dealer, 7/97, Charley Tuppen collection. Graded About Uncirculated-55 by NGC.

• New Jersey collection, ex: Doug Winter/Lee Minshull, Spectrum Numismatics 1/99, Jason Carter/CNL 10/98, Heritage Rare Coin Galleries inventory, 6/98. Graded About Uncirculated-55 by NGC.

• Superior 3/00: 958 (unsold). Graded About Uncirculated-53 by PCGS.

• Tennessee collection, ex: Bowers and Merena 11/00: 725 ($17,250), Harry Bass collection, Kreisberg 9/71: 1160. Graded About Uncirculated-53 by PCGS.

5 (tie). A group of approximately five to seven examples that grade About Uncirculated-50. These include the following:

• Private collection, ex: The Mint (Jay Parrino), Bowers and Merena 10/99: 1566 ($13,800), Harry Bass collection, Kosoff Shuford collection sale (4/68): 2308. Graded About Uncirculated-50 by PCGS.

- Heritage 1/99: 8197 ($18,400). Graded About Uncirculated-50 by PCGS.

- Chicago collection, ex: Doug Winter/Lee Minshull. Graded About Uncirculated-50 by PCGS.

- National Gold Exchange inventory, 7/97. Graded About Uncirculated-50 by PCGS.

- Bowers and Merena 9/94: 3230 ($14,850). Graded About Uncirculated-50 by PCGS.

Two examples have been graded About Uncirculated-53 by NGC as of January 2001.

A Mint State-63 has appeared for at least two years in the NGC Census Report but I do not believe that this coin exists.

The 1878-CC eagle is a rare coin in all grades. It is usually seen in Very Fine grades. Average quality Extremely Fine pieces are actually a bit more available than one might believe but this is not the case with properly graded high end Extremely Fine coins. The number of encapsulated About Uncirculated-50 to About Uncirculated-53 1878-CC eagles is swelled by coins that are, in my opinion, only Extremely Fine and this is a truly rare issue in any About Uncirculated grade. There are currently no 1878-CC eagles known in Mint State.

1879-CC

MINTAGE: 1,762
RARITY RANKINGS:
   Overall Rarity: 2nd of 19
   High Grade Rarity: 8th of 19

The 1879-CC eagle has the lowest mintage figure of any gold coin ever produced at the Carson City mint. In the past, there have been exaggerated claims regarding the rarity of this date. While unquestionably a genuinely rare coin, previous claims that as few as "10-12 survive" (as per Walter Breen in his "Encyclopedia of United States Coins") are grossly inaccurate.

STRIKE: The strike is similar to that seen on the 1878-CC eagle. Most are somewhat weakly struck at the centers but this softness tends to be limited to the curls below BER in LIBERTY and on the eagle's neck feathers. It is not uncommon to find some weakness on the hair and bun of Liberty and on the inner feathers of the eagle, near the shield. All 1879-CC eagle have a mint-made die scratch through BER in LIBERTY and extreme die polishing on the banner above and below the word IN.

A very interesting 1879-CC eagle was sold by Stack's as lot 1239 in the March 1990 sale and later appeared as Lot 5447 in Heritage's February 1994 sale. This piece either represented the terminal die state for this issue or it was simply the poorest struck Carson City eagle of any date. It was nearly free of wear and very lustrous but was exceedingly weak at the centers; perhaps due to die failure. It is possible that others exist.

SURFACES: The surfaces are often heavily abraded but tend not to be as extensively marked as on the 1875-CC through 1878-CC eagles. I have seen a few 1879-CC eagles without numerous marks but those few present were extremely deep and located in obvious positions, such as the face of Liberty or in the left field in front of the profile.

LUSTER: On higher grade pieces, the luster is somewhat above average. It is frosty in texture. Most 1879-CC eagles are either worn to the point that they have no luster or the original luster has been affected by dipping and/or cleaning.

COLORATION: The natural coloration is a very attractive warm orange-gold or, less often, medium green-gold. Few 1879-CC eagles have not been cleaned or dipped and pieces with attractive, original color are accorded a strong premium by knowledgeable collectors of Carson City gold.

EYE APPEAL: Very few Carson City eagles from the 1870's can be found with good eye appeal and this date is certainly no exception. Most 1879-CC eagles have some weakness of strike, a number of detracting marks, little remaining luster, and the original color long since been removed through ill-advised cleanings. The few relatively appealing pieces that exist are greatly coveted by specialists.

DIE VARIETIES: There is just one variety known to exist.

Variety 1-A: The date is spaced midway between the base of the neck and the denticles. There is some filling in the area below the loop of the 9. This is not an overdate. The reverse is a reuse of that seen on 1878-CC eagles. The same reverse clashmarks as described for the 1878-CC are found on the 1879-CC and on the late die state these clashmarks become very prominent. Light machine doubling is sometimes seen on the mintmark.

RARITY:
Total Known: 40-50

BY GRADE:

VF	EF	AU	MINT STATE
20-25	12-15	8-10	0

CONDITION CENSUS

1 (tie). Private collection, ex: Bowers and Merena 10/99: 1573 ($48,300), Harry Bass collection, Stack's 12/70: 362. Graded About Uncirculated-55 by PCGS.

• Northern California collection via Doug Winter, ex: Bowers and Merena 11/00: 729 ($28,750), Harry Bass collection, Bowers and Ruddy 10/77: 1823, Arthur Lamborn collection. The Akers plate coin graded About Uncirculated-55 by PCGS.

3. Private collection ex: Doug Winter/Lee Minshull 5/99, Nevada collection, Winthrop Carner, Stack's 3/95: 621 ($30,800), James Stack collection. Graded About Uncirculated-58 by NGC.

4 (tie). A group of six pieces graded About Uncirculated-53 by the two services. These are as follows:

• Bowers and Merena Stetson sale (5/93): 2080 ($25,300). Graded About Uncirculated-53 by PCGS.

• Private collection, ex: Heritage 10/95: 6400 ($26,400), Stack's/Superior Kramer sale (12/88): 614. Graded About Uncirculated-53 by PCGS.

• Private collection, ex: Heritage Rare Coin Galleries, Dale Williams, Northern California estate. Graded About Uncirculated-53 by PCGS.

• Superior 6/98: 2302 ($19,800), ex: National Gold Exchange inventory, 7/97. Graded About Uncirculated-53 by NGC.

• Private collection, ex: Eastern dealer, 7/97, Charley Tuppen collection. Graded About Uncirculated-53 by NGC.

• Stack's 10/00: 1820, ex: Goldberg 9/99: 1835 ($21,850). Graded About Uncirculated-53 by NGC.

5 (tie). Other About Uncirculated examples include the following:

• Chicago collection, ex: Doug Winter/Lee Minshull, Dr. Larry Cutler collection. *The plate coin in the book "Gold Coins of the Old West."* Graded About Uncirculated-50 by PCGS.

• Eastern dealer, 11/97. Graded About Uncirculated-50 by PCGS.

• Heritage 1/01: ($14,375), ex: Heritage 11/00: 7196 (unsold). Graded About Uncirculated-50 by PCGS. Possibly the same as the last.

• Orange County collection. Graded About Uncirculated-50 by PCGS.

• Heritage 1999 ANA: 8129 (unsold). Graded About Uncirculated-50 by NGC.

The 1879-CC is certainly a rare coin in all grades, but it is not as rare as the 1870-CC eagle as has been claimed. Most survivors fall in the Very Fine to lower end Extremely Fine range and choice Extremely Fine coins are about the best quality that is generally available. There are fewer than a dozen known in About Uncirculated with most of these in the lower range of that grade. No Uncirculated 1879-CC eagles are currently known.

1880-CC

MINTAGE: 11,190
RARITY RANKINGS:
  Overall Rarity: 15th of 19
  High Grade Rarity: 14th of 19

Beginning with this issue, Carson City eagles take on an entirely different complexion in terms of overall and high grade rarity. The survival rate of these issues is much higher than their predecessors from the 1870's and, clearly, they did not remain in circulation as long. The 1880-CC is scarce compared to some of the Carson City eagles from the 1890's but is considerably more available than any of the 1870's dates.

STRIKE: This is a very well struck issue. The obverse is sharply struck with the exception of the lock of hair above Liberty's ear which is often flat. In addition, there may be some minor weakness on the curls around the face. The reverse is sharp with the eagle's feathers well defined. The arrow feathers are sometimes flat and the left claw may be softly impressed as well.

SURFACES: The Carson City eagles from the 1880's are often found with less abraded surfaces than their counterparts from the 1870's. The typical 1880-CC eagle shows medium to heavy marks on its surfaces. It is among the hardest Carson City eagles from this decade to find without marks and I have seen a number of coins with very detracting marks located on the face and/or neck of Liberty.

LUSTER: The luster is most often satiny in texture. There are some semi-prooflike or even fully prooflike 1880-CC eagles known but these are often very heavily abraded and unattractive as a result.

COLORATION: The natural coloration ranges from light to medium green-gold all the way to a rich orange-gold. There are still a fair number of 1880-CC eagles with original coloration but these are getting harder to find as more are cleaned or dipped.

EYE APPEAL: The level of eye appeal is usually slightly above average. Most are reasonably well struck, liberally abraded, and have acceptable luster and color. If the collector is patient, he should be able to locate a pleasing 1880-CC eagle in the lower to middle range of About Uncirculated.

DIE VARIETIES: There are three die varieties known.

Variety 1-A: On the one obverse die seen on 1880-CC eagles, the date is very slightly low in the field. On the first reverse, the mintmark is placed close together with the first C above the space between the E and N of TEN and the second over the right side of the N. Die cracks are sometimes seen through the reverse legend.

Variety 1-B: On this variety, the mintmark is placed more to the left. The first C is located mostly above the E in TEN while the second C is directly above the middle of the N. The C's are placed more widely apart than on Reverse A. On this reverse, there are often extensive die cracks through the legend.

Variety 1-C: On this variety, the mintmark is level and closely spaced. The arrowfeather points to the space between the two C's unlike on the other two varieties where it points to the center of the second C. The first C is positioned between the E and the N in TEN while the second is over the left side of the right of the N in TEN. This variety is most easily distinguishable by a die scratch close to the second S in STATES and the absence of any cracks through the reverse legend.

RARITY:
Total Known: 175-225+

BY GRADE:

VF	EF	AU	MINT STATE
60-78	65-85	45-55	5-7

CONDITION CENSUS

1. Private collection, ex: Eastern dealer, 7/97, Charley Tuppen collection. Graded Mint State-61 by NGC.

2 (tie). Dr. Nathan Sonnheim collection, ex: Doug Winter/Lee Minshull 11/98, Casey Noxon, Jeff Garrett. Graded Mint State-61 by NGC.

• Orange County collection 10/95, ex: Doug Winter/Lee Minshull. Graded Mint State-61 by NGC.

• Nevada collection, ex: Doug Winter/Lee Minshull, Goldberg 10/00: 1045 ($10,925; as NGC MS-60). Graded Mint State-61 by NGC.

3 (tie) A group of four or more coins have been certified as Mint State-60. These include the following:

• Private collection via Blanchard & Co., 10/99, Doug Winter, Nevada collection. Graded Mint State-60 by PCGS. *The plate coin in this book.*

• Heritage 10/95: 6406 ($8,800), ex: Warren Miller collection. Graded Mint State-60 by PCGS.

• Private collection, ex: Long Island dealer, National Gold Exchange, Martin Paul. First seen at the 1996 ANA convention. Graded Mint State-60 by NGC.

The 1880-CC is the first eagle from the Carson City mint that can not truly be called a scarce coin in any grade. It is not hard to locate in Extremely Fine and even lower quality About Uncirculated specimens can be found without considerable effort. In the middle to upper range of About Uncirculated, however, this is a scarce issue and the 1880-CC is a rare coin in Uncirculated. There are only a half dozen or so known in Mint State and not a single one of these approaches the Choice level.

1881-CC

MINTAGE: 24,015
RARITY RANKINGS:
  Overall Rarity: 16th of 19
  High Grade Rarity: 16th of 19

The 1881-CC is the most available Carson City eagle struck prior to 1890. This is especially true in higher grades; primarily on account of a fairly substantial hoard of About Uncirculated and Uncirculated specimens that appears to have been located sometime between the end of 1997 and the end of 1998.

STRIKE: The strike seen on 1881-CC eagles is reasonably sharp although most do have some weakness on the hair around the face and above the ear. The reverse is always much sharper with strong detail except on the neck feathers of the eagle. Generally speaking, this is among the better struck Carson City eagles produced during the 1880's and the collector should expect a sharp, well-detailed example.

SURFACES: As with nearly all Carson City eagles, the surfaces on most 1881-CC's are very noticeably abraded. The fields are normally deeply abraded and this will tend to affect the luster. A number of specimens have copper spots or mint-made grease stains which appear as black streaks in the planchet.

LUSTER: The luster is slightly above average and is usually frosty and somewhat satiny in texture. There are still a fair amount of original 1881-CC eagles that have unimpaired luster but these are becoming harder to find all the time.

COLORATION: The natural coloration ranges from medium yellow-gold to a deeper orange-gold with coppery overtones. Examples with undisturbed, original color have become hard to locate.

EYE APPEAL: The 1881-CC has better eye appeal than any other Carson City eagle produced during the 1880's. The surfaces, while noticeably abraded, tend to be less extensively marked than on the 1880-CC and the 1882-CC through 1884-CC issues. It is possible to locate a visually pleasing piece with decent surfaces, nice color and sharp detail and the date collector should hold out for the "right" coin.

DIE VARIETIES: There is one die variety currently known as well as a second that has been rumored to exist.

Variety 1-A: The date is large and placed somewhat low in the field. It slants downwards very slightly. A few pieces have been seen with light repunching on the base of the first 1. The mintmark is tall and widely spaced with the first C higher than the second. The first C is between the E and the N in TEN while the second is over the middle of the N. Late die states show thin cracks through the 81 and off to the right of the date.

RARITY:

Total Known: 300-400+

BY GRADE:

VF	EF	AU	MINT STATE
60-70	90-100	120-180	30-50 (?)

CONDITION CENSUS

1. Private collection, ex: Heritage 10/85: 1192 ($6,600). Mint State-63 or better.

2. Private collection, ex: Bowers and Ruddy 10/82 Eliasberg sale: 768 ($3,850), John Clapp Jr. and John Clapp Sr., Bradford Bank, 1895. Graded Mint State-63 by NGC.

3. Private collection, ex: Heritage 10/95: 6411 ($10,725), Warren Miller collection, Eastern dealer. Graded Mint State-62 by PCGS; choice for the grade.

4 (tie). A large group has been graded Mint State-62. As of March 2001, PCGS had graded four while NGC had graded fifty-seven as of January 2001. Since very few of these have been seen in the market, it is not certain exactly how many individual coins this represents.

The 1881-CC is the most common pre-1890 eagle from the Carson City mint. It is easily located in any circulated grade and appears to be fairly available in the lower Uncirculated grades. It remains a mystery as to the whereabouts of the numerous PCGS and NGC graded Mint State-62 examples as few of these have been seen. In any grade above Mint State-62, the 1881-CC eagle is very rare.

1882-CC

MINTAGE: 6,764
RARITY RANKINGS:
 Overall Rarity: 10th of 19 (tie)
 High Grade Rarity: 11th of 19

After two years of relatively high production, the mintage figure for Carson City eagles dropped considerably in 1882. The 1882-CC is the scarcest post-1879 issue from this mint in terms of overall rarity and compares favorably to such better known, more highly priced early issues as the 1871-CC and the 1874-CC.

STRIKE: The 1882-CC is not as well struck as the 1880-CC eagle but is generally found with better detail than the 1883-CC and 1884-CC issues. Many are weak on the hair of Liberty; especially on the curls above and below the ear of Liberty. Some of the stars are weak at the centers and the first three at the left may show noticeable weakness. The reverse is prone to display weakness on the neck feathers, the wingtips, and the claws.

SURFACES: This issue was clearly used in local commerce and most 1882-CC eagles show very deep, concentrated abrasions on the surfaces. This is true for both well-worn and higher grade pieces. Any example that has minimal marks is rare and desirable.

LUSTER: This issue does not have good luster. On high grade pieces, the luster is often grainy in its texture. A few 1882-CC eagles are known that are semi-prooflike. These are often extremely heavily abraded and very unattractive due to the reflectiveness of the fields accentuating the marks.

COLORATION: The natural coloration is a rather deep green-gold or medium coppery-orange shade. Lower to medium grade 1882-CC eagles are sometimes available with original color but most higher grade specimens have been dipped or cleaned at one time.

EYE APPEAL: The level of eye appeal for the typical 1882-CC eagle is below average. Most show considerable wear, deep abrasions and softness of strike at the centers. Examples that grade About Uncirculated-55 or better and that have good eye appeal are extremely hard to locate.

DIE VARIETIES: There is just a single die variety known for this year.

Variety 1-A: The date is level and placed about midway in the field. The mintmark is tall and evenly spaced. The two C's are level with the first above the far right side of the E in TEN and the second C above the middle of the N.

Variety 2-A: Misplaced date in dentils. There are two curves in the dentils close to the rim which are the remnants of an errantly placed logotype punch. The two 8's are below and slightly to the left of the correctly placed digits. The reverse appears to be the same as used on the first variety. It is possible that Variety 2-A represents the very early Die State of Variety 1-A.

This variety was first publicized by Bowers and Merena in their description of the Bass IV: 742 coin, sold in November 2000.

RARITY:
Total Known: 125-150

BY GRADE:

VF	EF	AU	MINT STATE
40-53	54-62	30-33	1-2

CONDITION CENSUS

1. Private collection, ex: Eastern dealer, 7/97, Charley Tuppen collection. Graded Mint State-61 by NGC. This coin is possibly ex: Superior Auction '88: 419 and Eliasberg: 772. If it is, than the 1882-CC eagle may well be unique in Mint State.

2 (tie). A group of approximately a half dozen coins exist which grade About Uncirculated-58. Some of these are as follows:

• Superior 2/98: 3497 ($6,600), ex: various dealers, Doug Winter, Pennsylvania collection, New York dealer. Graded About Uncirculated-58 by PCGS.

• Northern California collection, ex: Doug Winter, Nevada Collection. Graded About Uncirculated-58 by PCGS. *The plate coin in this book.*

• Dr. Nathan Sonnheim collection, ex: Bowers and Merena 10/99: 1595 ($6,900), Harry Bass collection, Douglas Weaver 8/73. Graded About Uncirculated-58 by PCGS.

• One other coin has been graded About Uncirculated-58 by PCGS as of March 2001.

• Alaska collection, ex: Doug Winter/Lee Minshull, Cutler collection. Graded About Uncirculated-58 by NGC.

• Private collection, ex: Doug Winter/Lee Minshull 7/00, Spectrum Numismatics. Graded About Uncirculated-58 by NGC.

• Washington D.C. collection 12/96, ex: Doug Winter/Lee Minshull. Graded About Uncirculated-58 by NGC.

• Heritage 10/95: 6414 ($4,290), ex: Warren Miller collection. Graded About Uncirculated-58 by NGC.

• Private collection ex: Blanchard & Co., Doug Winter/Lee Minshull 1/99, Spectrum Numismatics, 9/98. Graded About Uncirculated-58 by NGC.

• Fourteen other coins have been graded About Uncirculated-58 by NGC as of January 2001. This number is significantly inflated by resubmissions.

The 1882-CC has become somewhat more available in the last decade due to a hoard of approximately thirty to forty examples ranging in grade from Extremely Fine-40 to About Uncirculated-55 that reached the market in the mid-1990's. This issue remains rare in the higher About Uncirculated grades and it is extremely rare in Mint State with just one or two pieces currently known.

1883-CC

MINTAGE: 12,000
RARITY RANKINGS:
  Overall Rarity: 12th of 19 (tie)
  High Grade Rarity: 12th of 19

The 1883-CC is the second most available Carson City eagle from the 1880's. But even though this is a fairly easy date to find in lower grades, choice higher grade pieces with good eye appeal are among the scarcest of the post-1880 eagles from this mint.

STRIKE: This issue is generally well struck with the exception of one die variety (see below). On the typical piece, the centers are somewhat weak with lack of detail evident on the innermost part of the curls around the face and above the ear. The reverse is better struck with all of the detail relatively sharp with the exception of the neck feathers and the right claw which are often not complete.

SURFACES: The surfaces seen on nearly every surviving 1883-CC eagle are very heavily abraded. With the exception of the 1881-CC, the same can be said for all of the Carson City eagles from the 1880's. These coins were roughly treated in daily commerce and were probably shipped from the mint loose in bags where they acquired numerous contact marks. I have seen a number of 1883-CC eagles with mint-made black streaks or spots in the planchet.

LUSTER: The luster on the issue is a bit better than on other Carson City eagles from this era. Most higher grade 1883-CC eagles have a satiny texture. A few are known that are semi-prooflike but these tend to either be very heavily abraded or they were struck from Reverse C (see below) and have an odd, "rippled" texture.

COLORATION: The natural coloration is a warm medium to deep orange-gold. This coloration can be extremely attractive but there are not many higher grade pieces remaining that have not been dipped or cleaned.

EYE APPEAL: The 1883-CC eagle is a very hard coin to find with good eye appeal. While most have relatively good detail, the surfaces are usually very heavily abraded. Uncleaned, original pieces do exist and these tend to have very pleasing color.

DIE VARIETIES: Three die varieties are known.

Variety 1-A: All three varieties of this year share the same obverse. The date is large and well-centered. On this first reverse, the mintmark is small and very widely spaced. The first C is over the space between the E and the N in TEN while the second C is over the right side of the N.

Variety 1-B: On this variety, the mintmark is taller and spaced more closely. The first C, which is higher than the second, is mostly above the left side of the N in TEN while the second C is over the right side of the N.

Variety 1-C: The third variety has a very closely spaced mintmark with both of the C's showing double punching. In addition, the C's are closed with the tops touching the bottoms. The first C is entirely above the left side of the N in TEN while the second C is above the middle portion of the right side of the N. There is slight machine doubling seen on the beak of the eagle, the left wingtip near OF and on certain letters in STATES OF. The most interesting feature of this variety is a peculiar wavy texture in the periphery around the legend. This texture slightly resembles the "orange peel" surfaces seen on many Proof gold coins of this era and it is not found on any other Carson City gold coins. This variety is always seen with a poor quality of strike. It is by far the rarest of the three varieties for this year.

RARITY:

Total Known: 150-175

BY GRADE:

<u>VF</u>	<u>EF</u>	<u>AU</u>	<u>MINT STATE</u>
68-80	51-58	29-34	2-3

CONDITION CENSUS

1. Private collection, ex: Heritage 10/95: 6419 ($9,350), Warren Miller collection. Graded Mint State-60 by PCGS. This coin had earlier been graded Mint State-61 by NGC.

2. Northern California collection, ex: Doug Winter 5/99, Nevada Collection, Stack's 10/94: 1331 ($5,775), James Stack collection. Graded Mint State-60 by PCGS. *The plate coin in this book.*

3 (tie). An example graded Mint State-60 by NGC. It is possible that this coin is ex: Superior's session of Auction '88: 420 and earlier Superior 1/86: 3217.

• Bowers and Merena 3/01: 207 ($9,545). Graded Mint State-60 by NGC.

4 (tie). A group of approximately six to eight pieces exist which grade About Uncirculated-58. I am aware of the following accurately graded examples:

• Heritage Rare Coin Galleries inventory, 10/00. Graded About Uncirculated-58 by PCGS.

• Bowers and Merena 10/99: 1600 ($4,830), ex: Harry Bass collection, Douglas Weaver 8/30/73. Graded About Uncirculated-55 by PCGS.

• Washington D.C. collection, ex: Doug Winter, Eastern dealer, Charley Tuppen collection. Graded About Uncirculated-58 by NGC.

• Orange County collection. Graded About Uncirculated-58 by PCGS.

• Chicago collection, ex: Doug Winter/Lee Minshull, Dr. Larry Cutler collection. Graded About Uncirculated-58 by NGC.

• Southern California collection, ex: Doug Winter/Lee Minshull 10/00, Spectrum Numismatics. Graded About Uncirculated-58 by NGC.

• Eight other coins have been graded About Uncirculated-58 by NGC as of January 2001. This figure is inflated by resubmissions.

A hoard of approximately two to three dozen 1883-CC eagles entered the market in the mid-1990's and made this date slightly more available in the Extremely Fine-40 to About Uncirculated-53 range. The 1883-CC eagle remains rare in About Uncirculated-55 and it is very rare in properly graded About Uncirculated-58. There are only two or three Uncirculated pieces currently known and these all grade Mint State-60.

1884-CC

MINTAGE: 9,925
RARITY RANKINGS:
  Overall Rarity: 10th of 19 (tie)
  High Grade Rarity: 13th of 19

The 1884-CC is similar to the 1882-CC and 1883-CC eagles in terms of its overall rarity. It is somewhat more available in high grades than these other two dates.

STRIKE: The 1884-CC is the most difficult Carson City eagle from the 1880's to locate with a good strike. Most are seen with noticeable weakness on the obverse, especially on the curls around the face of Liberty, the top of the bun, and many of the stars. The reverse is sharper although there is almost always weakness on the neck of the eagle and, less often, on the arrow feathers.

SURFACES: Almost every known 1884-CC eagle has deep, detracting abrasions on the obverse and the reverse. I have seen a number that have unsightly mint-made black spots in the planchet. Even the highest grade survivors tend to be heavily marked and it is extremely difficult to find a piece with acceptable surfaces. Every known 1884-CC eagle shows a number of mint-made "chisel marks" on the obverse. For more information on these, see "Die Varieties," below.

LUSTER: The luster is slightly below average in comparison to the other Carson City eagles from the 1880's. The luster is frosty in texture.

COLORATION: The natural coloration is a medium to deep coppery-orange or deep green-gold hue. This coloration can be very attractive. Unfortunately, there are not many 1884-CC eagles remaining that have original coloration as most have been cleaned or dipped.

EYE APPEAL: This is a difficult issue to find with good eye appeal since so many have been heavily abraded. There are, however, a few truly exceptional 1884-CC eagles known to exist and these are greatly admired by collectors.

DIE VARIETIES: There is one variety known.

Variety 1-A: The date is large and well centered. Every known 1884-CC eagle has a number of unusual "chisel marks" on the neck of Liberty, through the hair, and through LI and T in LIBERTY. These appear to have been done intentionally in an effort to "cancel" or deface the obverse die. It is possible that this die was not going to be used and was later resurrected. Perhaps there were not going to be any eagles struck at Carson City in 1884 and a sudden order for them produced a desperate hunt for a usable obverse die. The canceled die that was used could well have been the only one that was available and it was used despite its condition. The reverse is the same as that used on the 1883-CC Variety 1-B eagles.

Another explanation is offered in the description of an 1884-CC eagle sold as Lot 749 in the November 2000 Bass IV sale conducted by Bowers and Merena. It is suggested here that these are, in fact, heavy die lapping lines.

"Following heavy filing (also called lapping), to remove clashing or die rust, dies were typically "finished" with a much finer series of files and abrasives to remove vestiges of the heavier conditioning. This obverse die merely missed the finishing step in its preparation before placed into coinage service."

RARITY:
Total Known: 125-150

BY GRADE:

VF	EF	AU	MINT STATE
40-50	53-63	27-32	5

CONDITION CENSUS

1. Private collection, ex: Bowers and Merena 11/00: 749 ($25,300), Harry Bass collection, Paramount 1969 ANA: 2150. Graded Mint State-63 by PCGS.

2. Orange County collection 5/99, ex: Doug Winter, Nevada collection via Doug Winter, Superior 2/99: 1765 ($17,250; as NGC Mint State-62), New York collection, Doug Winter (8/97), Eastern dealer, Charley Tuppen collection. Graded Mint State-62 by PCGS. *The plate coin in this book.*

3. Upstate New York collection. Graded Mint State-60 by PCGS.

4. Private collection, ex: Heritage 10/95: 6424 ($8,250), Warren Miller collection. Graded Mint State-60 by PCGS.

5. Alaska collection, ex: Superior 5/95: 3724 ($6,600). Graded Mint State-60 by NGC.

The 1884-CC eagle is most often seen in Very Fine and Extremely Fine grades. It is only marginally scarce in the lower About Uncirculated grades but it becomes very scarce in About Uncirculated-55 and rare in About Uncirculated-58. This is a very rare coin in Mint State with around a half dozen pieces currently known.

1890-CC

MINTAGE: 17,500
RARITY RANKINGS:
 Overall Rarity: 17th of 19
 High Grade Rarity: 18th of 19

Beginning with this issue, the grade distribution of Carson City eagles changes noticeably. Unlike the dates from the 1870's and the 1880's, which are usually seen well-worn and are almost never available in Mint State, the 1890-CC is seldom seen in grades below Extremely Fine-45 and it is often seen in About Uncirculated and the lower Mint State grades.

STRIKE: On most examples, the obverse is not as well detailed as the reverse. The curls that surround the face and ear show weakness and the bun is not fully impressed. In addition, some of stars have weakness on the radial lines. The reverse is generally sharp with the exception of the eagle's neck feathers, which invariably show weakness.

SURFACES: The surfaces are usually very heavily abraded with clusters of deep marks visible in the fields and on the devices. A number of 1890-CC eagles have mint-made black spots in the planchet and others have copper spots.

LUSTER: This issue is noted for very good luster. The type of luster seen on most pieces is frosty. A few semi-prooflike and even fully prooflike pieces are known. These are popular with collectors and generally command a premium.

COLORATION: The natural coloration of the 1890-CC can be among the most attractive found on any eagle from this mint. I have seen hues that range from light green and rose-gold to deep orange-gold. A reasonable number of pieces still have their original color.

EYE APPEAL: The 1890-CC eagle is generally seen with average to slightly above-average eye appeal. The luster and color on many uncleaned, original pieces is very good but tempered by numerous deep, detracting marks. The collector should be able to locate a very acceptable example without considerable effort.

DIE VARIETIES: A single die variety is known.

Variety 1-A: The mintmark is tall and heavy. The first C is positioned above the second and it is located over the left side of the N in TEN. The second C is entirely to the right of the arrowfeather and it is placed over the right side of the N in TEN.

RARITY:

Total Known: 350-400

BY GRADE:

VF	EF	AU	MINT STATE
30-35	75-85	190-215	55-65

CONDITION CENSUS

1. Private collection, ex: Liz Arlin, 5/95. This coin was once graded Mint State-63 by PCGS but it has since been removed from its holder.

2 (tie). Five coins have been graded Mint State-63 by NGC as of January 2001. These include the following:

• Private collection, ex: Eastern dealer, Charley Tuppen collection.

• Bowers and Merena 10/00: 2480 ($9,775).

• Private collection via unknown dealer, Lee Minshull, Heritage Rare Coin Galleries 8/99.

3 (tie). A group of approximately twelve to fifteen examples have been graded Mint State-62 by PCGS or NGC. Some of these include the following:

• Private collection, ex: Doug Winter, Heritage Rare Coin Galleries 6/95. Graded Mint State-62 by NGC.

• Orange County collection, ex: Doug Winter, Bowers and Merena 8/95: 361 ($3,520). Graded Mint State-62 by PCGS.

• Superior 2/99 ($6,900), ex: New York collection, Doug Winter/Lee Minshull, 6/96. Graded Mint State-62 by PCGS.

• Washington, D.C. collection, ex: Doug Winter/Lee Minshull, 10/96, Dr. Larry Cutler collection. Graded Mint State-62 by NGC.

• Chicago collection, ex: Doug Winter/Lee Minshull, 4/97. Graded Mint State-62 by NGC.

• Spectrum Numismatics 5/99, ex: Doug Winter, Nevada collection. Graded Mint State-62 by PCGS.

The 1890-CC eagle is almost never seen in grades below Extremely Fine-45. Low-end to medium quality About Uncirculated examples are common. In Uncirculated, the 1890-CC is the second most available eagle from this mint. It is usually seen in Mint State-60 to Mint State-61. Examples grading Mint State-62 are very scarce and Mint State-63's are very rare. I have never seen or heard of a piece grading higher than this.

1891-CC

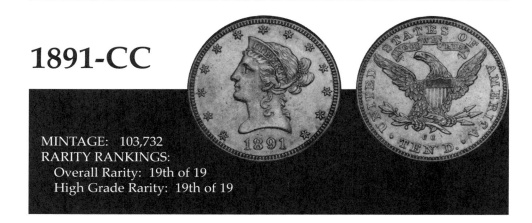

MINTAGE: 103,732
RARITY RANKINGS:
  Overall Rarity: 19th of 19
  High Grade Rarity: 19th of 19

The 1891-CC is, by a huge margin, the most common Carson City eagle. Nearly as many examples are known as for all of the other Carson City eagles combined. The availability of the 1891-CC in relatively high grades makes it a popular type coin as well.

STRIKE: 1891-CC eagles are often seen with good strikes. While most have some minor weakness on the curls surrounding the face of Liberty, it is possible to locate examples that are quite sharply detailed at the centers.

SURFACES: Nearly every known 1891-CC has heavily abraded surfaces. Some higher grade pieces display more moderately marked surfaces but even these tend to have clusters of small but deep marks. This date is more likely to show copper spots than any other Carson City eagle. If these spots are light and situated inconspicuously, they do not affect the value. But some 1891-CC eagles are so heavily spotted that they are not considered desirable by collectors and sell at discounted levels.

LUSTER: This issue is notable for having better luster than nearly any other Carson City eagle. This luster tends to be frosty in texture. Some 1891-CC eagles are known with semi-prooflike or even fully prooflike surfaces. These are very scarce.

COLORATION: The coloration on original, uncleaned 1891-CC eagles can range from rose-gold to pale green-gold. When undisturbed, this coloration is extremely attractive.

EYE APPEAL: The 1891-CC eagle is plentiful in Uncirculated and there are a number of attractive pieces available in the Mint State-61 to Mint State-63 range. It is very hard to locate an example that does not have heavily abraded surfaces.

DIE VARIETIES: There are at least three varieties currently known. I am reasonably certain that other varieties exist.

Variety 1-A: The date is level and placed about midway between the base of the neck and the denticles. The mintmark is fairly far to the left with the first C noticeably higher than the second. The first C is above the right serif of the E in TEN while the second is above the center of the N. The base of the arrowfeather points to the center of the second C.

Variety 2-B: The date is slightly higher than on variety 1-A and it appears to be less level. The mintmark is even and close with the left C above the left side of the N in TEN and the right C above the right side of the N in TEN.

Variety 3-C: "Repunched Mintmark." The date position is very similar to that seen on Variety 2-B but there is a small mint-made spine extending down from Liberty's chin. Cracks develop through the stars and they become heavy on late die states. The reverse shows obvious repunching on both C's in the mintmark with the first punches too far to the right. The first C is positioned above the far left side of the N in TEN while the second is above the middle of the right serif of the N. This variety should sell for a premium as it is easily visible below light magnification.

RARITY:
Total Known: 1500-2000+

BY GRADE:

VF	EF	AU	MINT STATE
50-100	150-200	900-1100	500-600 +

CONDITION CENSUS

As of January 2001, NGC had graded a total of six coins in Mint State-64 with none better. PCGS had, as of March 2001, graded just one 1891-CC eagle in Mint State-64. The roster of Mint State-64 pieces includes the following:

• A coin graded Mint State-64 by PCGS early in 2000.

• Private collection, ex: Doug Winter/Lee Minshull, 9/98. Graded Mint State-64 by NGC.

• Chicago collection, ex: Doug Winter/Lee Minshull, 6/98. Graded Mint State-64 by NGC.

• Private collection. Graded Mint State-64 by NGC in 1994.

• Private collection, possibly ex: Norweb III: 2252. Graded Mint State-64 by NGC.

• Two other examples sold by Heritage Rare Coin Galleries to dealers, one in 1995 and the other in 1998. Both were graded Mint State-64 by NGC.

The 1891-CC is the most common Carson City eagle by a substantial margin. It is common in all circulated grades and it is readily available in the lower Uncirculated grades. It becomes slightly scarce in properly graded Mint State-63 and it is rare in Mint State-64. I have never seen a Gem 1891-CC eagle but would not be surprised if one or two exist.

1892-CC

MINTAGE: 40,000
RARITY RANKINGS:
  Overall Rarity: 18th of 19
  High Grade Rarity: 17th of 19

The 1892-CC is the second most available Carson City eagle in terms of overall rarity. It is a considerably scarcer coin in high grades, however, than the 1890-CC.

STRIKE: This is usually one of the most sharply struck Carson City eagles. Most are quite well struck on the obverse with just a bit of weakness noted on the curls around the face. The hair curl behind the ear is often soft and the lowest portion of the hair bun may not be fully detailed. The reverse is usually very sharply impressed.

SURFACES: Almost every known 1892-CC eagle shows surface abrasions that range from fairly significant to extensive and detracting. Mint-made copper spots are seen on the surfaces of many pieces. This is a fairly common occurrence on Carson City eagles from the 1890's.

LUSTER: The quality of the luster seen on original, uncleaned examples tends to be excellent and is among the best on any eagle from this mint. The texture is very frosty.

COLORATION: The natural coloration ranges from medium green-gold to orange-gold. This coloration can be extremely attractive. It is becoming more and more difficult to locate 1892-CC eagles that have original coloration.

EYE APPEAL: This is generally a well-produced issue that shows a good strike and that has good luster. Most have extensive marks and it is becoming difficult to locate original pieces that have not been cleaned or dipped.

DIE VARIETIES: There are two die varieties currently known. I would not be surprised if another reverse was used to produce 1892-CC eagles.

Variety 1-A: The date is centered. The 189 in the date show light repunching with the 8 and the 9 more visibly repunched than the 1. On late die states, there are varying cracks through the stars. The mintmark is evenly spaced and medium in size. The first C is positioned at the far left side of the N in TEN while the second C is above the right serif of the N in TEN. The bottom of the arrowfeather points past the left side of the second C.

Variety 2-A: The date is placed further to the left than on Variety 1-A. In addition, there is no repunching on the date. On the reverse, there are clashmarks that run from the eagle's right wing to its beak and from the left wing of the eagle to its neck. These clashmarks are similar to the ones seen on the reverse of the 1878-CC and 1879-CC but this is not a reuse of this earlier die.

RARITY:

Total Known: 400-500

BY GRADE:

VF	EF	AU	MINT STATE
50-60	170-200	150-200	30-40

CONDITION CENSUS

1. Private collection, ex: Bowers and Ruddy 1989 ANA: 606 ($12,100), Bowers and Merena Eliasberg collection (10/82): 798 ($9,900), Clapp (1942), Bradford Bank (1895). Graded Mint State-64 by PCGS and NGC.

2. Orange County collection, ex: Doug Winter/Lee Minshull. Graded Mint State-63 by PCGS.

3 (tie) A group of approximately five or six coins are known that grade Mint State-62. Some of these include the following:

- Superior 5/99: 3693 ($4,025). Graded Mint State-62 by PCGS.

- Superior 2/99 ($4,370), ex: New York collection 4/97, Doug Winter/Oregon collector. Graded Mint State-62 by NGC.

- Superior 9/97: 3015 ($3,520). Graded Mint State-62 by NGC.

- Superior 1/94: 2614 ($6,600). Graded Mint State-62 by PCGS.

PCGS had graded four others in Mint State-62 as of March 2001 while NGC had graded three others in Mint State-62 as of January 2001.

The 1892-CC is the second most available eagle from the Carson City mint. It is common in all circulated grades although nice, original About Uncirculated-58 pieces are becoming hard to locate. This is a scarce coin in Uncirculated and most of the coins known to exist grade no better than Mint State-60 to Mint State-61. A Mint State-62 1892-CC eagle is in the Condition Census for the date and I know of just two pieces that grade higher than this.

1893-CC

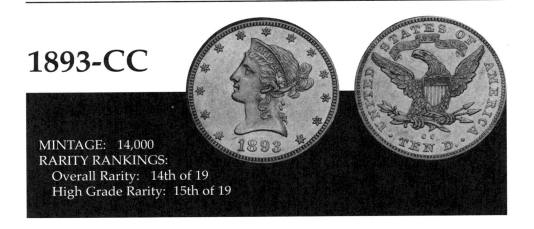

MINTAGE: 14,000
RARITY RANKINGS:
  Overall Rarity: 14th of 19
  High Grade Rarity: 15th of 19

The overall and high grade rarity of this date is much more similar to an 1880's Carson City eagle than one from the 1890's. And unlike the other 1890's issues, which are more often seen in high grades than circulated ones, the 1893-CC is very rare in Mint State and not often seen above About Uncirculated-55.

STRIKE: This is the worst struck Carson City eagle from the 1890's but it is still a better produced issue than any from the 1880's. Most 1893-CC eagles have noticeable weakness on the curls around the face and above the ear of Liberty. The stars often are weakly impressed on their radial lines. The reverse is better struck with good overall sharpness. It is not unusual to see some weakness on the wingtips and on the neck feathers of the eagle.

SURFACES: The surfaces always show a large number of deep, detracting marks. Unlike the other Carson City eagles from the 1890's, the 1893-CC is not prone to mint-made copper spots.

LUSTER: The luster is below average and many are worn to the point that they have little original mint luster remaining. On higher grade examples, the luster is frosty and slightly grainy in its texture.

COLORATION: The natural coloration is a medium to deep orange-gold. A number of 1893-CC eagles show dark, smudgy coloration that is not attractive.

EYE APPEAL: This is a very hard coin to find with good eye appeal. Most 1893-CC eagles are well-worn, heavily abraded and have been cleaned. Those few with good eye appeal are much coveted by specialists.

DIE VARIETIES: A single variety is known.

Variety 1-A: The date is large and placed somewhat low in the field. It slants downward from left to right. The reverse is from the same die used to strike 1892-CC eagles.

RARITY:
Total Known: 165-215

BY GRADE:

VF	EF	AU	MINT STATE
50-70	63-80	46-57	6-8

CONDITION CENSUS

1. Private collection, ex: Eastern dealer, Charley Tuppen collection. Graded Mint State-62 by PCGS.

2. Northern California collection, ex: Eastern dealer, Superior 2/99: 1787 ($12,075; as NGC MS-62), New York collection, Doug Winter/Lee Minshull. Graded Mint State-62 by PCGS.

3 (tie). New Jersey collection 5/99, ex: Doug Winter, Nevada collection. Graded Mint State-61 by PCGS.

• Orange County collection, ex: Silvertowne 9/95. Graded Mint State-61 by PCGS.

4. Private collection, ex: Heritage inventory, 12/96. Graded Mint State-62 by NGC.

5 (tie). Private collection, ex: Eastern dealer, Heritage 1994 ANA: 5910 ($2,200). Graded Mint State-60 by NGC.

• Private collection, ex: Heritage Rare Coin Galleries, Heritage 10/94: 7005 ($1,650). Graded Mint State-60 by NGC.

• Chicago collection, ex: Doug Winter/Lee Minshull, 10/95. Graded Mint State-60 by NGC.

The 1893-CC eagle is easily the rarest Carson City eagle from the 1890's and it compares favorably to the 1880's issues in terms of its overall and high grade rarity. The typical example grades Extremely Fine-40 to About Uncirculated-50. This date becomes very scarce in the middle range of About Uncirculated and it is rare in the high end of this range. Uncirculated 1893-CC eagles are very rare and I have never seen one that graded higher than Mint State-62.

RARITY SUMMARY: CARSON CITY EAGLES

DATE	GRADES				
	VF	**EF**	**AU**	**MINT STATE**	**TOTAL**
1870-CC	22-30	9-11	4	0	35-45
1871-CC	53-57	26-29	10-12	1-2	90-100
1872-CC	47-55	9-10	4-5	0	60-70
1873-CC	43-48	8-10	4-5	0	55-65
1874-CC	96-104	42-57	10-12	2	150-175
1875-CC	47-54	12-14	6-7	0	65-75
1876-CC	47-52	17-20	6-8	0	70-80
1877-CC	30-34	18-22	6-8	1	55-65
1878-CC	28-34	10-12	7-9	0	45-55
1879-CC	20-25	12-15	8-10	0	40-50
1880-CC	60-78	65-85	45-55	5-7	175-225
1881-CC	60-70	90-100	120-180	30-50(?)	300-400+
1882-CC	40-53	54-62	30-33	1-2	125-150
1883-CC	68-80	51-58	29-34	2-3	150-175
1884-CC	40-50	53-63	27-32	5	125-150
1890-CC	30-35	75-85	190-215	55-65	350-450
1891-CC	50-100	150-200	900-1100	500-600+	1500-2000+
1892-CC	50-60	170-200	150-200	30-40	400-500
1893-CC	50-70	63-80	46-57	6-8	165-215

II. CARSON CITY EAGLES: OVERALL RARITY

RANKING	DATE	TOTAL KNOWN
1.	1870-CC	35-45
2.	1879-CC	40-50
3.	1878-CC	45-55
4.	1873-CC	55-65
4 (tie).	1877-CC	55-65
6.	1872-CC	60-70
7.	1875-CC	65-75
8.	1876-CC	70-80
9.	1871-CC	90-100
10 (tie).	1882-CC	125-150
10 (tie).	1884-CC	125-150
12.	1874-CC	150-175
12 (tie).	1883-CC	150-175
14.	1893-CC	165-215
15.	1880-CC	175-225
16.	1881-CC	300-400+
17.	1890-CC	350-450
18.	1892-CC	400-500
19.	1891-CC	1500-2000+

III. CARSON CITY EAGLES: HIGH GRADE RARITY

RANKING	DATE	TOTAL KNOWN
1.	1870-CC	4
2.	1872-CC	4-5
2 (tie).	1873-CC	4-5
4.	1875-CC	6-7
5.	1876-CC	6-8
6.	1877-CC	7-9
6 (tie).	1878-CC	7-9
8.	1879-CC	8-10
9.	1871-CC	11-14
10.	1874-CC	12-14
11.	1882-CC	31-35
12.	1883-CC	31-37
13.	1884-CC	32-37
14.	1880-CC	50-62
15.	1893-CC	52-65
16.	1881-CC	150-230
17.	1892-CC	180-240
18.	1890-CC	245-280
19.	1891-CC	1400-1700+

CARSON CITY DOUBLE EAGLES:
AN INTRODUCTION AND OVERVIEW

Carson City twenty dollar gold pieces or double eagles are the most available Carson City gold coins. Only one date in the series, the 1870-CC, can be called truly rare, although other dates are very rare in high grades. Amassing a complete collection with an example of each date (with the exception of the 1870-CC which is out of the price range of most collectors) is an enjoyable undertaking.

A collector of average means can put together a nice set of Carson City double eagles with the average coins grading choice Very Fine to About Uncirculated. The collector will find that only the 1870-CC presents a great challenge in terms of availability. Just 35-45 examples of this famous issue are believed to exist. Thus, no more than 35-45 complete collections of Carson City double eagles exist. In comparison, the maximum number of Carson City half eagle collections which could exist is 50-60 while 35-45 eagle sets could exist. In each series, the 1870-CC is the "stopper" date.

The completion of a Carson City double eagle set is somewhat easier than a comparable half eagle or eagle set, provided that the collector is willing to accept coins which do not grade Mint State. There are only 19 dates required to form a complete collection. Carson City double eagles tend to be among the most popular of all United States gold coins. The large size of these pieces, combined with their romantic history, renders them irresistible to many collectors. This fervent collector base is most evident when one examines the great popularity of the 1870-CC double eagle. This issue has grown so popular in status that it has become nearly impossible to buy in today's market. In fact, nearly every known piece is in a tightly-held collection and is regarded as one of the "favorites" in its owner's set.

As with the other Carson City series, it is very challenging to pursue the double eagles in About Uncirculated and Mint State grades. It becomes even more of a challenge when the collector demands clean, original coins with an absolute minimum of bagmarks and/or abrasions. As a rule, the Carson City double eagles are less rare in higher grades than their half eagle and eagle counterparts. This means that locating really choice examples of most dates (i.e., coins which grade About Uncirculated-50 or better) is not nearly as difficult as it is with the other two denominations from this mint.

More than most other Liberty Head double eagles, the Carson City issues have tended to remain popular and increase in value over the course of time. One of the major reasons for this has to do with the great story behind these coins. Carson City double eagles are reasonably easy to promote due to their availability (especially in lower grades) and their wonderful history. These coins have proven very easy to sell to non-collectors and investors. Interestingly, the Japanese were a major consumer of Carson City double eagles in the 1980's. The Japanese have always been fascinated with the legends and history of the Old West and Carson City double eagles were an affordable, tangible souvenir of this era. I am aware of several dealers who sold a considerable number of Carson City double eagles to the Japanese and other Asians.

At the present time, it is impossible to complete a set of Carson City double eagles containing only Mint State coins. At least one out of the 19 dates is unknown in full Mint State. However, many more dates in the double eagle series exist in Mint State than in the half eagle and eagle series (both of which contain a host of issues either unknown or excessively rare in Mint State).

The 1870-CC double eagle is unknown in any Uncirculated grade. The 1871-CC, 1872-CC, 1878-CC, and 1879-CC issues are excessively rare in Mint State with five or fewer examples of each date known to exist. It is estimated that a dozen or fewer examples of the 1873-CC and 1891-CC double eagles are currently known. Other very rare dates in Mint State include the 1885-CC (12-15 known), 1874-CC (also with 12-15 known) and the 1877-CC (around 18-20 known). Conversely, a few dates are relatively plentiful in Mint State. These include the 1875-CC, 1890-CC, and 1893-CC. For each of these dates, it is felt that between 200 and 300 Uncirculated coins are in existence. It should be pointed out that the great majority of them grade Mint State-60 or slightly better and that any Carson City double eagle (regardless of date) grading Mint State-62 or above is legitimately rare and very desirable.

Carson City double eagles which grade Mint State-63 or Mint State-64 by today's strict interpretations are extremely rare. I estimate that fewer than a dozen exist. It is doubtful that a single Mint State-65 Carson City double eagle of any date exists. As of early 2001, neither PCGS or NGC had graded a Carson City double eagle higher than Mint State-64 and just a tiny number at that level. The majority of very choice pieces are either dated 1875-CC or are from the 1890's.

It is easy to explain why these coins are so hard to find in the upper ranges of Mint State. There was probably not a single coin collector alive in the Carson City area during the time period in which coins were struck there. The few very choice coins which still exist were preserved by good fortune or sheer happenstance. Many were stored in the vaults of European, Central American, and South American banks after they had been shipped there as payment for international debts. While stored in these overseas banks, they were protected from the American gold recall of 1933 and the wholesale meltings which took place during this period. Many of these coins have worked their way back to the United States since the 1960's as their numismatic value has increased. Despite the fact that literally thousands have been repatriated, more Carson City double eagles are still being found in Europe, Central America and South America.

An examination of this series reveals some interesting rarity trends. Survival statistics depend, to some extent, on the original mintage figures. But they vary widely according to the year of issue.

The rarity trends for Carson City double eagles do not break down as neatly as the half eagles and eagles from this mint. Unlike these other two denominations, the double eagles are not easily categorized as "rare early dates" and "common later dates." One of the rarest double eagles is the 1891-CC while the most common is the 1875-CC. After studying the half eagles and eagles from this mint, I can state that the rarity of the Carson City double eagles is based less on mintages and actual use than on mintage values and subsequent shipment overseas. The collector who studies the tables presented in this book on the survival statistics of Carson City double eagles will note the following very general trend: the lower a coin's mintage and the older its date, the rarer it is in terms of pieces known to exist today.

The 1870-CC double eagle had the lowest mintage figure of any Carson City double eagle: a scant 3,789 coins. In the entire 57 coin Carson City series, only the mintages of the 1877-1879 eagles were lower. As with the other 1870-CC issues, the comparably high survival rate of the double eagle (on a percentage basis) is most probably due to a few pieces being saved as first-year-of-issue keepsakes. The fact that no About Uncirculated or better specimens exist implies that these coins went directly into circulation and saw very active use.

The next rarest date is the 1891-CC with an estimated surviving population of 150-200 coins. In comparison to the half eagle and eagle series (with many issues having surviving populations of 75 or fewer coins), the 1891-CC double eagle is not a really hard coin to locate. But due to the popularity of the double eagle denomination, the demand for this coin tends to exceed the supply.

The next lowest mintages--and among the next rarest dates--are the 1878-CC, the 1879-CC, and the 1885-CC. Each of these dates is represented by about 300-400 survivors. The relative rarity of the other dates is listed in the Rarity Summary at the end of the Double Eagle section of this book.

The 1892-CC and 1893-CC double eagles (like the 1891-CC) appear to have been shipped overseas and then subsequently stored. This enabled these two dates to survive in higher quantities than the original mintage figures would have suggested.

As with the other gold denominations, a general rule is that the older the coin, the lower the average grade of surviving specimens. This intuitive statement is not nearly as easy to predict for the double eagle series. As an example, the 1879-CC is tied for fourth in terms of its overall relative rarity but it ranks as the third rarest Carson City double eagle for coins grading About Uncirculated or better. This strongly suggests that this date was released into circulation and was not hoarded and/or stored in banks.

Carson City double eagles served two primary functions. They were meant to circulate but they were also regarded as a storehouse of value. The large $20 denomination was a most convenient form in which to coin, transport, and trade the large quantities of gold which had recently been mined in Nevada. During the western gold rushes, paper money was viewed with suspicion. This made gold coins an important factor in daily commerce, which quickly became the accepted mode of payment in the Old West. Thus, it is not surprising to learn that Carson City double eagles can be found in very low grades. These low grade coins are often very heavily marked from years of intense commercial usage. Conversely, most of the known Uncirculated coins are also heavily marked, the result of loose coins striking against each other while being transported in bags. It is not uncommon to see Carson City double eagles with no real wear but so extensively abraded that they must be downgraded in the commercial marketplace to the About Uncirculated level.

The greatest challenge for the Carson City double eagle collector is not finding specific dates but, rather, locating clean, problem-free coins. As mentioned above, the "typical" piece, whether it grades Very Fine or Mint State-61, tends to have mediocre eye appeal due to excessive surface marks, scuffing or mint-made copper spotting. Coins which have truly good eye appeal are quite rare and deserve a strong premium over average quality specimens. The collector is urged to "stretch" for uncommonly clean examples.

Most of the pieces struck from 1870 to 1875 are not sharply impressed. This is most evident in the central portion of the coin where the greatest amount of pressure is needed to raise the metal of the planchet and bring out the details. On the obverse, the weakest area is usually on the hair of Liberty. On the reverse, this weakness is most often seen on the neck feathers of the eagle, in the radial lines of the shield and on E PLURIBUS in the motto. This weakness of strike is very often confused with wear. Still, Carson City double eagles of this era tend to be sharper (and easier to grade) than their half eagle and eagle counterparts.

The survival estimates given in this book are based on information current as of 2001. In time, it is inevitable that more coins will surface, possibly including large hoards of certain dates, which will, in turn, lead to radical changes in both survival estimates and individual Condition Census listings. As one can note from comparing the population figures in this book versus those in 1994's "Gold Coins of the Old West," these numbers can--and will continue to--change dramatically.

Due to the sheer numbers of Carson City double eagles which exist, I have always found it much more difficult to estimate surviving populations for these coins than for comparable half eagles and eagles. I anticipate that my current estimates for double eagle survival rates are conservative. Even if the exact figures were revised upwards, the relative rarity and the in-grade rarity figures would probably be similar. It should also be noted that the grading standards in effect in 2001 are bound to change over the course of time. Coins I viewed as being a certain grade in this book may rise or fall to another grade level a few years from now.

As I studied auction data, private treaty records and dealer advertisements, the difficulty of amassing a complete collection of Carson City double eagles in a short period became very evident. In an average year, the number of 1870-CC double eagles offered ranged from zero to two. For dates such as the 1871-CC and the 1891-CC, the number of pieces offered each year averaged from two to six. Dates such as the 1872-CC, 1873-CC, 1878-CC, 1879-CC and the 1885-CC are offered for sale at a rate of six to ten times per year. Obviously, the rarer the date and the higher the grade desired, the harder it will be to find an acceptable example. Carson City double eagles are especially cherished by their owners and many years may pass before Condition Census-quality pieces are offered for sale.

The budget conscious collector can form a complete set of Carson City double eagles (excluding the 1870-CC) in grades ranging from Very Fine to Extremely Fine. A number of the dates in this series can be obtained in lower grades for a relatively small premium over their melt value, which gives them very little downside risk. The true collector will still appreciate the historic nature of low grade Carson City double eagles.

The collector with a slightly larger budget will probably focus on coins grading Extremely Fine or better. With the exception of the 1870-CC, none of the dates in this series are prohibitively expensive or hard to locate in this grade range. Such a set can be assembled in two years or less.

A connoisseur with a large budget will focus on coins which grade About Uncirculated and better. For the 1870-CC, a coin grading Extremely Fine-40 should prove satisfactory. A collector such as this will probably prefer coins with minimal marks. Since many of the early issues are so rare in Mint State, finding even About Uncirculated-55 coins is difficult. Given normal market forces, a collection of this magnitude could probably be assembled in three or four years.

An even more impressive collection would be one focusing on Uncirculated coins. Such a set is possible to complete with the exception of the 1870-CC, 1871-CC and 1872-CC. Given typical market conditions, a collection of this sort might take more than a decade to complete.

Collecting Carson City double eagles is very enjoyable and the number of collectors currently working on sets will attest to this. The following pages give the collector more specific information of each Carson City double eagle.

SECTION THREE

DOUBLE EAGLES

I. LIBERTY HEAD, TYPE TWO REVERSE, WITH MOTTO, VALUE SPELLED AS TWENTY D. (1870-1876)

1870:	3,789
1871:	17,387
1872:	26,900
1873:	22,410
1874:	115,085
1875:	111,151
1876:	138,441

Total Mintage, TYPE TWO......................... 435,163

II. LIBERTY HEAD, TYPE THREE REVERSE, WITH MOTTO, VALUE SPELLED AS TWENTY DOLLARS (1877-1879, 1882-85, 89-93)

1877:	42,565
1878:	13,180
1879:	10,708
1882:	39,140
1883:	59,962
1884:	81,139
1885:	9,450
1889:	30,945
1890:	91,209
1891:	5,000
1892:	27,265
1893:	18,402

Total Mintage, TYPE THREE...................... 428,965

Total Mintage, All Types............................ 864,128

1870-CC

MINTAGE: 3,789
RARITY RANKINGS:
   Overall Rarity: 1st of 19
   High Grade Rarity: 1st of 19

The 1870-CC is the rarest Carson City double eagle and also the best-known and most highly-prized gold coin from this mint. Since the publication of the first edition of this book in 1994, the price of the 1870-CC has soared due to very strong demand from Carson City collectors, double eagle specialists, and first-year-of issue collectors.

STRIKE: This is not a well struck issue. The obverse is always seen with less detail than the reverse. The stars, especially on the left, are flat while the hair shows very little detail. The denticles are fairly well defined although those from 5:00 to 7:00 may have some weakness. On the reverse, the wing feathers are relatively well defined. The stars encircling the motto are weak and never show central detail. The tail feathers are especially weak and have a blunt appearance at the bottom.

The uneven wear pattern seen on the 1870-CC double eagle seems to be the result of technical difficulties at the Carson City mint. When these coins were struck, they were not properly centered within the collar. As a result, the left obverse rim and the corresponding reverse are narrower and more weakly impressed than the rims at the right. This characteristic is found on all known examples and is a good test for the authenticity of any 1870-CC double eagle.

SURFACES: Every 1870-CC double eagle that I have ever seen has excessive abrasions on the surfaces. These are usually very deep and conspicuous. In addition, the rims frequently have noticeable bumps or bruises. It is clear that this issue went directly into circulation. If an 1870-CC double eagle were to be discovered with clean, smooth surfaces, it would sell for a very strong premium to a knowledgeable specialist.

LUSTER: On the small handful of pieces that show any luster, the fields tend to be very slightly prooflike. I have never seen or heard of an 1870-CC double eagle that had more than a tiny fraction of its original mint luster.

COLORATION: Most have been cleaned and lack any natural coloration. Only a few exist that are original and on these the color is either a dark green-gold or a slightly orange-gold hue. An 1870-CC double eagle with original color is worth a substantial premium over the "typical" example.

EYE APPEAL: The traditional concept of eye appeal does not apply to this issue. Nearly every known example is poorly struck, heavily bagmarked, cleaned and/or well-worn. Because of its fame and rarity, most collectors are content to make do with whatever 1870-CC double eagle they are able to locate and can afford.

DIE VARIETIES: Two die varieties are known.

Variety 1-A: The date is large and well impressed. The 1 is close to the neck of Liberty but does not touch it. This digit is much closer to the neck than to the denticles. The mintmark is small and rather compact and is placed high and near to the tailfeathers of the eagle. It is located over the space between the NT in TWENTY. A few have minor doubling noted on the reverse lettering. This is the more available of the two varieties.

Variety 2-B: The date is large but not quite as well impressed as on Variety 1-A. It is placed slightly lower in the field with more space noted between the top of the 1 and the neck. The first C in the mintmark is placed over the right upright stroke of the N in TWENTY while the second is over the top of the T in TWEN-TY. This variety was discovered by New York dealer Anthony Terranova in 1993. It appears to be rarer than Variety 1-A.

RARITY:
Total Known: 35-45

BY GRADE:

VF	EF	AU	MINT STATE
23-30	9-11	3-4	0

CONDITION CENSUS:

1 (tie). Private collection via Universal Coin and Bullion, 1999, ex: Doug Winter, Nevada collection. Graded About Uncirculated-50 by PCGS. *The plate coin in this book.*

• Private collection via Universal Coin and Bullion, 1998, ex: Doug Winter/Lee Minshull, eastern dealer. Graded About Uncirculated-50 by PCGS.

• Private collection via Universal Coin and Bullion, 1996, ex: Lee Minshull/Casey Noxon, Sotheby's 6/96: 196 ($60,500). Graded About Uncirculated-50 by PCGS.

- Private collection via Universal Coin and Bullion, 1999, ex: Doug Winter/Lee Minshull/Casey Noxon, Bowers and Merena 10/99: 1804 ($97,750; as PCGS EF-45), Harry Bass collection, Bowers and Merena 10/87: 2054 ($21,450).

2 (tie). The nicest Extremely Fine examples of this date that I am aware of include the following:

- Goldberg 6/00: 1756 ($109,250). Graded Extremely Fine-45 by PCGS.

- Midwestern collection, ex: Bowers and Ruddy Eliasberg collection 10/82: 925 ($22,000). Graded Extremely Fine-45 by PCGS.

- Southern collection via Universal Coin and Bullion, 1996. Graded Extremely Fine-45 by PCGS.

- Heritage 1999 ANA: 8220 ($92,000), ex: Lloyd's of London, Paul Nugget. Identifiable by a reverse planchet defect below WE. Graded Extremely Fine-45 by PCGS.

- Wyoming collection. Graded Extremely Fine-45 by NGC.

- Eagle collection. Graded Extremely Fine-45 by NGC.

The 1870-CC is the rarest and most popular Carson City double eagle. Most of the survivors are owned by serious collectors and, as a result, a number of years may pass before a piece is available. The great majority grade Very Fine or so and an accurately graded Extremely Fine is a very rare coin. I have seen just a small handful that grade About Uncirculated by today's standards and none of them were better than About Uncirculated-50.

1871-CC

MINTAGE: 17,387
RARITY RANKINGS:
    Overall Rarity: 2nd of 19
    High Grade Rarity: 2nd of 19

The 1871-CC is the second rarest Carson City double eagle, both in terms of overall rarity and high grade rarity. For most collectors, a nice example of this date represents their single greatest expenditure on a Carson City double eagle.

STRIKE: The strike seen on the 1871-CC is usually considerably better than that found on the 1870-CC. The obverse stars are often fully defined with complete radial lines at the centers. The hair has surprisingly good definition and is sharper than on most San Francisco--and even some Philadelphia--double eagles of this era. The edges are square and sharp and the centering is excellent. The reverse is sharply struck as well with strong wing and tail feathers seen on higher grade coins. Weakness can sometimes be seen on the scroll outlining E PLURIBUS.

SURFACES: The surfaces on virtually every known 1871-CC are very heavily abraded. These marks are often deep and detracting. The obverse fields are usually the most heavily abraded area. There are a few known with relatively clean surfaces and these are worth considerably more than a typical bagmarked example.

LUSTER: On some high grade 1871-CC double eagles, the luster is satiny. Others are more reflective with semi-prooflike tendencies noted in the fields. It is extremely hard to locate a piece with good luster due to the fact that many have been cleaned and/or the amount of abrasions on the surfaces have caused a disturbance in the luster.

COLORATION: The natural coloration is a medium to deep green-gold. This coloration tends to be very attractive. Unfortunately, it is very hard to find an example with natural coloration due to the fact that most have been cleaned or dipped.

EYE APPEAL: This is a hard issue to locate with good eye appeal. While most show good detail due to sharp strikes, the typical 1871-CC double eagle is very heavily abraded with an unoriginal appearance. A small number of pleasing, original About Uncirculated coins are known and, when available, these sell for significant premiums.

DIE VARIETIES: There appears to be just one variety for this issue.

Variety 1-A: The date is large and closely spaced. The first 1 is close to the base of the neck but it does not touch. The 7 and the second 1 are also close and they do not touch. The mintmark is placed fairly far to the left with the second C about halfway over the serif of the N in TWENTY. The first C is slightly higher.

RARITY:
Total Known: 200-250

BY GRADE:

VF	EF	AU	MINT STATE
60-80	93-112	45-55	2-3

CONDITION CENSUS:

1. Private collection via Universal Coin and Bullion 2000, various dealer intermediaries, eastern collector, David Akers Auction '88: 977 ($46,200), Superior 1/88: 4414, private collection, Ed Shapiro, ca. 1978. Graded Mint State-63 by NGC.

2. Private collection via Universal Coin and Bullion 1999, ex: Doug Winter/Lee Minshull, Jason Carter/Chris Napolitano, private collection. Graded Mint State-61 by NGC.

3 (tie). Five coins have been graded About Uncirculated-58 by NGC as of January 2001. These include the following:

- Heritage 8/00: 7450 (unsold), ex: Dr. Barry Southerland collection.

4 (tie). Four coins have been graded About Uncirculated-55 by PCGS as of March 2001. These are as follows:

- Tahoe collection 6/96, ex: John McIntosh.

- Heritage 1999 ANA: 8223 ($16,675).

- Superior 1/95: 1645 ($8,800).

- Frank Sanders collection.

The 1871-CC is the second rarest Carson City double eagle. When available, the typical piece grades Very Fine to Extremely Fine. This is a very scarce date in About Uncirculated and most of the pieces known in this grade range are no better than About Uncirculated-50. The 1871-CC becomes rare in About Uncirculated-55 and it is very rare in About Uncirculated-58. This is an extremely rare coin in Uncirculated with just two or three pieces currently known.

1872-CC

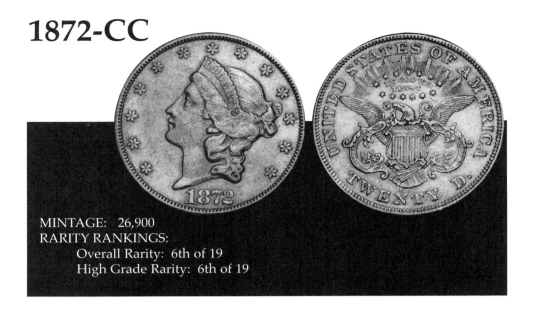

MINTAGE: 26,900
RARITY RANKINGS:
    Overall Rarity: 6th of 19
    High Grade Rarity: 6th of 19

The 1872-CC double eagle is a reasonably scarce issue but it is much more available than the 1871-CC. It remains extremely scarce in the higher range of About Uncirculated and it is very rare in Mint State.

STRIKE: The 1872-CC double eagle is generally seen with a good strike and a high overall quality of manufacture. This is surprising when one considers that the similarly-dated half eagles and eagles from this mint are among the worst struck branch mint gold issues from the second half of the 19th century. On the obverse, the strike is quite sharp with some of the stars showing full radial line detail and the hair is well detailed as well. The reverse is also sharply impressed although it is not uncommon to find some weakness on the stars around the motto and the horizontal lines in the shield.

SURFACES: Almost every known 1872-CC double eagle shows numerous deep abrasions on the surfaces. The small number of reasonably clean higher grade examples known are always in demand among collectors.

Some 1872-CC double eagles show test marks on their edges. These are reminders of a scandal that rocked the mint in 1873 when it was learned that some lightweight, debased coins dated 1872-CC and 1873-CC had been struck. These test marks are usually unobtrusive and do not adversely affect the grade or value of a coin.

LUSTER: The luster is good, most often with a soft, satiny texture. Many 1872-CC double eagles have disturbed luster as a result of excessively abraded fields or aggressive cleaning(s). An example with unimpaired luster is very scarce.

COLORATION: The natural coloration for the 1872-CC double eagle is either a medium to deep green-gold or an appealing light rich yellow-gold. This coloration can be especially attractive but the number retaining their original coloration is rapidly dwindling.

EYE APPEAL: The typical 1872-CC double eagle has below-average eye appeal, primarily due to excessive marks, considerable wear and a lack of originality. Pleasing, original coins are scarce, especially in higher grades.

DIE VARIETIES: There are two die varieties currently known.

Variety 1-A: The date is large and well spaced with the 1 close to but not touching the neck. The 2 is somewhat low and close to the denticles. The mintmark is very similar in its placement and this reverse appears to be a reuse of the one seen on 1871-CC double eagles.

Variety 1-B: The obverse is the same as on the last variety. The mintmark is more widely spaced with the right side of the second C at about the midway point between the N and the T in TWENTY.

RARITY:
   Total Known: 350-400

BY GRADE:

VF	EF	AU	MINT STATE
55-65	193-210	100-115	2-3

CONDITION CENSUS:

1. Private collection, ex: eastern dealer, Charley Tuppen collection. Graded Mint State-61 by NGC.

2. A coin graded Mint State-60 by NGC. I am not aware of this coin's location or pedigree.

3 (tie). As of March 2001 PCGS had graded four examples in About Uncirculated-58. They include the following:

• Eastern collection via Universal Coin and Bullion, ex: Bowers and Merena 1/96: 2083 ($8,360).

• Midwestern collection.

• Country Lane Rarities, ex: Doug Winter, Heritage 2/01: 7173 ($9,775; as PCGS AU-50).

4 (tie). As of January 2001, NGC had graded eighteen examples in About Uncirculated-58. This number is greatly inflated by resubmissions. Accurately graded pieces include the following:

• Heritage 8/00: 7451 (unsold), ex: Dr. Barry Southerland collection.

• Eagle collection.

• Heritage 1999 ANA: 8224 ($12,650).

• Spink America 5/99: 158 ($14,300; as "EF/AU"). Graded About Uncirculated-58 by NGC.

• Washington, D.C. collection.

• Bowers and Merena 3/95: 2461 ($13,200).

• Bowers and Merena 1/94: 3391 ($9,075; as "AU.").

The 1872-CC is a reasonably scarce issue in all grades, although it is sometimes available in Extremely Fine. About Uncirculated coins are not easily located and most examples in this grade range are no better than marginal About Uncirculated-50 quality. This is a very scarce coin in About Uncirculated-55 and a rare one in accurately graded About Uncirculated-58. Uncirculated 1872-CC double eagles are extremely rare with just two or three currently known.

1873-CC

MINTAGE: 22,410
RARITY RANKINGS:
    Overall Rarity: 8th of 19
    High Grade Rarity: 7th of 19

The 1873-CC double eagle has a mintage figure very similar to the 1872-CC. When the first version of this book was published in 1994, it was believed that the 1873-CC was a scarcer coin than the 1872-CC. But the discovery of a number of small groups of this date during the 1990's has rendered the 1873-CC more available.

STRIKE: The 1873-CC shows a slightly better strike than the 1872-CC and it is probably the second best manufactured of the Type Two Carson City double eagles, after the 1875-CC. The stars are mostly sharp and on a number of coins the majority of the radial line definition is clear. The hair is reasonably well detailed although it is typical to find pieces that lack detail on the central curls. On the reverse, the details are mostly sharp with the exception of stars around the motto and the tips of the tailfeathers.

SURFACES: Nearly every known 1873-CC double eagle shows noticeable abrasions on the surfaces. These marks are typically deep and detracting. In addition, some have mint-made defects on the surfaces. A number of 1873-CC's have been seen with dark smudges on the surfaces. These smudges are not mint-made but they are very hard to properly remove and are detracting.

LUSTER: The quality of luster seen on the 1873-CC is not as good as on the other dates of this era. It tends to have a "washed out" appearance, even on those that have not been cleaned or dipped. Some do have appealing rich, satiny luster and these generally command a premium. A small number of semi-prooflike 1873-CC double eagles are known. These are almost always very heavily bag-marked and unappealing.

COLORATION: A broad range of natural coloration has been observed on this date. I have seen such hues as bright yellow-gold, orange-gold, and medium green-gold. This coloration is generally attractive. Locating an 1873-CC double eagle with original color is becoming difficult as many have been cleaned or dipped.

EYE APPEAL: The eye appeal on the typical 1873-CC double eagle is slightly below average, most often due to the presence of numerous marks on the surfaces. There are some very appealing middle to upper range About Uncirculated pieces with good eye appeal and these are avidly sought by collectors.

DIE VARIETIES: I am currently aware of just a single die variety. However, I suspect that at least one or two others may exist.

Variety 1-A: The date is large with the 1 very close to the base of the neck but not touching it. All 1873-CC double eagles have a Closed 3 in the date, unlike the Philadelphia and San Francisco double eagles of this year which have both a Closed 3 and an Open 3 variety. The mintmark is widely spaced with the first C over the right side of the left upright of the N in TWENTY and the second C over the middle part of the right upright of the N.

RARITY:

Total Known: 400-500

BY GRADE:

VF	EF	AU	MINT STATE
62-115	195-235	135-150	8-10

CONDITION CENSUS:

1. Texas collection via Universal Coin and Bullion, 1998, ex: U.S. Coins (Kenny Duncan). Graded Mint State-63 by PCGS.

2. Kingswood 6/98: 738 ($45,650), ex: various dealers, Oregon collection, New York dealers, Bowers and Merena 5/93: 2239 ($34,100). Graded Mint State-62 by PCGS.

3. Heritage 1999 ANA: 8968 ($20,700). Graded Mint State-60 by PCGS.

4. Bowers and Merena 5/94: 1492 ($13,200). Graded Mint State-60 by PCGS.

5 (tie). As of January 2001, NGC had graded nine examples in Mint State-60. These include the following:

• Eagle collection.

• Sotheby's 9/96: 147 ($9,900).

• At least four have been sold by Universal Coin and Bullion to collectors since 1996.

The 1873-CC has become more available in recent years due to the presence of some small hoards that were located in the 1990's. This issue is still scarce in the lower to middle About Uncirculated grades and accurately graded About Uncirculated-58's are very scarce. Full Mint State coins are quite rare with most of these showing numerous bag-marks and grading no better than Mint State-60. I have only seen two that I would grade higher than Mint State-60.

1874-CC

MINTAGE: 115,085
RARITY RANKINGS:
    Overall Rarity: 16th of 19
    High Grade Rarity: 15th of 19

After four years of comparably low mintage figures, production of double eagles at the Carson City mint increased greatly in 1874. In fact, the 1874-CC has the second highest mintage figure of any Carson City double eagle.

STRIKE: The 1874-CC double eagle does not usually show as sharp a strike as the 1872-CC and 1873-CC. On the obverse, the hair behind the ear of Liberty and above her brow is often very flat. The top of the hair and the bun tend to be sharper but may also show some flatness as well. The stars range in sharpness from flat to well-defined and, on most coins, some stars will be sharp while others will be flat. The reverse is sharper with the exception of the center which shows similar weakness as described above for the obverse. The arrowheads appear to be extremely weak but this is actually die lapping that has eradicated some of this design element.

SURFACES: It seems that this issue's high mintage figure was due to an acute need for large denomination gold coins in the West in the mid-1870's, which is probably why the typical 1874-CC double eagle shows numerous deep abrasions on its surfaces. These coins were actively used in commerce and were roughly handled as well. It is extremely hard to locate a piece that is not extensively bag-marked and any reasonably clean 1874-CC double eagle has a strong level of demand among collectors.

LUSTER: The luster seen on 1874-CC double eagles is very different in appearance from other Carson City dates from this era. It is an unusual grainy, semi-prooflike texture, sometimes unfairly mistaken for cleaning. Some are known with a more frosty texture and these are more desirable due to their better eye appeal.

COLORATION: The natural coloration can be very attractive with green-gold or bright yellow-gold hues often seen. It is becoming hard to locate 1874-CC double eagles with original color since many have been cleaned or dipped in recent years.

EYE APPEAL: The typical 1874-CC double eagle shows weakness of strike at the centers, below-average luster, and numerous marks on the surfaces. It has never been easy to find an example with good eye appeal, which has been compounded in recent years by many dealers' and collectors' compulsion to clean or dip coins in order to make them "bright and shiny." A piece with good eye appeal is very scarce and it commands a strong premium among knowledgeable specialists.

DIE VARIETIES: I am aware of only a single die variety but I would not be surprised if a number of others did not exist, especially given the relatively high original mintage figure of this date.

Variety 1-A: The date is large and placed high with the 1 close to but not touching the base of the neck. The mintmark is somewhat widely spaced with the second C slightly higher than the first. The first C is placed over the middle of the left serif of the N in TWENTY while the second is over the middle half of the right serif of the N.

RARITY:
   Total Known: 1500-2000+

BY GRADE:

VF	EF	AU	MINT STATE
200-275	708-1000	580-710	12-15

CONDITION CENSUS:

1. Midwestern collection, ex: Stack's 10/91: 1085 ($10,450). Graded Mint State-62 by PCGS.

2. Private collection, ex: Bowers and Merena 5/93: 2242 ($15,400). Graded Mint State-62 by NGC.

3 (tie). The following coins grade Mint State-61:

• Kingswood 6/98: 739 ($11,220), ex: Heritage 2/95: 5945. Graded Mint State-61 by PCGS.

• One other has been graded Mint State-61 by PCGS as of March 2001.

• Two coins have been graded Mint State-61 by NGC as of January 2001.

4 (tie). The following coins grade Mint State-60:

• Eagle collection. Graded Mint State-60 by NGC.

• Two other coins have been graded Mint State-60 by NGC as of January 2001.

- Oregon collection, ex: Bowers and Merena 1/96: 2085. Graded Mint State-60 by PCGS.

- Two other coins have been graded Mint State-60 by PCGS as of March 2001.

The 1874-CC double eagle has become a readily available coin in grades up to and including About Uncirculated-50 due to the release of a number of significant hoards during the past decade. It remains hard to find in the middle About Uncirculated grades and is rare and underrated in About Uncirculated-58. In Mint State, the 1874-CC double eagle is a very rare coin. Of the dozen or so that exist, nearly all of these are very heavily bagmarked Mint State-60's.

1875-CC

MINTAGE: 111,151
RARITY RANKINGS:
    Overall Rarity: 17th of 19 (tie)
    High Grade Rarity: 18th of 19

The 1875-CC has a mintage similar to the 1874-CC but it is a more available coin, especially in high grades. It is easily the most obtainable Carson City double eagle in Mint State from the 1870's and is the only issue from this decade sometimes seen even in the higher Uncirculated grades (i.e., Mint State-63 and above).

STRIKE: The quality of strike found on the 1875-CC double eagle varies greatly. Some show good overall detail with individual strands of hair noted on the hair, well-defined radial lines in the stars, and sharp feathers in both wings. Many others have weakness on the hair of Liberty, stars that have considerable flatness, incomplete definition on the shield, and weakness on the tips of the feathers. Overall, this is the best struck Type Two issue from the Carson City mint. The edges are sometimes rounded and have a slightly bevelled appearance.

SURFACES: Most 1875-CC double eagles show numerous abrasions on the surfaces. However, it is possible to find an example that is relatively clean, with just a few small, scattered marks. I have seen a fairly large number with mint-made copper spots. These sometimes are very heavy and in this case are considered detracting.

LUSTER: The luster tends to be among the best seen on any Carson City double eagle. It ranges in texture from very frosty to almost fully prooflike. The majority of the very high end 1875-CC double eagles tend to have especially nice thick, frosty luster.

COLORATION: A wide spectrum of natural coloration has been observed on the 1875-CC double eagle, ranging from an intense yellow-gold to orange-gold to medium green-gold. It is easier to locate an 1875-CC double eagle with original color than any other Carson City date from the 1870's but more and more are being enhanced in an attempt to gain a high grade from one of the grading services and are being destroyed as a result.

EYE APPEAL: The level of eye appeal is typically better than any other Carson City double eagle struck prior to 1882. While most 1875-CC double eagles do show numerous abrasions, it is possible to find a reasonably clean piece with good luster and pleasing coloration. This makes the 1875-CC a favorite among types wishing to obtain an attractive Type Two issue for their collections.

DIE VARIETIES: I am aware of two die varieties, but I am virtually certain that others exist.

Variety 1-A: The date is quite large with the 1 fairly close to the base of the neck. The left edge of this digit is positioned over the center of a denticle. The mintmark is very closely spaced. The first C is over the inside edge of the right serif of the N in TWENTY while the second is between the N and the T and does not lie over any part of this second letter.

Variety 2-B: The date is positioned somewhat differently with the 1 not as close to the neck and it is positioned over the right side of a denticle. The mintmark is more widely spaced with the first C over the right side of the N and the second over the left side of the T. Some show light machine doubling on TWENTY D.

RARITY:

Total Known: 2500-3000+

BY GRADE:

VF	EF	AU	MINT STATE
250-350	950-1100	1100-1300	200-250

CONDITION CENSUS:

1 (tie). There are approximately ten to twelve known that grade Mint State-63. Some of these include the following:

• Private collection, ex: unknown dealer, Heritage Rare Coin Galleries, 6/99. Graded Mint State-63 by PCGS.

• Heritage 2/99: 5583 ($11,788). Graded Mint State-63 by PCGS.

• Bowers and Merena 8/98: 371 ($13,225; as PCGS MS-62). Graded Mint State-63 by NGC.

• Stack's 5/97: 941 ($14,300). Graded Mint State-63 by NGC.

• Heritage 6/95: 5943 ($9,900). Graded Mint State-63 by NGC.

• Eagle collection. Graded Mint State-63 by NGC.

• Three coins graded Mint State-63 by NGC were sold privately by Heritage Rare Coin Galleries between July 1997 and December 1998.

As of March 2001, PCGS had graded a total of eleven in Mint State-63 while NGC had graded thirteen in Mint State-63 as of January 2001. These figures are inflated by resubmissions.

The 1875-CC is the most available Carson City double eagle from the 1870's and it is the single most available Type Two issue from this mint. It is easily located in all circulated grades and can be found in the lower Uncirculated grades without much effort. It becomes scarce in Mint State-62 and rare in Mint State-63. I have never seen one grading higher, although I have seen some Mint State-63's that were clearly very high end.

1876-CC

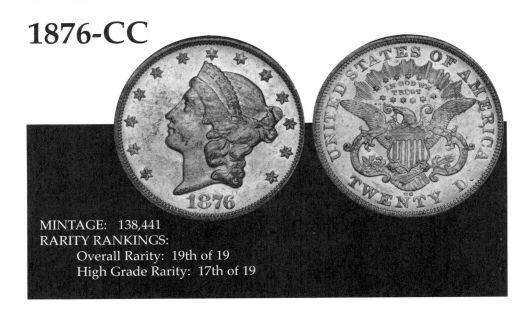

MINTAGE: 138,441
RARITY RANKINGS:
 Overall Rarity: 19th of 19
 High Grade Rarity: 17th of 19

The 1876-CC has the highest mintage figure of any Carson City double eagle. It is a relatively obtainable issue but it is not the most common double eagle from this mint. In fact, until a hoard of three to four dozen Uncirculated examples was released in 1993-94, the 1876-CC was almost unobtainable in high grades.

STRIKE: The 1876-CC is generally found with a better overall quality of strike than the 1875-CC. The obverse is relatively well detailed although there is often weakness on the curls around the face and on the radial lines in a number of the stars. The reverse is always seen with better detail than the obverse, with nearly complete definition on the feathers and the shield.

SURFACES: Most 1876-CC double eagles show numerous deep abrasions on the surfaces. This is an extremely hard issue to locate with clean surfaces and the few reasonably unmarked coins that exist are always in strong demand among collectors. A number have mint-made copper spots and these can sometimes be heavy and detracting. Others have dark smudges on the surfaces that appear to be the result of storage. These smudges can sometimes be removed but, other times, they are permanent and are considered detracting.

LUSTER: This issue generally shows good luster which can range from frosty to semi-prooflike. A few 1876-CC double eagles are known that are almost fully prooflike and these have very impressive visual appeal, provided that they are not abundantly abraded.

COLORATION: The natural coloration of the 1876-CC double eagle is usually bright yellow-gold or medium to deep green-gold. It is still possible to locate an example with original coloration but many have been cleaned or dipped in recent years.

EYE APPEAL: The level of eye appeal for this date is usually below average. This is due to the fact that most 1876-CC double eagles are very heavily abraded. On the positive side, it is possible to locate a piece that, while "choppy," has nice coloration, good detail and excellent luster.

DIE VARIETIES: I am aware of two varieties. I feel certain that others exist.

Variety 1-A: The date is somewhat compact and well spaced between the neck and the denticles. The mintmark is uneven with the second C clearly higher than the first. The first is positioned over the far left side of the right serif of the N while the second C is very slightly over the far right side of the right serif of the N and it extends to between the N and the T. There are often fine, faint die cracks through the reverse legend.

Variety 1-B: The obverse is the same as the last. The mintmark is even and appears somewhat more squat in shape. The first N is placed over the center of the right serif of the N in TWENTY while the second is over the left side of the T.

RARITY:
   Total Known: 2750-3250+

BY GRADE:

VF	EF	AU	MINT STATE
350-450	1350-1500	950-1175	100-125

CONDITION CENSUS:

1. Private collection, ex: Winthrop Carner, 1994. Graded Mint State-63 by NGC.

2. Texas collection via Universal Coin and Bullion, ex: Doug Winter/Lee Minshull, Heritage 5/00: 7856 ($17,250). Graded Mint State-63 by NGC.

3. A number are known that grade Mint State-62. Some of these include the following:

   • Superior 5/99: 3789 ($13,800). Graded Mint State-62 by PCGS.

   • Heritage 1998 ANA: 7865 ($14,375). Graded Mint State-62 by NGC.

   • Bowers and Merena 11/95: 2150 ($5,280). Graded Mint State-62 by NGC.

   • Private collection, ex: Heritage Rare Coin Galleries 4/95. Graded Mint State-62 by PCGS.

   • Bowers and Merena 9/94: 1437 ($8,250). Graded Mint State-62 by PCGS.

As of March 2001, PCGS had graded thirteen in Mint State-62.

As of January 2001, NGC had graded twenty-six in Mint State-62. This figure is inflated by resubmissions.

The 1876-CC has the highest mintage figure of any double eagle from the Carson City mint. It is a relatively common coin in all circulated grades and it can be located in the lower Uncirculated grades without much effort. In Mint State-62, this issue becomes rare and it is extremely rare in Mint State-63. Nearly every known Uncirculated 1876-CC double eagle shows very heavily abraded surfaces and clean, choice examples--in any Mint State grade--are extremely hard to locate.

1877-CC

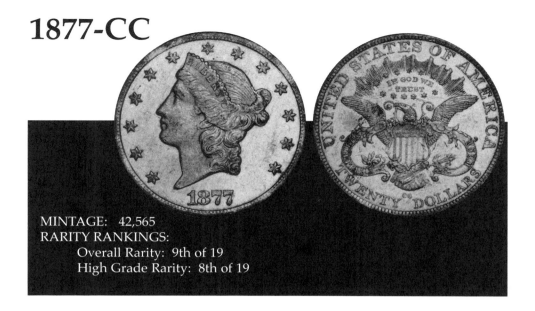

MINTAGE: 42,565
RARITY RANKINGS:
   Overall Rarity: 9th of 19
   High Grade Rarity: 8th of 19

In 1877, the design of the double eagle was modified by changing the value from TWENTY D. to TWENTY DOLLARS. These coins are known to collectors as "Type Three" double eagles. This is especially relevant to Carson City collectors as it presents the only significant design change for the gold coinage from this mint.

The mintage figure for the 1877-CC is considerably lower than for the 1874-CC, 1875-CC, and 1876-CC double eagles and it is a much scarcer coin in terms of its overall and high grade rarity.

STRIKE: As a rule, Type Three double eagles are much better struck than their Type Two counterparts, particularly on the obverse hair detail. The 1877-CC shows much sharper hair than the 1876-CC (or any of the other Type Two issues) with good individual definition noted. The reverse also shows good detail with sharp feathers and stars on most coins. The obverse rim often shows areas of weakness

SURFACES: The surfaces on most 1877-CC double eagles show very extensive abrasions. This seems to be especially true for higher grade coins (i.e., About Uncirculated and Uncirculated) as these pieces are often marred by clusters of deep, detracting marks. I have seen a few higher coins with reasonably clean surfaces but even these tend to shows some "choppiness" in the fields. A number are known with mint-made copper spotting.

LUSTER: The quality of luster on this issue is very good with the typical higher grade example displaying thick, frosty luster. A small number of semi-prooflike pieces are known. A few are almost fully prooflike, but these are usually very heavily marked and, as a result, have poor visual appeal.

COLORATION: The natural coloration ranges from bright yellow-gold to a deeper orange-gold hue. This coloration can be very attractive. Many examples that were released into the market in the mid-1990's had very deep coloration and a number were subsequently cleaned or dipped.

EYE APPEAL: The 1877-CC double eagle is a hard coin to locate with good eye appeal. This is due to the fact that most are very heavily abraded. Any example that is reasonably clean, lustrous and which has natural coloration is quite scarce and deserving of a premium price.

DIE VARIETIES: I am aware of just a single variety. I would not be surprised if at least one or two others exist.

Variety 1-A: The date is small, compact, and placed low in the field. The mint-mark is tall and compact with the second C slightly higher than the first. Both C's are placed between the Y in TWENTY and the D in DOLLARS.

RARITY:
Total Known: 500-600

BY GRADE:

VF	EF	AU	MINT STATE
82-115	275-300	125-175	18-20

CONDITION CENSUS:

1. Private collection, ex: Eastern dealer 1997 ($27,500), Charley Tuppen collection via private treaty at the 1993 ANA convention. Graded Mint State-62 by NGC.

• Two other coins have been graded Mint State-62 by NGC as of January 2001.

2. Private collection, ex: Robert Leece, Bowers and Merena 5/93: 2251 ($23,100). Graded Mint State-62 by PCGS.

3 (tie). A group of approximately four to six pieces are known that grade Mint State-61. These include the following:

• Eagle collection, graded Mint State-61 by NGC.

• Private collection, ex: Heritage Rare Coin Galleries, 4/98. Graded Mint State-61 by PCGS.

• PCGS had graded four others Mint State-61 as of March 2001.

4 (tie) The remainder of the Uncirculated 1877-CC double eagles grade Mint State-60. The most current population figures are as follows:

• PCGS had graded nine coins Mint State-60 as of March 2001.

• NGC had graded eight coins Mint State-60 as of January 2001.

NOTE: Most of the high grade 1877-CC double eagles trace their origin from a hoard that entered the market in the mid-1990's. A number were sold in the July 1995 Bowers and Merena sale.

> *The 1877-CC double eagle is usually found in Extremely Fine to lower end About Uncirculated grades. This issue becomes hard to locate in the middle range of About Uncirculated and properly graded About Uncirculated-58 pieces are scarce. This is a very scarce coin in Uncirculated with most of the known pieces grading Mint State-60. I have seen two that grade Mint State-62 and only one that, in my opinion, has claims to a higher grade.*

1878-CC

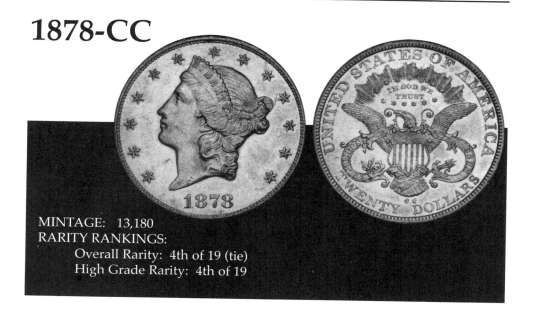

MINTAGE: 13,180
RARITY RANKINGS:
    Overall Rarity: 4th of 19 (tie)
    High Grade Rarity: 4th of 19

Production of double eagles at the Carson City mint dropped dramatically in 1878. The 1878-CC has the lowest mintage figure since the 1870-CC and it is among the scarcest double eagles from this mint.

STRIKE: This issue is usually seen with a very sharp strike. The hair detail is quite bold with many of the hair strands separated and individually defined. The one area on the obverse not found sharp is the word LIBERTY on the headdress which is usually softly impressed. The borders are sharp as well with full--or nearly full--radial lines noted in most of the stars. The reverse shows nearly complete detail on the feathers, shield and claws. The rims are usually somewhat beveled in appearance.

SURFACES: As on all of the Carson City double eagles from the 1870's, the 1878-CC is typically seen with heavily abraded surfaces. For some reason, the abrasions on this issue are not as extensive or detracting as on many from the earlier part of this decade. Some 1878-CC double eagles have dark mint-made grease stains or lighter copper spots in the surfaces. I have seen a fair number that had small mint-made laminations or other planchet problems as well.

The great majority of 1878-CC double eagles show a long, thin vertical die scratch on the neck of Liberty. This should not be mistaken for damage.

LUSTER: The luster is above average with two distinctive textures seen. Most high grade pieces are frosty with a slightly grainy texture noted around the borders. A few are semi-prooflike and there are even some fully prooflike pieces, which can have spectacular eye appeal. Because so many 1878-CC double eagles have been cleaned, it is hard to find examples that have original, undisturbed luster.

COLORATION: The natural coloration tends to be excellent with rich orange-gold and medium to deep yellow-gold hues most often seen. Circulated coins tend to have a darker green-gold hue. It has become very difficult to locate high grade 1878-CC double eagles with natural coloration and those that have attractive natural hues are beginning to sell for very strong premiums among knowledgeable collectors and dealers.

EYE APPEAL: The level of eye appeal on the 1878-CC double eagle is generally slightly above average. It is not hard to find an example that is well-detailed and free of deep, detracting marks. A few truly spectacular, fully prooflike pieces with good color and choice surfaces are known, and these bring hefty premiums when they are available.

DIE VARIETIES: Two die varieties are currently known to exist.

Variety 1-A: The date is small and level and placed somewhat low in the field. There is a long, thin vertical die scratch on the neck of Liberty that can be seen even on well-worn examples. On the reverse, there are two small die lumps near the second T in TWENTY, a die scratch below the D in DOLLARS and a number of other small die scratches below the value. The mintmark is wide and squat and positioned fairly far to the right. The first C, which is higher than the second, is almost exactly midway between the edge of the Y in TWENTY and the D in DOLLARS while the second C is over the left edge of the D. This is by far the more available of the two varieties.

Variety 2-B: The date appears to be slightly higher than on Variety 1-A. The vertical die scratch seen on the first variety is not present but there is a noticeable raised die dot close to a denticle above the eleventh star. On the reverse, there are no die lumps near the second T in TWENTY or lines around the D in DOLLARS. There is a faint die line through the M in AMERICA and a second running through the E in that word. There is a patch of roughness in the field after the second A in AMERICA and a number of spikes protruding from the right side of the S in DOLLARS. The first C is lower than the second and positioned midway between the Y in TWENTY and the D in DOLLARS. I am aware of just two examples of this variety: the Bass III: 874 coin and an example in a Washington D.C. collection.

RARITY:
Total Known: 300-350

BY GRADE:

VF	EF	AU	MINT STATE
80-90	150-170	66-84	4-6

CONDITION CENSUS:

1. Midwestern collection, ex: Stack's 3/90: 1426 ($17,600). Graded Mint State-62 by PCGS.

2. Another coin has been graded Mint State-62 by PCGS. It is possible that it is the same as one of the pieces listed below.

3. Texas collection via Universal Coin and Bullion, ex: Doug Winter, Nevada collection, New York dealer, Charley Tuppen collection. Graded Mint State-61 by PCGS.

4. Private collection, ex: Superior 1/96: 2529 ($15,400; as PCGS MS-60), Heritage 2/94: 6539 ($15,400). Graded Mint State-61 by PCGS.

5. Washington D.C. collection 1/95, ex: Doug Winter, Paul Nugget. Graded Mint State-61 by NGC. Possibly ex: Bowers and Merena 5/93: 2294 ($9,350).

The 1878-CC is among the scarcest Carson City double eagles. It is most often seen in Extremely Fine. It is not often found in grades higher than About Uncirculated-53 and an accurately graded About Uncirculated-55 coin is quite rare. Uncirculated 1878-CC double eagles are extremely rare and many years may go by before an example is made available to collectors.

1879-CC

MINTAGE: 10,708
RARITY RANKINGS:
     Overall Rarity: 4th of 19 (tie)
     High Grade Rarity: 3rd of 19

The mintage figure for this date is even lower than for the 1878-CC and it is the fourth lowest of any Carson City double eagle. While rare in high grades, the overall level of rarity for the 1879-CC has been exaggerated in the past and it is actually comparable in rarity to the 1878-CC. A hoard of Extremely Fine and About Uncirculated pieces entered the market in the early-to-mid 1990's. These were quickly absorbed by collectors.

STRIKE: The 1879-CC is usually seen with a sharp strike, and the typical example is as boldly detailed as the 1878-CC, if not sharper. On the obverse, the hair of Liberty shows nearly complete detail with the exception of the back curls which tend to show moderate weakness. The stars are very sharp with nearly full radial lines. The reverse is also well struck with good detail noted on the eagle's feathers and claws as well as on the shield. The rims show noticeable beveling.

SURFACES: Every Carson City double eagle issue is plagued by excessively abraded surfaces, the result of rough handling and hard circulation. For some reason, the 1879-CC is generally found with fewer deep, detracting surfaces marks than other issues of this era. This does not mean that it is easy to locate a clean piece; merely that the typical example shows fewer serious marks than on such issues as the 1877-CC and 1878-CC. A number show mint-made copper spots on the surfaces.

A small area of die rust can be seen on the obverse below the 1 and the 9 in the date while there is reverse rust below the W in TWENTY. The die rust pattern appears on all 1879-CC double eagles that I have seen.

LUSTER: The quality of luster varies greatly. Some 1879-CC double eagles have an impressive rich, frosty texture but many others have an unappealing somewhat grainy finish that gives the impression of the coin having been overdipped or "washed out." A small number of fully prooflike pieces are known as well.

COLORATION: The natural coloration seen most often is a rich yellow-gold hue. Lower grade 1879-CC double eagles tend to be darker with a medium dirty green-gold or orange color. It is very hard to find higher grade pieces with original coloration as many have been cleaned or dipped.

EYE APPEAL: Most 1879-CC double eagles have somewhat above average eye appeal, due to their reasonably clean surfaces and sharp details. A small number of very high grade pieces (in this case About Uncirculated-58 and above) have extremely good eye appeal and these are held in high regard by specialists.

DIE VARIETIES: A single variety is known to exist.

Variety 1-A: The date is well spaced and even with a slightly low placement in the field between the truncation and the denticles. As mentioned above, there is a spot of die rust below the 1 and the 9. The first C in the mintmark is slightly higher than the second and is placed a bit closer to the Y in TWENTY than to the D in DOLLARS. The second C is positioned over the far left edge of the D in DOLLARS.

RARITY:
Total Known: 300-350

BY GRADE:

VF	EF	AU	MINT STATE
65-75	170-190	62-81	3-4

CONDITION CENSUS:

1. Private collection, possibly ex: Stack's 7/86: 443, Stack's 9/81: 293. The Akers plate coin. Graded Mint State-62 by NGC.

2 (tie). A group of approximately five to seven pieces that grade Mint State-60 to Mint State-61. These include the following:

• Superior 5/99: 3794 ($18,975). Graded Mint State-60 by NGC.

• Heritage 8/00: 7467 (unsold), ex: Dr. Barry Southerland collection, Heritage 1998 ANA: 7871 ($20,700). Graded Mint State-61 by NGC.

• Midwestern collection, ex: Winthrop Carner, Bowers and Merena 5/93: 2257. Graded Mint State-61 by PCGS.

• Texas collection via Universal Coin and Bullion, ex: Doug Winter, Nevada collection, New York dealer. Graded Mint State-61 by PCGS.

• Charley Tuppen collection. Graded Mint State-61 by PCGS.

As of March 2001, PCGS had graded two other examples Mint State-61 and one coin Mint State-60.

As of January 2001, NGC had graded one other example Mint State-61 and one coin Mint State-60.

The 1879-CC double eagle is not as scarce as its low mintage figure would suggest. It is most often seen in Very Fine to Extremely Fine grades. Low end About Uncirculated examples are moderately scarce but this issue becomes rare in About Uncirculated-55 and very rare in properly graded About Uncirculated-58. Uncirculated 1879-CC double eagles are extremely rare.

1882-CC

MINTAGE: 39,140
RARITY RANKINGS:
    Overall Rarity: 11th of 19
    High Grade Rarity: 10th of 19

Production of double eagles resumed at the Carson City mint after a two-year hiatus. The 1882-CC is among the more available issue of this decade but it is rarer in high grades than such dates as the 1883-CC, 1884-CC, and 1889-CC.

STRIKE: The 1882-CC is among the best struck double eagle produced at the Carson City mint. The obverse is usually very well detailed with sharp hair curls and nearly full radial lines noted on the stars. On some there may be minor weakness at the top of the hair and the rear of the hair bun. The reverse is also seen with good detail including sharp feathers and a bold shield. The unevenness of strike seen on this issue makes it a hard coin to evaluate and many, as a result, are improperly graded.

SURFACES: The surfaces on most 1882-CC double eagles show heavy abrasions. This appears to be the rule on both circulated and Uncirculated pieces. I have seen a number that had mint-made copper spots or dark areas in the planchet. These are not generally considered detracting unless they are plentiful or poorly located.

LUSTER: There are two distinctive types of luster seen on this issue. Most have a somewhat subdued grainy texture that occasionally exhibits a slight amount of semi-prooflike reflectiveness in the fields. A smaller number have attractive, frosty luster.

COLORATION: A wide range of natural coloration has been observed on the 1882-CC double eagle. These hues range from rich orange-gold to medium green-gold. It is very hard to find an example that has undisturbed, original color as many have been cleaned or dipped.

EYE APPEAL: The level of eye appeal tends to be slightly below average. This is a result of heavy surface abrasions and subdued luster. There are a small number of very choice 1882-CC double eagles known and these command strong premiums when offered for sale.

DIE VARIETIES: There are currently two varieties known. I would not be surprised if at least one other awaits discovery.

Variety 1-A: The date is somewhat large, well centered and even. The mintmark is upright with the two C's closely spaced and the first higher than the second. The right side of the second C is over the center of the left upright of the D in DOLLARS.

Variety 2-B: The obverse is very similar to Variety 1-A except that the 1 is placed slightly more to the right. The mintmark leans slightly to the left and is closely spaced with the first C lower than the second. The right side of the second C is over the center of the left upright of the D in DOLLARS. This variety is found with varying reverse cracks. On the late state, this crack encircles the periphery.

RARITY:
Total Known: 800-900

BY GRADE:

VF	EF	AU	MINT STATE
150-160	420-440	200-265	30-35

CONDITION CENSUS:

It is difficult to create an accurate Condition Census for this issue as most of the Uncirculated survivors are not noticeably different in terms of quality. I have seen two or three Mint State-62's that were clearly above-average for the issue but most Uncirculated pieces are very similar.

1 (tie). As of March 2001, PCGS had graded four coins in Mint State-62 while NGC, as of January 2001, had graded four in Mint State-62. Some of these are as follows:

• Heritage 1999 ANA: 8239 ($8,337). Graded Mint State-62 by PCGS.

• Midwestern collection. Graded Mint State-62 by PCGS.

• Texas collection via Universal Coin and Bullion, ex: Doug Winter, Nevada collection. Graded Mint State-62 by PCGS.

• Private collection via Universal Coin and Bullion 11/98, ex: Lee Minshull. Graded Mint State-62 by NGC.

2 (tie). As of March 2001, PCGS had graded fifteen coins in Mint State-61 while NGC, as of January 2001, had graded twelve in Mint State-61. These figures are inflated by resubmissions. Some of these are as follows:

• Bowers and Merena 5/00: 881 ($6,900), ex: Harry Bass collection. Graded Mint State-61 by PCGS.

- Heritage 4/99: 6184 ($7,130). Graded Mint State-61 by NGC.

- Bowers and Merena 8/98: 376 ($7,590). Graded Mint State-61 by PCGS.

- Superior 1/94: 2701 ($8,058). Graded Mint State-61 by PCGS.

The 1882-CC is a reasonably common coin by the standards of Carson City double eagles. It can be located in Extremely Fine and lower-end About Uncirculated grades without much effort. It becomes scarce in the higher About Uncirculated grades and it is very scarce in Uncirculated. Almost every 1882-CC double eagle that is known in Mint State is at the low end of this range and examples that grade Mint State-62 are very rare and are the best available quality currently known for this date.

1883-CC

MINTAGE: 59,962
RARITY RANKINGS:
    Overall Rarity: 14th of 19
    High Grade Rarity: 12th of 19

The 1883-CC is one of the more obtainable Carson City double eagles. Its relative availability and high quality of manufacture make it a popular choice among type collectors seeking one nice Carson City double eagle for their set.

STRIKE: Most 1883-CC double eagles do not come as well struck as the 1882-CC but the overall quality of strike is still above average for a Carson City double eagle of this era. On the obverse, the areas most likely to show weakness are the brow and the hair above the ear of Liberty. Some of the stars may have incomplete radial line definition as well. On the reverse, the eagle's neckfeathers and the outline of the shield may show some weakness.

SURFACES: This is an issue that is almost always seen with heavily abraded surfaces. It is very hard to find an 1883-CC double eagle relatively free of marks but a few such pieces do exist. These generally bring strong premiums from knowledgeable collectors.

LUSTER: The quality of luster seen on this issue is of average quality. Many have somewhat dull frosty luster while a few are semi-prooflike. There are a few fully prooflike pieces known and these are very impressive from a visual standpoint. Many technically Uncirculated 1883-CC double eagles have impaired luster due to excessive bagmarks and are typically "net graded" down to the About Uncirculated-55 to About Uncirculated-58 level by the major grading services.

COLORATION: The natural coloration most often seen is either a medium green-gold or a deep yellow-gold hue. Some 1883-CC double eagles have dark, smudgy coloration that is unappealing. This seems to be a slightly easier date than others of this era to locate with nice original color but attractive, uncleaned examples are becoming harder to find.

EYE APPEAL: Despite the relative availability of the 1883-CC double eagle in higher grades, it is not easy to locate an example that has good eye appeal. Most show extremely heavily bagmarked surfaces. A small number of very choice pieces are known in the Mint State-62 to Mint State-63 range. Such coins show superior eye appeal and when available are actively sought by collectors.

DIE VARIETIES: At least two varieties currently known. Given the mintage figure for this issue, it would not be surprising if another one or two exist.

Variety 1-A: The date is well spaced and even. Some small, raised die lines can be seen between the eleventh and the twelfth stars on the obverse. On the reverse, the mintmark is closely spaced with some filling noted between the top and bottom loops of both C's. The first C is centered about midway between the edge of the Y in TWENTY and the front of the D in DOLLARS while the second C is above the far left edge of the D.

Variety 2-A: The 1 in the date is positioned slightly differently in relationship to the denticle immediately below it. There is a noticeable raised die dot to the right of the middle of the 3.

RARITY:
Total Known: 900-1000+

BY GRADE:

VF	EF	AU	MINT STATE
125-150	410-450	300-325	65-75

CONDITION CENSUS:

1 (tie). As of March 2001, PCGS and NGC had each graded two 1883-CC double eagles in Mint State-63. These include the following pieces:

• Texas collection via Universal Coin and Bullion 1999, ex: Doug Winter, Nevada collection. Graded Mint State-63 by PCGS.

• Private collection, ex: Bowers and Merena 5/93: 2266 ($16,500). Graded Mint State-63 by NGC.

2 (tie). As of March 2001, PCGS had graded three examples in Mint State-62 while NGC had graded eight as of January 2001. These include the following:

• Private collection, ex: unknown dealer, Heritage Rare Coin Galleries 10/98. Graded Mint State-62 by PCGS.

• Midwestern collection, ex: Winthrop Carner 9/93. Graded Mint State-62 by PCGS.

The 1883-CC is one of the more available Carson City double eagles. It can be located in any circulated grade without much difficulty and is not that hard to find a bagmarked Mint State-60 example. It becomes very scarce in Mint State-62 and properly graded Mint State-63's are extremely rare. I have only seen one or two that qualified as such and have never seen or heard of one that graded higher.

1884-CC

MINTAGE: 81,139
RARITY RANKINGS:
    Overall Rarity: 15th of 19
    High Grade Rarity: 11th of 19

The 1884-CC is one of the more common Carson City double eagles and it is the most available Type Three issue in high grades struck prior to 1890.

STRIKE: This is among the best struck gold issue of any denomination produced at the Carson City mint. The typical 1884-CC double eagle is very sharp with most of the hair individually defined and full radial lines within the stars. The reverse is also sharp with strong feather and wingtip detail. Some pieces have minor weakness noted at the top of Liberty's hair and on the rear of the bun.

SURFACES: The surfaces are nearly always abraded, but it is possible to locate an 1884-CC not so heavily marked that its eye appeal is impacted. Copper spots or small areas with deep copper-hued coloration are not uncommon and I have seen a number of 1884-CC double eagles with mint-made black grease stains on the surfaces.

LUSTER: This issue has above-average luster. The majority of higher grade pieces are frosty with a slightly grainy texture noted in the fields. A small number of semi-prooflike coins are known. These are usually not especially appealing due to overly bagmarked surfaces.

COLORATION: The natural coloration is a medium to deep green-gold. Some show a pronounced orange-gold hue. It is easier to locate an 1884-CC with natural color than most any other double eagle from this mint. However, original pieces are becoming harder to locate with each passing year. Coins with extremely nice color are generally accorded premiums by knowledgeable collectors.

EYE APPEAL: The 1884-CC has much better eye appeal than most Carson City double eagles. The typical piece is well struck and lustrous with decent color but heavily abraded surfaces. Since this issue is generally seen with good eye appeal, it is a very popular type issue among collectors seeking a single, high grade double eagle from the Carson City mint.

DIE VARIETIES: I am aware of just one variety. I would not be surprised if one or two others exist.

Variety 1-A: The date is compact, somewhat small and placed slightly low in the field. The mintmark is tall, placed slightly high and close together. The first C is almost midway between the Y in TWENTY and the D in DOLLARS while the second C is over the left side of the D in DOLLARS.

RARITY:

Total Known: 1250-1500+

BY GRADE:

VF	EF	AU	MINT STATE
200-250	700-750	250-350	100-150

CONDITION CENSUS:

1 (tie). As of March 2001, PCGS and NGC had each graded two examples in Mint State-63. None have ever appeared at auction.

2 (tie). As of March 2001, PCGS has graded sixteen examples in Mint State-62 while NGC had graded thirty-five as of January 2001. These numbers are inflated by resubmissions. Some of these include the following:

- Heritage 8/00: 7483 (unsold), ex: Dr. Barry Southerland collection. Graded Mint State-62 by NGC.

- Kingswood 2/99: 986 ($6,490). Graded Mint State-62 by PCGS.

- Kingswood 6/98: 743 ($5,820). Graded Mint State-62 by PCGS.

- Bowers and Merena 1/96: 2097 ($4,730). Graded Mint State-62 by PCGS.

> *The 1884-CC is among the more common Carson City double eagles. It is readily available in all circulated grades and can be located in the lower Mint State grades without much difficulty. It becomes quite scarce in accurately graded Mint State-62 and it is very rare in any grade higher than this. At the present time, I have never seen one better than Mint State-63 and only a small number at this level.*

1885-CC

MINTAGE: 9,450
RARITY RANKINGS:
    Overall Rarity: 6th of 19 (tie)
    High Grade Rarity: 9th of 19

The mintage figure for the 1885-CC is considerably lower than for any other Carson City double eagle produced during the 1880's. It is the rarest Carson City double eagle from this decade, both in terms of overall and high grade rarity.

STRIKE: The 1885-CC is not as well struck as the 1882-CC, 1883-CC or 1884-CC double eagles. Liberty's hair shows relatively good overall definition but there tends to be scattered areas of weakness including the curls below the ear and the top portion of the bun. On some, the lower part of the obverse is not as sharp as the upper part and the rim may show minor weakness from 4:00 to 7:00. The stars in this area show weakness as well. The reverse has a better overall strike with the exception of the words TWENTY DOLLARS which are sometimes weak. The edges on both the obverse and reverse have a noticeably beveled appearance.

SURFACES: Nearly every known 1885-CC double eagle shows excessive bag-marks on the surfaces. These are often very poorly situated--i.e., on the face of Liberty or in the field directly before the face. An example that has relatively smooth surfaces commands a strong premium among knowledgeable collectors. Some show mint-made copper spots or other impurities in the planchet.

LUSTER: The quality of the luster is slightly below average. Textures range from frosty to fully prooflike. I have seen at least a half dozen 1885-CC double eagles that had a fully prooflike obverse coupled with a frosty reverse. Locating a piece with undisturbed original luster is very difficult due to the fact that most have been cleaned or dipped at one time.

COLORATION: The natural coloration found on the 1885-CC double eagles ranges from medium green-gold to a rich coppery-orange hue. Other pieces, typically in the Extremely Fine-40 to About Uncirculated-50 grade range, have dark, smudgy coloration. This is a very hard date to find with attractive, original color.

EYE APPEAL: This is one of the more difficult Carson City double eagles to locate with good eye appeal. The typical 1885-CC shows some weakness of strike, very heavily abraded surfaces, impaired luster due to these marks, and repeated cleanings or dippings. An example that is original and attractive is worth a very strong premium.

DIE VARIETIES: A single variety is currently known to exist.

Variety 1-A: The date is somewhat small and deeply impressed. The mintmark is widely spaced and squat with the two letters even in height. The first C is placed to the left and its edge is over the far right of the Y in TWENTY. The second C is placed to the right and its edge is over the left side of the D in DOLLARS.

RARITY:
Total Known: 350-400

BY GRADE:

VF	EF	AU	MINT STATE
70-80	110-120	158-185	12-15

CONDITION CENSUS:

1. Heritage 3/99: 6822 ($23,000), ex: Bowers and Merena 1/97: 351 ($19,800). Graded Mint State-62 by PCGS.

2. A second coin has been graded Mint State-62 by PCGS as of March 2001.

3. Heritage 9/99: 6808 ($17,250). Graded Mint State-62 by NGC.

4 (tie). As of March 2001, PCGS had graded six examples of this date in Mint State-61 while NGC had graded one as of January 2001. Some of these include the following:

• Eagle collection. Graded Mint State-61 by NGC.

• Private collection, ex: Stack's 6/94: 761 ($8,800). Graded Mint State-61 by PCGS.

• Private collection 1999 via Universal Coin and Bullion, ex: Doug Winter/Lee Minshull, California collection. Graded Mint State-61 by PCGS.

• Private collection 1997 via Universal Coin and Bullion, ex: Lee Minshull, Heritage Rare Coin Galleries. Graded Mint State-61 by PCGS.

The 1885-CC double eagle is a relatively scarce date although the total number of examples known has probably doubled since the early 1990's, due to the discovery of some hoards. It is most often seen in Extremely Fine grades and a nice medium quality About Uncirculated is generally as nice as it is found. The 1885-CC becomes rare in properly graded About Uncirculated-58 and it is very rare in full Mint State with only a dozen or so currently known.

1889-CC

MINTAGE: 30,945
RARITY RANKINGS:
  Overall Rarity: 11th of 19 (tie)
  High Grade Rarity: 14th of 19

When "Gold Coins of the Old West" was released in 1994, the 1889-CC was already considered among the more available Carson City double eagles. Today, it is even more available, thanks to the release of a significant hoard(s) during the middle of the 1990's.

STRIKE: Some 1889-CC double eagles show sharp strikes while others are not that well struck. Most are well detailed at the centers with nearly full hair and feathers. The peripheral details, however, are more likely to have some weakness. On the obverse, stars six through ten are often weak on their radial lines and the lower portion of the rim, from 5:00 to 7:00, is not well struck with some of the denticles showing blurriness. On the reverse, TWENTY DOLLARS is sometimes not fully impressed.

SURFACES: As with nearly all double eagles from this mint, the 1889-CC is generally seen with very heavily bagmarked surfaces. In addition, some show either mint-made copper spots or dark imperfections in the surfaces. Some are available in higher grades with comparably clean surfaces and the date collector is urged to wait for the right coin before he purchases an example.

LUSTER: The luster is average quality. Most examples have somewhat subdued grainy luster that is slightly reflective in the fields. A small number of 1889-CC double eagles have superb rich, frosty luster and such pieces are always in demand among knowledgeable collectors.

COLORATION: The natural coloration found on the 1889-CC ranges from medium golden-orange to deep green-gold. There are a larger number with original coloration available than other Carson City double eagles of this era, but more and more show signs of having been cleaned or dipped.

EYE APPEAL: The typical 1889-CC double eagle has average to above-average quality eye appeal. Most are somewhat weakly struck at the lower obverse and have noticeable bagmarks in the fields. Some extremely attractive pieces are known, including a small number in the Mint State-62 to Mint State-63 range.

DIE VARIETIES: I am aware of a single variety. It is possible that at least one other exists.

Variety 1-A: The date is small, widely spaced and placed fairly low in the field. On the early die state of this variety, the base of the 1 shows repunching. The mintmark is large, compact and placed to the right. The first C is slightly more than midway between the Y in TWENTY and the D in DOLLARS while the second C is over the far left edge of the D. Die cracks are often seen in the legends.

RARITY:
Total Known: 800-900+

BY GRADE:

VF	EF	AU	MINT STATE
75-85	225-250	420-465	80-100

CONDITION CENSUS:

1. Midwestern collection. Graded Mint State-64 by PCGS.

2 (tie). A pair of coins have been graded Mint State-63 by PCGS as of January 2001 2000. These are as follows:

• Texas collection via Universal Coin and Bullion, 1999, ex: Doug Winter, Nevada Collection. *The plate coin in this book.*

• Private collection, ex: Bowers and Merena 5/93: 2278 ($12,650).

3 (tie). As of March 2001, PCGS had graded twenty-seven examples of this date in Mint State-62 while NGC had graded eight as of January 2001. These figures are inflated by resubmissions.

The 1889-CC double eagle can be located in any circulated grade without difficulty. In the lower Uncirculated grades, it is only moderately scarce. It becomes very scarce in Mint State-62 and it is very rare in Mint State-63. There is currently just one example known that grades higher than Mint State-63.

1890-CC

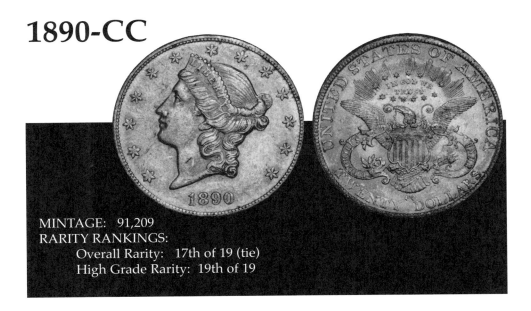

MINTAGE: 91,209
RARITY RANKINGS:
   Overall Rarity: 17th of 19 (tie)
   High Grade Rarity: 19th of 19

The 1890-CC is, along with the 1875-CC and the 1876-CC, one of the three most common Carson City double eagles. Its population has increased in the past decade by the introduction of a substantial number of pieces into the numismatic market in the mid-1990's. 1890-CC double eagles are still being found in Europe, although not as often as in the past.

STRIKE: This is a reasonably well struck issue, but not as well detailed as those produced during the early part of the 1880's. The central obverse is mostly well defined with sharp hair strands and curls while the stars are usually nearly full at the radial lines. The reverse is also well struck. What appears to be weakness on the eagle's tailfeathers at the far right is probably the result of a very light impression into the working die.

SURFACES: Most show deep, detracting abrasions in the fields. These abrasions can be detracting enough that some 1890-CC double eagles that have no actual wear are net graded to the About Uncirculated-55 or About Uncirculated-58 level as a result of an overabundance of abrasions. Copper spots on the surfaces are not uncommon and some 1890-CC double eagles have detracting mint-made grease spots or areas of dark discoloration.

LUSTER: The 1890-CC has better luster than just about any double eagle from this mint. Many higher grade pieces have deep, rich mint frost. A few are known with semi-prooflike fields while a small number are fully prooflike.

COLORATION: The natural coloration ranges from orange-gold to a medium green-gold hue, which can be extremely attractive. I have seen some 1890-CC double eagles with especially attractive multi-hued colors. There are still a number of original pieces available but their number is dwindling.

EYE APPEAL: This is an issue that the date collector should be able to locate with good eye appeal. Many are well struck and very lustrous with nice color. While most 1890-CC double eagles are significantly bagmarked, enough reasonably clean pieces exist so it should be possible to locate one not covered with detracting marks.

DIE VARIETIES: I am aware of just one variety. I expect that a few other minor positional varieties exist.

Variety 1-A: The date is small, compact, and placed slightly to the right. The 1 is twice as far from the truncation as from the denticles and the left edge of the lower serif is over the center of a denticle. The mintmark is small and very round with close spacing between the two letters. The first C is left of the midway point between the Y in TWENTY and the D in DOLLARS while the second C is just over the far left side of the D. Pieces are known with varying die cracks through the reverse legend.

RARITY:

Total Known: 2500-3000+

BY GRADE:

VF	EF	AU	MINT STATE
300-400	800-900	1200-1400	200-300

CONDITION CENSUS:

1. Midwestern collection, ex: Bowers and Merena 5/93: 2281 ($13,200). Graded Mint State-63 by PCGS.

2 (tie). There are approximately fifteen pieces known that grade Mint State-62. As of March 2001, PCGS had graded eleven while NGC had graded twelve as of January 2001. These numbers are inflated due to resubmissions. Some of these include the following:

- Bowers and Merena 8/99: 2282 ($8,050).

- Bowers and Merena 5/94: 1504 ($8,250).

- Heritage 1990 ANA: 717 ($7,260). Later graded Mint State-62 by PCGS.

The 1890-CC is one of the two most common Carson City double eagles in terms of the total number that exist. It is readily available in all circulated grades and can be obtained in the lower Uncirculated grades without difficulty. It becomes quite scarce in accurately graded Mint State-62 and it is extremely rare in Mint State-63 and better with just one currently known.

1891-CC

MINTAGE: 5,000
RARITY RANKINGS:
    Overall Rarity: 2nd of 19
    High Grade Rarity: 5th of 19

Unlike the Carson City half eagles and eagles of this date, the 1891-CC double eagle is a rare, low mintage issue. In fact, its original production of just 5,000 pieces is the second lowest for any Carson City double eagle, trailing only the 1870-CC.

STRIKE: The strike seen on this issue varies. Most have well defined centers with very sharp hair and feathers. But it is not unusual to find weakness on the first three and the final three stars, the lower portion of the date, and on some of the obverse denticles from 4:00 to 7:00. This weakness does not generally correspond to the reverse.

SURFACES: I can not recall having seen more than a handful of 1891-CC double eagles that did not have excessively abraded surfaces. As a rule, this is one of the most heavily abraded of all Carson City gold coins (regardless of denomination) and any piece with only moderately abraded surfaces is in great demand. Copper spots are frequently seen and a number have mint-made grease stains as well.

LUSTER: This issue has above-average luster. Most high grade 1891-CC double eagles are frosty, although this luster tends to be interrupted by the excessive bagmarks described above. A few are semi-prooflike and I have even seen a small number that are significantly reflective. These tend to have poor eye appeal as the reflectiveness magnifies the marks on the surfaces.

COLORATION: The natural color for the 1891-CC double eagle is a medium to deep orange-gold. It is very hard to locate an example with original color as most have been cleaned or dipped at one time.

EYE APPEAL: This is one of the most difficult Carson City double eagles to find with good eye appeal. The typical coin shows some weakness on the lower obverse, has extremely heavily abraded surfaces and no longer has its natural color. An example with even slightly above-average eye appeal is very desirable.

DIE VARIETIES: A single variety is known.

Variety 1-A: The date is evenly spaced and medium in size. The mintmark is tall, closely spaced and somewhat uneven with the second C higher than the first. The first C is slightly more than midway in the field between the edge of the Y and the D. The second C is placed directly above the left side of the D in DOL-LARS.

RARITY:
   Total Known: 150-200

BY GRADE:

<u>VF</u>	<u>EF</u>	<u>AU</u>	<u>MINT STATE</u>
30-40	40-50	70-95	10-15

CONDITION CENSUS:

1. Private collection via Universal Coin and Bullion, ex: U.S. Coins. Graded Mint State-63 by PCGS.

2. Midwestern collection, ex: Charley Tuppen collection. Graded Mint State-62 by PCGS.

3 (tie). Four coins have been graded Mint State-62 by NGC as of January 2001.

4 (tie). Three coins have been graded Mint State-61 by PCGS as of March 2001.

• Seven coins have been graded Mint State-61 by NGC as of January 2001.

In the past, the 1891-CC has been regarded as a rare coin in all grades. While certainly a hard issue to locate, the 1891-CC is only moderately scarce in Very Fine to Extremely Fine grades. It is quite scarce in About Uncirculated and most are in the lower end of this range. In Mint State, the 1891-CC continues to be a rare coin and any piece grading higher than Mint State-60 is very rare.

1892-CC

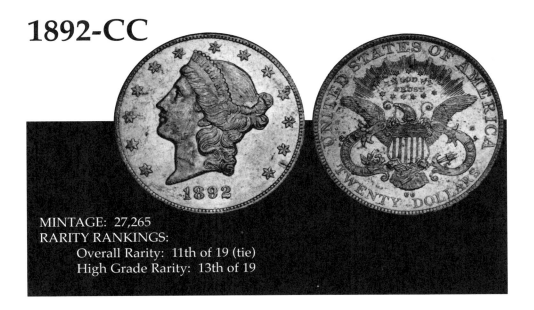

MINTAGE: 27,265
RARITY RANKINGS:
    Overall Rarity: 11th of 19 (tie)
    High Grade Rarity: 13th of 19

Of all the Carson City double eagles produced during the 1890's, the 1892-CC has had its overall and high grade rarity levels most adversely affected by hoards discovered since the 1994 publication of "Gold Coins of the Old West." Today, this is among the more available double eagles from this mint.

STRIKE: This is a reasonably well struck issue. The obverse is sharp at the center with strong hair. The border is less well struck. It is not uncommon to find noticeable weakness on a number of the stars and on scattered areas along the denticles as well. The reverse is usually very sharp at the center and the border tends to be better defined than the obverse.

SURFACES: The surfaces are nearly always seen with deep, dense abrasions. A few coins known are relatively clean and these bring strong premiums. Some 1892-CC double eagles show light to moderate copper spotting.

LUSTER: 1892-CC double eagles are found with a number of different types of luster. The most commonly seen texture is frosty. Some coins are prooflike and I have seen a few that have had deep, fully reflective surfaces on both sides. The overall quality of the luster seen on this date is among the best on any Carson City double eagle.

COLORATION: The natural coloration ranges from medium green-gold to a rich orange-gold shade. While it is not extremely hard to locate a piece with original color, it has become far more difficult as more and more have been cleaned or dipped.

EYE APPEAL: The level of eye appeal seen on the typical 1892-CC double eagle is slightly above average. Most show a good quality of strike and have good luster. It is very hard to find one with clean surfaces but the patient collector should be able to find a moderately abraded example.

DIE VARIETIES: A single variety is known. Others may exist.

Variety 1-A: The date is small, well spaced and placed fairly high in the field between the neck and the denticles. The mintmark is small and fairly compact. The first C is about midway between the right side of the Y in TWENTY and the left side of the D in DOLLARS. On most examples, the mintmark is filled.

RARITY:
Total Known: 800-900+

BY GRADE:

VF	EF	AU	MINT STATE
90-100	250-275	390-445	70-80

CONDITION CENSUS:

1 (tie). As of March 2001, PCGS had graded four examples in Mint State-63. These include the following:

- Private collection, ex: unknown dealer, Heritage Rare Coin Galleries 6/99. Graded Mint State-63 by PCGS.

- Heritage 4/99: 6202 ($20,700)

2 (tie). As of January 2001, NGC had graded three examples in Mint State-63. These include the following:

- Private collection, ex: Universal Coin and Bullion.

- Duquense collection.

- Bowers and Merena 10/99: 1909 ($14,950; as PCGS MS-62), ex: Harry Bass collection.

3 (tie). As of March 2001, PCGS had graded fifteen examples in Mint State-62 while NGC had graded sixteen in Mint State-62 as of January 2001. These numbers are inflated by resubmissions.

The 1892-CC double eagle is usually seen in Extremely Fine and About Uncirculated grades. It is moderately scarce in the lowest Uncirculated grades and it becomes very scarce in Mint State-62. In Mint State-63, the 1892-CC is a very rare coin and I have never seen one that I would grade higher than this.

1893-CC

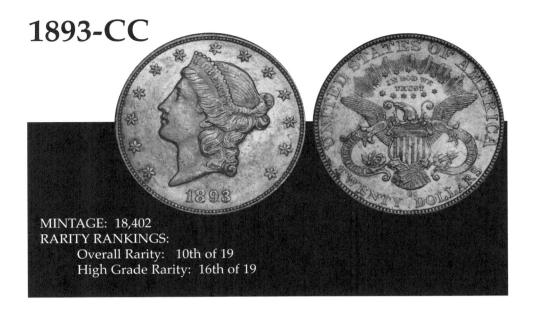

MINTAGE: 18,402
RARITY RANKINGS:
  Overall Rarity: 10th of 19
  High Grade Rarity: 16th of 19

The 1893-CC is the final double eagle produced at the Carson City mint. It is much more available than its low mintage figure would suggest. In fact, in high grades it is among the most readily available double eagles from this mint.

STRIKE: This is one of the best produced gold issues of any denomination from this mint. The strike is usually very bold with complete definition noted at the obverse and reverse centers. The borders are also well detailed although it is not uncommon for examples to show some weakness at the outer edge.

SURFACES: As with nearly all Carson City double eagles, the 1893-CC is usually very heavily bagmarked. Unlike many of these issues, the 1893-CC is sometimes seen with reasonably clean surfaces. A patient collector should be able to locate one that is not extensively abraded.

LUSTER: The luster is above-average. Many show nice frosty luster and a number are semi-prooflike with a decent amount of reflectiveness in the fields.

COLORATION: The natural coloration most often seen on 1893-CC double eagles is rich yellow-gold or medium orange-gold. I have seen a number of pieces that exhibited pleasing coppery hues. Many are extensively copper spotted; some detracting enough to lower the grade.

EYE APPEAL: The 1893-CC is found with better overall eye appeal than most Carson City double eagles, making it a popular choice as a type coin. While most are rather extensively abraded, it is possible to find an appealing piece with good color and luster as well as a sharp strike.

DIE VARIETIES: I am aware of two varieties. It is possible that at least one other reverse was used.

Variety 1-A: The date is small and closely spaced. The base of the 1 is very slightly closer to a denticle than the truncation. The left edge of the lower serif of the 1 is over the left edge of a denticle. The mintmark is short, closely spaced and distinguished by the backs of the letters being thicker than the fronts. The first C is over the right side of the space between the Y in TWENTY and the D in DOLLARS while the second is entirely over the D.

Variety 2-A: The date is small and closely spaced. The base of the 1 is further from the truncation than on Variety 1-A. The left edge of the lower serif of the 1 is over the center of a denticle. The reverse is the same as on Variety 1-A. There are often numerous fine die cracks in the reverse legends.

RARITY:

Total Known: 750-850+

BY GRADE:

VF	EF	AU	MINT STATE
25-30	125-150	350-395	250-275

CONDITION CENSUS:

1. Private collection, ex: Lee Minshull/Casey Noxon. Graded Mint State-64 by NGC.

2 (tie). There are approximately a dozen pieces known that grade Mint State-63. As of March 2001, PCGS had graded ten in Mint State-63 while NGC had graded eight as of January 2001. These figures are inflated by resubmissions.

The 1893-CC double eagle is almost never seen in grades below About Uncirculated-50, suggesting that this issue saw very little circulation. It is most often seen in About Uncirculated-55 to Mint State-60 and examples in this grade range are easily located. It becomes scarce in Mint State-62 and it is rare in Mint State-63, although more exist in this grade than nearly any other double eagle from this mint.

RARITY SUMMARY: CARSON CITY DOUBLE EAGLES

DATE	GRADES				
	VF	EF	AU	MINT STATE	TOTAL
1870-CC	23-30	9-11	3-4	0	35-45
1871-CC	60-80	93-112	45-55	2-3	200-250
1872-CC	55-65	193-210	100-115	2-3	350-400
1873-CC	62-115	195-235	135-150	8-10	400-500
1874-CC	200-275	708-1000	580-710	12-15	1500-2000+
1875-CC	250-350	950-1100	1100-1300	200-250	2500-3000+
1876-CC	350-450	1350-1500	950-1175	100-125	2750-3250+
1877-CC	82-115	275-300	125-175	18-20	500-600
1878-CC	80-90	150-170	66-84	4-6	300-350
1879-CC	65-75	170-190	62-81	3-4	300-350
1882-CC	150-160	420-440	200-265	30-35	800-900+
1883-CC	125-150	410-450	300-325	65-75	900-1000+
1884-CC	200-250	700-750	250-350	100-150	1250-1500
1885-CC	70-80	110-120	158-185	12-15	350-400
1889-CC	75-85	225-250	420-465	80-100	800-900+
1890-CC	300-400	800-900	1200-1400	200-300	2500-3000+
1891-CC	30-40	40-50	70-95	10-15	150-200
1892-CC	90-100	250-275	390-445	70-80	800-900+
1893-CC	25-30	125-150	350-395	250-275	750-850+

II. CARSON CITY DOUBLE EAGLES: OVERALL RARITY

RANKING	DATE	TOTAL KNOWN
1.	1870-CC	35-45
2.	1891-CC	150-200
3.	1871-CC	200-250
4.	1878-CC	300-350
4 (tie).	1879-CC	300-350
6.	1872-CC	350-400
6 (tie).	1885-CC	350-400
8.	1873-CC	400-500
9.	1877-CC	500-600
10.	1893-CC	750-850+
11.	1882-CC	800-900+
11 (tie).	1889-CC	800-900+
11 (tie).	1892-CC	800-900+
14.	1883-CC	900-1000+
15.	1884-CC	1250-1500+
16.	1874-CC	1500-2000+
17.	1875-CC	2500-3000+
17 (tie).	1890-CC	2500-3000+
19.	1876-CC	2750-3250+

III. CARSON CITY DOUBLE EAGLES: HIGH GRADE RARITY

RANKING	DATE	TOTAL KNOWN
1.	1870-CC	3-4
2.	1871-CC	47-58
3.	1879-CC	65-85
4.	1878-CC	70-90
5.	1891-CC	80-110
6.	1872-CC	102-118
7.	1873-CC	143-160
8.	1877-CC	143-195
9.	1885-CC	170-200
10.	1882-CC	230-300
11.	1884-CC	350-500
12.	1883-CC	365-400
13.	1892-CC	460-525
14.	1889-CC	500-565
15.	1874-CC	592-725
16.	1893-CC	600-670
17.	1876-CC	1050-1300
18.	1875-CC	1300-1550
19.	1890-CC	1400-1700

BIBLIOGRAPHY

Akers, David W. "United States Gold Coins: An Analysis of Auction Records, Volume IV: Half Eagles." Englewood, Ohio: Paramount Publications, 1979.

Akers, David W. "United States Gold Coins: An Analysis of Auction Records, Volume V: Eagles." Englewood, Ohio: Paramount Publications, 1980.

Akers, David W. "United States Gold Coins: An Analysis of Auction Records, Volume VI: Double Eagles." Englewood, Ohio: Paramount Publications, 1982.

"Auction Prices Realized: U.S. Coins." Iola, Wisconsin: Krause Publications, Inc. 1982-2000.

Bowers, Q. David. "Buyer's Guide to the Rare Coin Market." Wolfeboro, New Hampshire: Bowers and Merena Galleries, Inc., 1990.

Bowers, Q. David. "Buyer's Guide to United States Gold Coins." Wolfeboro, New Hampshire: Bowers and Merena Galleries, Inc., 1989.

Breen, Walter. "Varieties of United States Half Eagles, 1839-1929." Chicago, Illinois: Hewitt Brothers. 1967.

Breen, Walter. "Varieties of United States Eagles." Chicago, Illinois: Hewitt Brothers. Circa 1967.

Breen, Walter. "Walter Breen's Complete Encyclopedia of United States and Colonial Coins." New York, New York: Doubleday, 1988.

Cutler, Lawrence E. and Winter, Douglas. "Gold Coins of the Old West, The Carson City Mint 1870-1893. A Numismatic History and Analysis." Wolfeboro, N.H., Bowers and Merena Galleries, Inc., 1994.

Dannreuther, John and Garrett, Jeff. "United States Gold Coinage Significant Auction Records 1990-1999." Lexington, KY., Collectors Universe. First Edition, January 2000.

Davis, Sam P., ed. "The History of Nevada." 2 volumes, 1913 Reprint. Las Vegas, Nevada. Nevada Publications.

Hickson, Howard. "Mint Mark: 'CC' The Story of the United States Mint at Carson City, Nevada." Carson City, Nevada: The Nevada State Museum, 1972.

Locker, David J. "An Analysis of Mint State Carson City Coins." In The Numismatist (September 1992): 1250-1335.

Nielson Norm. "Tales of Nevada." Reno, Nevada: Tales of Nevada, 1989.

Nielson, Norm. "Tales of Nevada, Volume 2." Reno, Nevada: Tales of Nevada, 1990.

Numismatic Guaranty Corporation of America. "Census Report." Parsippany, New Jersey. Various issues, 1991-2001.

Paher, Stanley W. "Nevada Ghost Towns and Mining Camps.." Las Vegas, Nevada: Nevada Publications, 1970.

Taxay, Don. "The United States Mint and Coinage: An Illustrated History From 1776 to the Present." New York: Arco, 1966.

Professional Coin Grading Service. "Population Report." Newport Beach, CA. Various issues, 1991-2001.

White, Weimar W. "A Rarity Profile of Mint State Carson City Gold." In The Numismatist, (March 1991): 380-386.

White, Weimar W. "A Carson City Collection That Cannot Be Replaced." In Kingswood Galleries Franconia Sale, Auctions by Bowers and Merena, (August 1992): 93-96.

Winter, Douglas A. "Charlotte Mint Gold Coins: 1838-1861." Wolfeboro, N.H.: Bowers and Merena Galleries, Inc., 1987.

Winter, Douglas A. "New Orleans Gold Coins: 1839-1909." Wolfeboro, N.H.: Bowers and Merena Galleries, Inc., 1992.

Winter, Douglas A. " Gold Coins of the Dahlonega Mint 1838-1861." Dallas, TX.: DWN Publishing, 1997.

Winter, Douglas A. "Gold Coins of the Charlotte Mint: 1838-1861." Dallas, TX.: DWN Publishing, 1999.

Yeoman, R.S. "A Guidebook of United States Coins, 46th Edition." Racine, Wisconsin: Whitman Publishing. 1993.

Also, various numismatic auction catalogs including those produced by Bowers and Merena, Heritage, Superior, Mid-American, Stack's, David W. Akers and RARCOA.